W9-BXP-241

MINISTRY
IN THE
NEW TESTAMENT

OVERTURES TO BIBLICAL THEOLOGY

Editors

WALTER BRUEGGEMANN, McPheeters Professor of Old Testament, Columbia Theological Seminary, Decatur, Georgia

JOHN R. DONAHUE, S. J., Professor of New Testament, Jesuit School of Theology at Berkeley, California

SHARYN DOWD, Professor of New Testament, Lexington Theological Seminary, Lexington, Kentucky

CHRISTOPHER R. SEITZ, Associate Professor of Old Testament, Yale Divinity School, New Haven, Connecticut

MINISTRY
IN THE
NEW TESTAMENT

David L. Bartlett

FORTRESS PRESS   Minneapolis

MINISTRY IN THE NEW TESTAMENT

Copyright © 1993 Augsburg Fortress. All rights reserved. Except for brief quotations in critical articles or reviews, no part of this book may be reproduced in any manner without prior written permission from the publisher. Write to: Permissions, Augsburg Fortress, 426 S. Fifth St., Box 1209, Minneapolis, MN 55440.

Scripture quotations, unless otherwise noted, are from the New Revised Standard Version of the Bible, copyright © 1989 by the Division of Christian Education of the National Council of the Churches of Christ in the United States of America.

Library of Congress Cataloging-in-Publication Data

Bartlett, David Lyon, 1941–
    Ministry in the New Testament / David L. Bartlett.
        p.   cm.
    Includes bibliographical references and indexes.
    ISBN 0-8006-1565-4 (alk. paper)
    1. Clergy—Office—Biblical teaching.   2. Lay ministry—Biblical teaching.   3. Bible. N.T.—Criticism, interpretation, etc.
    I. Title.
    BS2545.C56B37   1993
    262'.1'09015—dc20   93-19849
                                                              CIP

The paper used in this publication meets the minimum requirements of American National Standard for Information Sciences—Permanence of Paper for Printed Library Materials, ANSI Z329.48-1984. ∞™

Manufactured in the U.S.A.   AF 1–1565

97   96   2   3   4   5   6   7   8   9   10

In Memory of Gene E. Bartlett

Contents

Editor's Foreword

For over two decades ministry has been the center of ferment in the family of Christian churches. Debates range not only over who can be ordained, but over the nature of ministry itself, and over its biblical and theological foundations. In 1982 the World Council of Churches issued the "Lima Statement" to underscore convergencies within the member churches and in hope that the document would further progress toward life "in communion with one another in continuity with the apostles and the teaching of the universal Church." Within Roman Catholicism, which appears to have changed least in its conception and practice of ministry, both new clerical ministries (e.g., married deacons) and new lay ministries are rapidly emerging, often "from below," in response to felt pastoral needs (e.g., laymen and laywomen as campus ministers and hospital chaplains).

David Bartlett's *Ministry in the New Testament* is a timely addition to the growing body of literature on ministry in the New Testament. Bartlett holds a Ph.D. in New Testament from Yale University; he has taught both New Testament and homiletics at the University of Chicago, the Graduate Theological Union, and Union Theological Seminary in Richmond; and he is now Lantz Professor of Preaching at the Yale Divinity School. He is, then, uniquely equipped to probe the New Testament with scholarly respect joined to sensitivity to different denominational readings.

After an opening chapter that highlights the understandings and challenges of ministry found in official church statements and in the writing of important twentieth-century theologians, Bartlett proposes an "overture" in two senses: first, as a contribution to conversation not only among biblical theologians but among practical theologians, including priests and pastors; second, as a contribution for "development in the ongoing symphony, drama, opera—as you will—of theological conversation and practice around the issues of ministry."

Bartlett's method is to survey the major blocks of literature in the New Testament. Adopting a historical sequence, he begins with Paul's undisputed letters; he continues with the Gospels of Matthew, Luke, and John (which is often neglected in studies of ministry) and the Acts of the Apostles; and he concludes with the Pastoral Epistles. By attending to the latest scholarly contributions on questions of dating and setting of different documents, Bartlett presents a panorama of the diverse practices and theology of ministry in the historical and literary context of each block of literature. The work's comprehensive character alone will make it a valuable contribution to discussions of ministry in seminaries and church life.

After finishing Bartlett's "overture," church leaders, working pastors, and people considering ministry might well recall the words of Karl Barth: "[The question,] What is within the Bible? has a mortifying way of converting itself into the opposing question, Well, what are you looking for, and who are you, pray, who make bold to look?"[1] Bartlett challenges the contemporary church to take a bold look at the New Testament. He comments that "every church structure we discover in or behind the New Testament documents stands far to the left of establishment American churches today—Catholic and Protestant alike." Any contemporary ecclesial body that wishes to define its identity in terms of the New Testament may paradoxically find there both a reflection of its life and practice and a challenge to its most deeply held tradition and convictions.

John R. Donahue, S.J.

---

1. Karl Barth, *The Word of God and the Word of Man,* trans. D. Horton (New York and Evanston: Harper and Row, 1957), 32.

Preface

I incurred innumerable debts in writing this book. I acknowledge some of them here.

George Stroup suggested that I write a book on ministry. John Hollar invited me to write such a book for Fortress Press and provided wise advice until his untimely death. Marshall Johnson has graciously and helpfully served as editor for Fortress on the project. John Donahue has been an invaluable series editor, critic, resource, and support.

I first presented much of the material that led to the book in the Crozer Lectures at Colgate Rochester Divinity School in 1987. President Larry Greenfield and Barbara Greenfield, President Emeritus Gene E. Bartlett and Jean Bartlett, and Dean Kenneth Smith were my gracious hosts. Many participants in that convocation made suggestions that have enriched the book. At Union Theological Seminary in Virginia, Sally Hicks and Martha Aycock Sugg provided invaluable assistance.

At various stages of this work Roger Nicholson, Ted Winter, Tom Schattauer, and Duane Harbin have all helped at the word processor. Peter Lampe and Ulrich Luz provided manuscripts and suggestions that broadened my understanding of the first-century church. Allen Hunt provided great help in the last stages of revision. Hank Schlau was the excellent copy editor. Carol, Benjamin, and Jonah provided best of all: their love.

In recording these acknowledgments, I began listing my own mentors in ministry, but the list grew longer and longer. Of the first and most significant, however, there was no doubt, and I dedicate this book to his memory.

David L. Bartlett

Abbreviations

AB	Anchor Bible
ATR	*Anglican Theological Review*
BEM	*Baptism, Eucharist, and Ministry*
CBQ	*Catholic Biblical Quarterly*
CBQMS	Catholic Biblical Quarterly—Monograph Series
ConBNT	Coniectanea biblica, New Testament
FRLANT	Forschungen zur Religion und Literatur des Alten und Neuen Testaments
HTR	*Harvard Theological Review*
IBC	Interpretation: A Bible Commentary for Teaching and Preaching
Int	*Interpretation*
JBL	*Journal of Biblical Literature*
JRH	*Journal of Religious History*
LG	*Lumen Gentium* (Vatican II)
NICNT	New International Commentary on the New Testament
NovT	*Novum Testamentum*
NTL	New Testament Library
RNT	Regensburger Neues Testament
SBLASP	SBL Abstracts and Seminar Papers
SBT	Studies in Biblical Theology
SNTSMS	Society for New Testament Studies Monograph Series
TDNT	*Theological Dictionary of the New Testament*
TS	*Theological Studies*

CHAPTER 1

Contemporary Views
of Ministry

Both institutionally and personally, we search for a richer understanding of the meaning of ministry. Institutionally, Protestants and Roman Catholics have been engaged in recent decades in a reappraisal of the origin, significance, and purpose of ordained leadership.

For Catholics, *Lumen Gentium* (Dogmatic Constitution on the Church), from the Second Vatican Council, sought to define in a positive way the role of ordained clergy in their relationship to the community of faithful church people. For Protestants, the study document *Baptism, Eucharist, and Ministry,* published by the World Council of Churches, seeks to provide the grounds for conversation as the various Protestant and Orthodox churches move toward greater unity.

A variety of books by theologians witnesses to the uncertainty of the church about our vocation as ministers, and to the eagerness of Christian thinkers to help us find our way. It does not take academic experts, however, to assure us of our uncertainty. In 1951 Karl Barth wrote of his friends who were just retiring from the pastorate:

It makes me think when I notice how my contemporaries, my former colleagues and fellow students are now one by one beginning to retire from their life's work. I can visualize what it means to spend forty years in giving instruction to first communicants, in seeking the right spiritual word at a grave side or for young married couples, in being pastor to every conceivable kind of folk, and above all in expounding the Gospel Sunday by Sunday and proclaiming the Word of salvation for the community and world of to-day, in face of all kinds of afflictions, irritations and hostilities, of the suspicion of the times and (not least, but above all) of all one's own unbelief.[1]

Apart from the acknowledgment of our own struggles with unbelief, an issue as vital now as it was in 1951, the above description of the pastoral role must raise in most of us envy for a job description that seems unbelievably simple and clear. Not simple in the depths of the demands, but simple in their focus. Like it or not, there is now considerable competition for the hearts and minds of believers or potential believers, competition with other communities of faith and competition with a whole different world of values and priorities. There is the legitimate demand that as Christian persons and as clergy we attend to the needs of the community in which we live and the national and international issues that weigh upon our conscience.

There is the sense, rightly or wrongly, that once upon a time clergy mattered more than we do now: mattered more to the community and even mattered more to the community of faith. We are bit players in the drama of our times, brought in to perform purely ceremonial functions, themselves perceived as aesthetically pleasing anachronisms. And in the meantime we have to keep the institution going: we are, after all, paid to worry about the church on the corner and its future, if it has one.

OFFICIAL STATEMENTS

The documents, Catholic and Protestant, and the books are exceedingly helpful as means toward the church's self-definition and as aids toward self-understanding for clergy and seminarians. The laments and the puzzlements of practicing clergy provide the data, or at least the feelings, to which any understanding of ministry must attend.

Yet another word must be added, a word about the visions of religious leadership found in the foundational documents for the life of the church and for the vocation of its clergy—the visions found in the Bible, and particularly in the New Testament. This book seeks to bring those visions into view, not as the end of our search, but as the beginning.

---

1. Karl Barth, *Church Dogmatics,* trans. G. W. Bromiley and T. F. Torrance (Edinburgh: T. and T. Clark, 1961), 3/4:xi.

LUMEN GENTIUM

With the blessing of Pope Paul VI, Vatican II approved and published the Dogmatic Constitution on the Church, known by its first Latin words, *Lumen Gentium*.[2]

Lumen Gentium begins its discussion of ministry not with the ordained clergy, but with the church as the whole people of God:

> The Church is a sheepfold whose one and necessary door is Christ (Jn. 10:1-10). She is a flock of which God Himself foretold that He would be the Shepherd (cf. Is. 40:11, Ez. 34:11 ff.). Although guided by human shepherds, her sheep are nevertheless ceaselessly led and nourished by Christ Himself, the Good Shepherd and the Prince of Shepherds (cf. Jn. 10:11; 1 Pet. 5:4), who gave His life for the sheep (cf. Jn. 10:11-15). (LG 1, 6)

Furthermore, priesthood belongs not exclusively to the clergy, but to the whole people of God:

> Christ the Lord, High Priest taken from among men (Heb. 5:1-5), "made a kingdom and priests to God his Father" (Apoc. 1:6; cf. 5:9-10) out of this new people. The baptized, by regeneration and the anointing of the Holy Spirit, are consecrated into a spiritual house and holy priesthood. Thus through all those works befitting Christian men they can offer spiritual sacrifices and proclaim the power of Him who has called them out of darkness into His marvelous light (cf. 1 Pet. 2:4-10). (LG 2, 10)

Nonetheless, when the document speaks of the gifts that the Spirit has given to the whole church, the order in which these gifts are mentioned suggests a priority of authority and value: "The Spirit...furnishes and directs her [the church] with various gifts both hierarchical and charismatic, and adorns her with the fruits of His grace (cf. Eph. 4:11-12; 1 Cor. 12:4; Gal. 5:22)" (LG 1, 4).

The sense that those with hierarchical gifts are given authority over those with only charismatic gifts is reinforced by the document's description of the church in the first century: "Among these gifts [mentioned in 1 Corinthians 12] stands out the grace given to the apostles. To their authority, the Spirit Himself subjected even those who were endowed with charisms (cf. 1 Cor. 14)" (LG 1, 7). The major portion of the document is given over to the discussion of the legitimacy and

2. All citations from *Lumen Gentium* (LG) are found in Walter M. Abbott, ed., *The Documents of Vatican II* (New York: Herder and Herder; Association Press, 1966), 14–96.

function of the hierarchical forms of ministry, and one senses that the unity and purpose of the church are most evident in the calling and functions of the clergy.

The bishops have primary authority for the life of the church because they succeed the apostles to whom Christ himself gave special authority. Foremost among the bishops is the pope, the bishop of Rome, the successor of Peter, who was foremost among the apostles (LG 3, 18).

The bishops are responsible for administering all the gifts of official ministry within the church: preaching, officiating at the sacraments, teaching, and governing. Through the bishops Christ himself preaches the word and administers the Eucharist and the other sacraments (LG 3, 21).

Priests, it is quite clear, do not have authority independent of the bishops, but derive their authority from those bishops whom it is their gift to assist. Indeed, priests serve as the apostles of the apostles, ambassadors for the bishop: "Associated with their bishop in a spirit of trust and generosity, priests make him present in a certain sense in the individual local congregations of the faithful, and take upon themselves, as far as they are able, his duties and concerns, discharging them with daily care" (LG 3, 28; see also 3, 21).

Above all, the priest's responsibility is to preside at the Eucharist. Here as host at the meal, the priest represents the presence of Christ himself:

> The ministerial priest, by the sacred power he enjoys, molds and rules the priestly people. Acting in the person of Christ, he brings about the Eucharistic Sacrifice, and offers it to God in the name of all the people. For their part, the faithful join in the offering of the Eucharist by virtue of their royal priesthood. They likewise exercise that priesthood by receiving the sacraments, by prayer and thanksgiving, by the witness of a holy life, and by self-denial and active charity. (LG 2, 10)[3]

Deacons are mentioned only rather briefly in *Lumen Gentium:* "At a lower level of the hierarchy are deacons, upon whom hands are imposed 'not unto the priesthood, but unto a ministry of service' " (LG 3, 29). A variety of possible assignments are suggested for deacons, including the administration of baptism, assisting at Eucharist, blessing marriages, reading Scripture, and teaching the faithful (LG 3, 29).

---

3. Here, of course, the ministerial priest refers to the bishop as well as to the priest or presbyter. See also 2, 17.

Toward the end of the document, *Lumen Gentium* turns again to the role of the laity:

> For their sacred pastors know how much the laity contribute to the welfare of the entire church. Pastors also know that they themselves were not meant by Christ to shoulder alone the entire saving mission of the Church toward the world. On the contrary, they understand that it is their noble duty so to shepherd the faithful and recognize their services and charismatic gifts that all according to their proper roles may cooperate in the common undertaking with one heart. (LG 4, 30)

It is perhaps not only Protestant bias that detects in these lines the sense that the hierarchy is called to condescend to share some of its proper ministry with lay people. The inference is strengthened by the further discussion of the proper role of laity in church deliberations:

> An individual layman, by reason of the knowledge, competence, or outstanding ability which he may enjoy, is permitted and sometimes even obliged to express his opinion on things which concern the good of the Church. When occasions arise, let this be done through the agencies set up by the Church for this purpose. Let it always be done in truth, in courage, and in prudence, with reverence and charity toward those who by reason of their sacred office represent the person of Christ. (LG 4, 37)

Lumen Gentium provides a clear and consistent understanding of the church and its ministry from a particular Roman Catholic perspective. Nonetheless, *Lumen Gentium* raises some questions that I can only mention now, questions to which I shall need to attend as this study proceeds.

First, what is the proper use of Scripture as a resource for understanding church and ministry? *Lumen Gentium* draws from every portion of the New Testament to provide illustration or proof texts for its points. The implication is that there is a uniform understanding of ministry in the New Testament and that every writer in the New Testament can be used to support the vision of every other writer. I shall argue, however, that different biblical texts suggest different and sometimes conflicting visions of ministry and that one cannot simply force them into one homogenized understanding.

Second, what is the relationship between biblical texts about the apostles or the twelve and the institution of the bishop? *Lumen Gentium* assumes that bishops are direct descendants of the apostles and that what Scripture says about the apostles the church can affirm about its bishops. This is a question that demands some exegetical attention.

Third, what is the relationship between the people of God and its leaders? Do the people depend exclusively on the authority of the clergy, or do clergy derive any authority from the whole body of Christ? Does the New Testament provide warrant for a hierarchical understanding of church leadership, or is there evidence for a greater reciprocity between people and leaders? Edward Schillebeeckx states a concern to which we shall need to attend:

> Moreover the church as an institution can be measured by the liberating power of the gospel. It can also be criticized. According to the New Testament there must be a fundamental solidarity and equality among Christians, without master-servant relationships, though this does not in any way exclude authority and leadership in the community.[4]

Fourth, how are we to evaluate the claim of *Lumen Gentium* that the fundamental role of the ordained clergy is to officiate at the Eucharist? While the New Testament suggests a variety of roles and functions for designated church leaders, presiding at the Eucharist is never explicitly mentioned as the responsibility of any particular group of Christians.[5]

Fifth, how does the understanding of the nature of ordination in *Lumen Gentium* relate to the rather sparse information on the appointment and choice of leaders and the laying on of hands in the New Testament?

BAPTISM, EUCHARIST, AND MINISTRY

The document *Baptism, Eucharist, and Ministry* (BEM), written by the Commission on Faith and Order of the World Council of Churches,[6] is an attempt to provide "theological support for the efforts the churches are making toward unity" (BEM, preface, 1). Since the fundamental purpose of the document is to promote unity, it is appropriate and commendable that the study seeks to find both in the New Testament and in church tradition those insights that might provide the basis of agreement. The point of the document is not to underline the radical

---

4. Edward Schillebeeckx, *The Church with a Human Face: A New and Expanded Theology of Ministry,* trans. John Bowden (New York: Crossroad, 1985), 41.

5. See ibid., 144–45.

6. *Baptism, Eucharist, and Ministry,* Faith and Order Paper no. 111, World Council of Churches, Geneva (St. Louis: Association of Evangelical Lutheran Churches, 1982).

differences in the application of the gospel that led to radical differences in church structure in the first century. The point of the document is to find in Scripture and in the tradition some vision of the church on which Christians, in our present diversity, might agree.

Both the section on baptism and the section on the Eucharist have implications for our study of the meaning of Christian ministry. In its study of baptism, the document states: "Baptism is normally administered by an ordained minister, though in certain circumstances others are allowed to baptize" (BEM, "Baptism," 5, 22, 16). The discussion of the Eucharist includes a paragraph that raises central questions for our reflection:

> In the celebration of the eucharist, Christ gathers, teaches and nourishes the Church. It is Christ who invites to the meal and who presides at it. He is the shepherd who leads the people of God, the prophet who announces the word of God, the priest who celebrates the mystery of God. In most churches, this presidency is signified by an ordained minister. The one who presides at the eucharistic celebration in the name of Christ makes clear that the rite is not the assemblies' own creation or possession; the eucharist is received as a gift from Christ living in his Church. The minister of the eucharist is the ambassador who represents the divine initiative and expresses the connection of the local community with other local communities in the universal Church. (BEM, "Eucharist," 3, 29, 27)

We note that both in the case of baptism and of Eucharist, the document suggests but does not require that an ordained person preside at the sacrament. What is striking is that when the ordained person does preside at Eucharist, he or she presides as a representative of the divine initiative, and therefore to some degree as a representative of Christ himself.

The section entitled "Ministry" spells out in greater detail a vision of the role of ordained persons in a united or uniting church. *Baptism, Eucharist, and Ministry,* like *Lumen Gentium,* begins its discussion of ministry by insisting that God calls all the people of God and gives to all Christians the gift of the Holy Spirit:

> The Holy Spirit bestows on the community diverse and complementary gifts. These are for the common good of the whole people and are manifested in acts of service within the community and to the world.... All members are called to discover, with the help of the community, the gifts they have received, and to use them for the building up of the Church and for the

service of the world into which the Church is sent. (BEM, "Ministry," 1, 5; cf. 1, 1–4, 29–30)

Within this understanding that all God's people are called and all are gifted by the Holy Spirit, the document seeks to understand the particular role of the ordained ministry.

Three reasons are given for the necessity of ordained ministers. First, the ordained ministers are "publicly and continually responsible for pointing to [the church's] fundamental dependence on Jesus Christ." Second, ordained ministers provide a focus for the church's unity. Third, "The Church has never been without persons holding specific authority and responsibility" (BEM, 2A, 8, 31).

The document supports this last claim by reference to the role of the apostles and of the twelve in the New Testament. It suggests that, on the one hand, the apostles "prefigure" both the whole church and its designated leaders, while, on the other hand, the apostles—as witnesses to the resurrection of Christ—were unique figures. Today's ordained ministers are not apostles, but their ministry is founded on that of the apostles (BEM, "Ministry," 2A, 10, 32). The role of ordained ministers is to serve as proclaimers of the gospel, leaders of the community, teachers, and pastors (BEM, "Ministry," 2A, 11, 32).

The commentary on the sections that relate contemporary ministry to that of the apostles is suggestive if not altogether compelling: "The basic reality of an ordained ministry was present from the beginning.... The actual forms of ordination and of the ordained ministry, however, have evolved in complex historical developments. The churches, therefore, need to avoid attributing their particular forms of ordained ministry directly to the will and institution of Jesus Christ" (BEM, "Commentary," in "Ministry," 32–33). What the passage at least implies is that the church *can* legitimately trace ordained ministry itself "directly to the will and institution of Jesus Christ."

When the document talks about the role of the clergy, especially in proclamation and sacrament, it claims the necessary interrelationship of clergy and people. Though all Christians depend upon each other, the clergy also apparently represent Christ to (and over against?) the people: "Their presence reminds the community of the divine initiative, and of the dependence of the Church on Jesus Christ, who is the source of its mission and the foundation of its unity" (BEM, "Ministry," 2A, 12, 33).

The succeeding commentary attempts to clarify the relationship between the responsibility of ordained persons and the gifts of all Christian people: "Any member of the body may share in proclaiming and teaching the Word of God, may contribute to the sacramental life of that body. The ordained ministry fulfills these functions in a representative way, providing the focus for the unity of the life and witness of the community" (BEM, "Commentary," in "Ministry," 2, 33).

The next passage, on the Eucharist, seeks to suggest the relationship between the clergyperson as focus of the church's unity and the clergyperson as representative of Christ. The claim here is descriptive rather than prescriptive, at least explicitly:

> It is especially in the eucharistic celebration that the ordained ministry is the visible focus of the deep and all-embracing communion between Christ and the members of his body. In the celebration of the eucharist, Christ gathers, teaches, and nourishes the Church. It is Christ who invites to the meal and who presides at it. In most churches this presidency is signified and represented by an ordained minister. (BEM, "Ministry," 2A, 14, 33)

The succeeding commentary recognizes that there is no New Testament evidence concerning who presided at Eucharist but suggests that, since ordained ministry is to provide a focus for the unity of the church, it is appropriate that an ordained person preside at the Lord's Table.

The section on the authority of the ordained ministry suggests that ministerial authority comes from Jesus Christ but is acknowledged within the community of faith. Those who are ordained possess their authority not for their own sakes, but for the building up of the community: "Therefore, ordained ministers must not be autocrats or impersonal functionaries. Although called to exercise wise and loving leadership on the basis of the Word of God, they are bound to the faithful in interdependence and reciprocity" (BEM, "Ministry," 2B, 15, 16, 34).

In section 3, "The Forms of the Ordained Ministry," *Baptism, Eucharist, and Ministry* argues for the recognition by the churches of the threefold form of ministry—bishop, presbyter, and deacon. The document acknowledges that there were a variety of patterns of church leadership witnessed in the New Testament; that the threefold pattern of ministry did not emerge until the second and third centuries; and that the responsibilities of those three offices have evolved from those early centuries until now. It does state, nevertheless, that "the threefold ministry of bishop, presbyter and deacon may serve today as an expression of the unity we seek and also as a means for achieving it" (BEM,

"Ministry," 3, 22, 38–39; see also 3, 19–21, 37–38). More directly, and more directively, *Baptism, Eucharist, and Ministry* argues that every church needs to maintain some form of *episkopē* (oversight), though it does not go so far as to argue that each church needs *episkopoi,* persons designated as "bishops" (BEM, "Ministry," 3A, 24, 39).

The document makes brief suggestions concerning the functions of the three forms of ministry. Bishops are to have pastoral oversight of a larger jurisdiction, while at the same time they preach the word and celebrate the sacraments. Presbyters preach the word and celebrate the sacraments with a local community of faith. The document does not seem quite clear about what deacons are to do, but their responsibilities will certainly include service and their attitude be marked by loving-kindness (BEM, "Ministry," 3C, 29–31, 41).

In the commentary on the issue of "Apostolic Tradition in the Church," *Baptism, Eucharist, and Ministry* seeks to understand the relationship between the apostles and contemporary ministry: "Within this apostolic tradition is an apostolic succession of the ministry which serves the continuity of the Church in its life in Christ and its faithfulness to the words and acts of Jesus transmitted by the apostles. The ministers, appointed by the apostles, and then the *episkopoi* of the churches, were the first guardians of this transmission of the apostolic tradition" (BEM, "Commentary," in "Ministry," 43).

In its discussion of ordination, *Baptism, Eucharist, and Ministry* acknowledges that the meaning of "ordination" or "appointment" in the New Testament is not altogether clear and may in fact differ from passage to passage. Nonetheless, the document does claim that ordination becomes a sign of the tie between the person being ordained and Christ and his apostles. It is a recognition of the call that the new minister has received from God and of the affirmation of that call by the church (BEM, "Ministry," 5A; "Commentary," 46, 5A, 39, 45; 5C, 45, 48).

Finally, the document calls for a more comprehensive ministry, drawing on both men and women, but leaves open for further discussion and conciliation the issue of whether women should be admitted to the ordained ministry (BEM, "Commentary," in "Ministry," 2D, 18, 36–37).

Baptism, Eucharist, and Ministry is a gift to the churches as they seek to grow in unity and understanding one with another. It is sober, careful, and conciliatory. Nonetheless, from the perspective of the biblical witness—and from the perspective of the church's mission today—there are questions to be raised:

1. As with *Lumen Gentium* we need to ask about the use of Scripture. Claims about the nature of ministry are drawn from Paul, from the Pastoral Epistles, from Luke-Acts, from Matthew, and from Mark. Does the attempt to bring together such diverse scriptural witnesses (and the perhaps inadvertent omission of others) do justice to the particularity and intractability of the New Testament witness to the meaning of ministry?

2. Again, though not without some modest disclaimer, it is assumed that one of the primary functions of the ordained clergyperson is to preside at the Eucharist, though again New Testament evidence for such a special function is scant.

3. The suggestion that some particular subgroup of Christians (the ordained ministers) is peculiarly representative of the lordship of Christ and the unity of the church at the very least needs scrutiny in the light of the New Testament witnesses.

4. The claim that early church officers, ministers, were somehow appointed by the apostles is at least open to discussion. Paul's Letter to the Romans, for instance, clearly recognizes church leaders who were not appointed by him. How was their authority recognized? Does the variety in the ways in which church leaders were chosen raise some question about any uniform description of lines of appointment and authority today?

5. As *Baptism, Eucharist, and Ministry* acknowledges, the forms of leadership in the early church emerged in part out of the social, religious, and ethical context in which Christian communities emerged. Different kinds of religious leadership were responsive to different needs and hopes. In our own situation, is it the case that the turn, or return, to the threefold form of ministry is responsive to the actual situation in which the church finds itself? It certainly responds to one pressing hope, the hope for deeper church unity. But does it neglect other equally important concerns?[7]

6. In particular, can we really stand with this document in its indecisiveness on the question of the ordination of women? May it not be that both the biblical witness and the issues of justice and reconciliation in our own time call us to say an unequivocal yes on that question, though the pace of Christian reunification be thereby slowed?

---

7. Here I am much influenced by Schillebeeckx, *Church;* See pp. 4–5 for an introductory statement, but the perspective informs this book throughout.

NEW MOVEMENTS AND DIRECTIONS:
THE SITUATION OF THE MINISTER TODAY

My reflections on the situation of the minister, the ministerial student, and the ministry today are highly subjective. On this question I have no word from the Lord and do not possess the wisdom of Vatican II or the Commission on Faith and Order. I have help from theologians both Catholic and Protestant. I speak from the practice of ministry for twenty-five years, from conversations with colleagues and students. I am assisted by specific studies that help to point out the problems and the possibilities.

MORE RECENT ROMAN CATHOLIC REFLECTIONS

Much of the more recent literature on ministry from American Roman Catholics acknowledges the helpfulness of some of the distinctions in *Lumen Gentium* but suggests that that official document may not go far enough in applying the larger aspirations of Vatican II to ordained ministry.

The Canon Law Society of America published a series of essays edited by James H. Provost entitled *Official Ministry in a New Age.*[8] The historical if not eschatological perspective of the title is a clue to the arguments of the book. The essayists look back and look around. They look back to the New Testament and the early history of the church to suggest that there are models of ministry less hierarchical and more charismatic and egalitarian than *Lumen Gentium* might suggest. They look around at contemporary Catholic practice and note the quite different possibilities for community and leadership suggested by the Latin American base communities, on the one hand, and by North American charismatic Catholic fellowships, on the other. Some of the essays further acknowledge that pressing questions about the place of women in ministry, about lay ministry, and about requirements for a celibate priesthood call for reevaluation of traditional views, even as those views were modified in the documents of Vatican II.

In his essay, Bernard Cooke raises the theological and biblical question that informs much of his and his colleagues' discussion:

> Vatican II's approach to episcopal power brings us immediately into contact with the tension between differing "models" for thinking about the Church.

8. James H. Provost, ed., *Official Ministry in a New Age* (Washington, D.C.: Canon Law Society of America, 1981).

Both New Testament scholarship and emphasis on the Church as a community that lives by faith have brought to the fore an "organic" model—the Church as body of Christ, animated by the Spirit, growing into eschatological fulfillment by increasing participation in the life of the risen Lord. Yet the "hierarchical" model, whether stressing its more political aspect or its "causation from above" aspect, is quite clearly what controlled the bishops' understanding of themselves at Vatican II.[9]

Nathan Mitchell seeks to help the Roman Catholic Church rethink the meaning of ordination, without, of course, simply abandoning traditional claims or understandings.[10] Again looking to biblical models, Mitchell suggests that the Roman Catholic emphasis on the sacramental role of the priest may have eclipsed the more fundamental New Testament emphasis on the leadership responsibilities of church officials:

> The New Testament thus never explicitly connects ministry with eucharist, probably because it was assumed that whoever possessed the charism of pastoral leadership would, *ipso facto,* be qualified to preside at the Lord's Supper. In short, the New Testament pattern places pastoral leadership before sacramental power—and assumes, indeed, that this leadership is the essential mark of a minister's authority and status in the church.[11]

Mitchell further reminds us that ordination is rooted in baptism, and—in a plea for ecumenical understanding—he argues that when churches accept each other's baptism they have already moved a long way toward accepting each other's ministry as well.[12]

The permanence of ordained ministry, therefore, is not the result of some indelible work in the life of the cleric accomplished at ordination. The permanence of ordained ministry depends on the permanence of baptism and the right of the baptized community to have leadership—in preaching, sacrament, and service. "The sacraments of the Christian community [including ordination] are small 'landmarks,' rough-hewn signs that point to the world itself as the place permeated by God's

---

9. Bernard Cooke, "Fullness of Orders," in Provost, *Official Ministry,* 157.
10. Nathan Mitchell, *Mission and Ministry: History and Theology in the Sacrament of Order* (Wilmington, Del.: Michael Glazier, 1982).
11. Ibid., 303–4.
12. Ibid., 305–6.

presence, permanently claimed by his love, and redeemed at its root by the cross of Christ."[13]

In his *Theology of Ministry,* Thomas Franklin O'Meara provides a definition of ministry. This may not represent a contemporary American Catholic (and ecumenical) consensus, but it provides a useful summary of a position that finds sympathetic response in many denominations: "Ordination is a *sacramental liturgy performed by a Christian community and its leaders during which a baptized, charismatically called and professionally prepared Christian is commissioned into a public ministry within and on behalf of the local church.*"[14]

PROTESTANT REFLECTIONS

Here I draw on an eclectic and impressionistic set of reflections based on readings and conversations that have helped set questions for this book. My suggestion is that the variety of images Protestant ministers and theologians use to understand their own office reflects the variety, and perhaps the confusion, of our sense of vocation.

The Minister as Professional

The concern in recent years to assert that ministers are to be understood as professionals emerges in part from our sense that our status and function in society are no longer as clear or as prestigious as once they were. Realistically or not we look back to the time of our parents or grandparents when clergy were held in highest regard, when Sunday's sermons were reported in Monday's papers, and when to be a parson was to be a person of note.

It is also true that the turn to the model of professionalism has roots more honorable and perhaps more perduring than our injured pride. On the one hand, in freer Protestant churches, at least, questions of ordination remain murky. We have tended to deny that there is any qualitative difference between the call to ministry and any other call. We define the clergy therefore not ontologically, or sacramentally, but functionally. Clergy are those who are paid, hired, to perform particular jobs for the congregation. We are professionals, not professional Christians, but

---

13. Ibid., 308–9.
14. Thomas Franklin O'Meara, *Theology of Ministry* (New York: Paulist Press, 1983), 190.

Christians whose profession is defined in relationship to the institutional church, which hires, pays, and sometimes lets us go.

On the other hand, the attempt to understand clergy as professionals emerges in part from the honorable attempt to understand the church in its present context, for our purposes, in twentieth-century North America. Joseph C. Hough, Jr., and John B. Cobb, Jr., argue that "the dominant leadership characters of the society in general will also appear as the dominant understanding of the leadership in churches." In our time the two forms of leadership that have prevailed in the definition of ministry are the minister as manager (for the sake of the institution) and the minister as therapist (for the sake of the individual believer).[15] (As we shall see, Hough and Cobb go on to argue for a new paradigm for the last part of the twentieth century.)

Yet what one senses in the shift to the professional model for ministry is an insufficient attention to our sources, to the foundational texts and experiences out of which the church emerged. What is missing is sufficient attention to Scripture. To be sure (as we shall see) even the earliest forms of Christian leadership drew upon the world outside the church for their titles and presumably for their functions. Yet what permeates the New Testament is the concern, indeed the passion, that the gospel be proclaimed, served, and preserved. In diverse ways the New Testament communities divulged to us in the New Testament texts held to the gospel as guide to the shape of ministry and as judge over against ministry's distortions. As we consider the question of ministers as professionals in our time we need that same conversation with the gospel; more, we begin the search for our identity there.[16]

The Minister as Practical Theologian

In recent years thoughtful theologians have called us to the renewal of practical theology. The task for the whole church in our time is to break down the dividing wall that has separated the classical theological

---

15. Joseph C. Hough, Jr., and John B. Cobb, Jr., *Christian Identity and Theological Education* (Chico, Calif.: Scholars Press, 1985), 16. See also the argument leading up to this point.

16. The concern with professionalism as one model of ministry is evident in some Catholic discussions as well. See James H. Provost, "Toward a Renewed Canonical Understanding of Official Ministry," in Provost, *Official Ministry*, 194–225, esp. 208–9; see also the definition of ministry in O'Meara, *Theology*, 190.

disciplines from the actual practice of Christian people. Now the actual practice of Christian people is to be part of the stuff on which theology reflects, the soil out of which theological fruit may grow.[17] The very helpful study by Hough and Cobb cited above seeks to move beyond the "professional" image of the minister as manager and therapist, without leaving that role entirely behind.

Drawing on recent management theory, Hough and Cobb suggest that even understood as professionals, ministers need to be more thoughtful and innovative than older pictures of executive leadership might suggest. Good managers must be adept at problem-solving, implementation, and path-finding. First, then, the minister should be a "practical Christian thinker." The role of the clergy will be to help enliven the Christian memory of Scripture and tradition and to elicit the congregation's faithful attention to the world.[18]

Second, the minister should be a "reflective practitioner." Drawing on the management theory of Donald Schoen, the authors say that the minister does not work most effectively or faithfully by assuming that there is a body of Christian (or psychological or sociological) theory to be applied to the congregational situation. The minister works by reflecting on the practice of ministry along with the parishioners.[19]

Third—and embracing both of the preceding categories—Hough and Cobb argue that the minister is called to be a "practical theologian":

> The focus on practical theology expresses our judgment as to the greatest current danger of the church in North America. This danger is that it conforms to expectations established for it by a bourgeois society that stems from the Enlightenment and that it thereby will lose its Christian identity.... What the church needs now is leadership in recovering its internal history, so that its identity in the world as the church is strengthened and clarified.[20]

---

17. A very helpful collection of articles on this subject is found in Lewis S. Mudge and James N. Poling, eds., *The Promise of Practical Theology: Formation and Reflection* (Philadelphia: Fortress Press, 1987). Also helpful is Don S. Browning, ed., *Practical Theology* (New York: Harper and Row, 1983). Browning's *A Fundamental Practical Theology* (Minneapolis: Fortress Press, 1991) looks to be a provocative next step in his thinking.

18. Hough and Cobb, *Christian Identity*, 81–84.

19. Ibid., 84–90. The description of this aspect of the minister's life is clearer in what it denies than in what it affirms.

20. Ibid., 93.

The rediscovery of practical theology as a legitimate field of reflection as well as action holds promise both for academic theology and for the practice of ministry.

We need only state the obvious. While Hough and Cobb acknowledge the necessity of drawing on formative Christian tradition, they do not engage in much conversation with Scripture or reflection on biblical models for ministry. How would such reflection enrich their models of professional leadership?

The "Maceration" of the Ministry

Beyond the analyses of the meaning of ministry are the problems faced by ministers. In his 1959 Lyman Beecher Lectures, Joseph Sittler pronounced a diagnosis that for many of us still comes painfully close to home:

> I have sought for a less violent term to designate what I behold, and mac-eration was the only one sufficiently accurate. Among the meanings of the term listed in the dictionary is this grim one: *to chop up into small pieces.* That this is happening to thousands of ministers does not have to be argued or established; it needs only to be violently stated. His time, his focused sense of vocation, his vision of his central task, his mental life, and his contemplative acreage—they are all under the chopper.[21]

Sittler goes on to write of pastors he has observed:

> These men are deeply disturbed because they have a sense of vocational guilt.... This sense of guilt has an observable content. A minister has been ordained to an Office; he too often ends up running an office. He was solemnly ordained to the ministry in Christ's church. Most of the men I know really want to be what they intended and prepared for. Instead they have ended up in a kind of dizzy occupational oscillation.[22]

The "maceration" is still evident among men and women in ministry. The fear of it haunts seminarians moving toward graduation and employment. In part it is a matter of guilt; in part a matter of frenzy.

It would be lovely if the minister felt responsible only to God, but that is a hope for heaven, not for this earth. Every minister feels and should feel responsible to and for the gospel, but also to and for the congregation, the denomination and its authorities, the community, and

21. Joseph Sittler, *The Ecology of Faith* (Philadelphia: Muhlenberg Press, 1961), 78.
22. Ibid., 84.

(to agree with Hough and Cobb) the future of humankind. Every minister feels and should feel obligation and commitment to his or her family or circle of friends. Most ministers, like it or not, will need to pay attention to the church budget, the repairs on the roof, and Sunday school attendance. To say that ministers are professionals means in part that no one else will have quite the stake we do in the day by day running of the institution we serve. No amount of longing for those bucolic days when the minister moved from the study to the homes of parishioners to the pulpit uninterrupted by the demands of the zoning commission, Alcoholics Anonymous, or a broken furnace will bring them back.

Nonetheless, our fragmentation as ministers does call us to radical rethinking and perhaps even to conversion. To say that the biblical stories and models can help with that rethinking and catalyze that conversion does not mean that we can or should return to any imaginary ideal. It is rather to say that the strength of the biblical stories and symbols lies in part in the sheer practicality with which they joined gospel to situation. We, with the same urgent need, can learn from our heritage.

It is guilt as well as frenzy that marks our ministerial incoherence. Sittler is right in that. But the guilt does not just derive from the fact that we have sold out the true gospel we learned in seminary to the practical corruptions of the real world. The guilt derives in part from the fact that the images we teach and learn in seminary and the books we read about the practice of ministry sometimes seem so far removed from what is really demanded of us "out there."

Much as I honor Sittler's work, there is a way in which he calls us back to a golden age. In the golden age, however, real ministers were undoubtedly complaining that too much was asked of them and doing what we are called to do—adjusting their vision of ministry to the new and uncomfortable world in which they lived.

TOWARD BIBLICAL VISIONS OF MINISTRY

It is my hope in this book to enter into conversation with the ecclesiological formulations of *Lumen Gentium* and *Baptism, Eucharist, and Ministry* and with those theologians and clerics who have sought to understand and broaden some of the implications of those documents. In particular the book will argue for the diversity of New Testament understandings of ministry and will argue that the diverse visions of ministry arise not only out of different understandings of the gospel but also out of different cultural, social, and historical situations. It may be that we shall discover that the unity of the church does not depend on a uniform style of religious leadership. It may be that we shall discover that, in our quite new situation, what we need to learn from the New Testament is not how to combine old traditions but how to adapt the ancient visions to our own needs. If we move toward a more unified (uniform?) vision of ministry, it will be a vision shaped by our own time as well as by the gospel's claim.

It is my hope in this book to provide a balance for the understandable interest of contemporary church people to understand ministers as professionals. While the danger in *Lumen Gentium* and *Baptism, Eucharist, and Ministry* may be that they attend insufficiently to the contemporary context, the danger in the professional vision of ministry may be that it lets the contemporary context control us. The models and visions of the tradition, however transmuted by the Spirit for our time, may correct and deepen a too narrow functional view of ministry, which claims that the pastor is to the church as the plumber is to the pipes.

It is my hope in this book to become part of the conversation on the emerging contribution of practical theology to the parish and the seminary. Taking seriously the claims of theologians that practical theology brings the "memories" or the "symbols" or the "classics" of faith to bear on our practice, and rethinks memories, symbols, and classics in the light of that practice, this book will seek once again to understand and appreciate some of the formative symbols for the meaning of Christian ministry.

Above all, it is my hope that this book will provide resource and reassurance for those who are engaged in the practice of ministry or for those students who anticipate entering ministry. It will almost certainly be the case that we will not be able to lead our people in just the way that New Testament leaders led; nor in the way that our own clerical mentors have done. But we can gain from the New Testament—as from our mentors—visions, questions, comfort, hope.

This book is an overture to biblical theology. It is an overture in two ways. First, it does not pretend to be a thorough study of models for ministry in Scripture. The Old Testament will get very short shrift, and even the New Testament will be surveyed selectively. Far more questions will be raised than answers given. The hope is that the book may contribute to conversation not only among biblical theologians but also among practical theologians, including especially priests and pastors. Second, the book is an overture because the themes we discover in Scripture should provide the basis for development in the ongoing symphony, drama, opera—as you will—of theological conversation and practice around the issues of ministry.

My method will be selective. The principle of selection is easily stated though not so easily explicated. I shall look at those scriptural passages that provide special help in moving toward a contemporary understanding of ministry. Some of the passages will suggest directions for development; some may represent approaches to be shunned. None will be studied simply out of historical curiosity.

My method will also be typological. I will look not only at the titles used for various offices or functions in the early church, but will look also at passages, stories, and symbols that give some clues to the way in which the first-century Christian communities understood leadership. My assumption is that these may provide models for our present understanding and practice, but only "typologically." The apostle is not a bishop, and John the elder is not really a member of the presbytery. No one in the New Testament went to seminary, and if there was real ordination for New Testament church leaders, it did not function as ours does or is apt to do. However, from the rich resources of the New Testament we can draw images, symbols, types, and models to help us shape ministry for our own time: led by the Spirit but informed by the word as well.

This study looks both at the texts as we have them and at guesses about the communities and histories behind the texts. It is of course Scripture that has authority for the church rather than critics' guesses about the history behind Scripture. Often the texts will provide the best guide to the possible meaning of ministry.[23]

We must not forget, though, that we live in a history that Scripture reflects as well as shapes. Behind the Pauline epistles we can, however imperfectly, see hints of disputes about apostleship and leadership in Corinth that are not fully articulated in the letters themselves. Behind John's Gospel we find evidence of a particular kind of community that does not explicitly define itself within the Gospel. We want to learn from the history as well as from the texts. Our view of biblical authority

---

23. Luke T. Johnson provides a helpful reminder of the validity of the *text* in *Decision Making in the Church* (Philadelphia: Fortress Press, 1983), 46–58.

does not provide for easy jumps from first-century texts to twentieth-century problems, even less from twentieth-century guesses about first-century situations back to the twentieth century again. Yet we seek to honor our fathers and mothers in the faith whose attempts to be church are evident in the texts and visible behind the text, however imperfect our vision. The texts and the communities behind them help us think about our communities, our ministry.

There are assumptions here about the authority of Scripture for the life of the church. I prefer to reflect on the nature of scriptural authority rather than to argue a particular doctrine of inspiration. For reasons both personal and practical, I ask not how Scripture originated but how it can be used faithfully.[24]

Scripture functions as authority for the church both de facto and de jure. That is, it is by the appeal to Scripture that we do *in fact* proceed with the business of Christian growth and Christian argument. For those of us who are committed to ecumenical dialogue, Scripture provides the necessary starting point, though not of course the only basis for discussion.

Moreover, Scripture *ought* to be our guide in matters of faith and practice. Commitment to Scripture comes with membership in the Christian community. The Bible is the charter out of which every church should read its life. That is not to say, however, that the Bible is an answer book to all our questions. We have questions the Bible does not answer, and when it does answer our questions the canon does not always speak with one voice. The Bible also has questions for us that may be better than the questions we started with.

Our interpretation of Scripture is conversational.[25] We acknowledge the conversations within Scripture itself. Matthew, we shall see, does not understand Torah the same way Paul does, and, not surprisingly,

---

24. Personally I have found this a more fruitful way of raising the question, as it does not require trying to guess what inspiration may have felt like to Paul or Matthew or the editors of the Pentateuch. Practically the question of authority *may* provide a way around some of the divisiveness that discussions of inspiration tend to provoke. For a much fuller discussion of these issues, see David L. Bartlett, *The Shape of Scriptural Authority* (Philadelphia: Fortress Press, 1983).

25. I know there are traces of Tracy here, and partly through him of Gadamer. See David Tracy, *The Analogical Imagination: Christian Theology and the Culture of Pluralism* (New York: Crossroad, 1981); idem, *Plurality and Ambiguity: Hermeneutics, Religion, Hope* (San Francisco: Harper and Row, 1987), esp. chap. 1. My debts and differences are sketched in *The Shape of Scriptural Authority*, 36–37. See also Hans-Georg Gadamer, *Truth and Method* (New York: Seabury Press, 1975).

neither does Matthew's Gospel present its hints about ministry exactly as Paul makes his claims. John's Christology is very different from Luke's; not surprisingly, so is his vision of church order. As interpreters we seek to understand that conversation.

We are also in conversation with Scripture. Christians have two thousand years of history, a complicated and sometimes frustrating contemporary scene, and strong personal and confessional commitments to bring to the conversation. Those who are Lutheran either denominationally or viscerally will not be surprised to find themselves cheered by Galatians and frustrated by James. It is not a coincidence that for the Roman Catholic Church, Matthew has been for centuries the first Gospel, and not in order only. Perhaps the claim that we find a canon within a canon is too provocative a way to confess that this side of the kingdom we all see God and God's purposes through a glass darkly, and some of us prefer one glass, some another. Part of the conversation is to know what perspective we bring; part of the conversation is to let Scripture question and criticize our perspectives. Lutherans may have something to learn from James; Catholics from the Gospel of John.

We are in conversation with each other. When mainline Christians learn from the Johannine epistles, they may also learn something of what motivates and inspires their more "sectarian" brothers and sisters, and when evangelicals ponder all that concern about order and orthodoxy in Acts 20, they may be open to conversation with those who are always puzzling about church in the world, not just over against the world.

This book is a modest contribution to an ecumenical conversation. I wear my own glasses, a free-church male cleric, ordained a generation ago, spending my life in and around divinity school faculties and university-related congregations. Looking from the beginning of the book to its end I am surprised, but should not be, at my enthusiasm for those biblical images of church leadership that sound free-church–like and, God help us, even professorial. I hope I have heard other voices sympathetically.

The diversity of the canon provides a warrant for the diversity of the one church. The unity of the canon—and the unity of the Spirit—provide hope that our ongoing conversations will be friendly, familial.

CHAPTER 2

Ministry in the
Letters of Paul

I have already suggested that the various writings of the New Testament provide evidence for a variety of forms of ministry in the first-century church. My hope is that by examining some of the major strains in the New Testament we will find clues that judge and shape our understanding of ministry today.

The letters of Paul are the earliest Christian writings. I will not argue here that Paul's vision of the church and its ministry is necessarily normative, either because it is early or because it is Paul's. Nor can we be sure that the descriptions of Pauline churches tell us much about other forms of church structure that may have existed at the same time. We can be sure that the actual churches Paul founded did not live up to his hopes for the community of faith. Paul's understanding of the church and its leaders does, however, give us clues both to Paul's hopes and frustrations and to the reality of community life in one group of churches very near the beginning of Christian history. By seeking to compare Paul's historical situation to our own, and Paul's understanding of ministry to our own, we may see what the Spirit has to teach us from the passion and wisdom of the apostle.

In studying Paul I wish to examine five issues, which will also provide a schema for my discussion of ministry in other strains of New Testament literature:

1. What is the historical, social, and theological situation for which these letters were written?

2. What is Paul's understanding of apostleship?

3. How are disputes settled within the Pauline congregations? (This will help us understand the nature of leadership and its authority.)[1]

4. What kinds of officers, or leaders, are present in the Pauline churches? What are the grounds of their authority?

5. What are the predominant images of the church for Paul?

THE HISTORICAL SITUATION FOR WHICH PAUL WRITES

Wayne A. Meeks has provided a helpful and persuasive study of the nature and structure of Pauline communities.[2] First, as we know by the addresses themselves, the Pauline churches are in urban centers. They therefore represent both the pressures and possibilities of a cosmopolitan and varied environment. Second, at least the "named" members of the Pauline churches were apparently moving ahead in the somewhat flexible urban environment: "The most active and prominent members of Paul's circle (including Paul himself) . . . are upwardly mobile; their achieved status is higher than their attributed status."[3] Third, the Pauline Christians were joined together in house churches, relatively small groups of Christians meeting in private homes. Almost certainly some of the structure of the Christian community reflected the structure of the households in which they met.[4]

What is immediately striking about the communities behind Paul's letters is this: The letters that Paul writes suggest a diversity of church structure and church leadership in the churches that he founded (or in the case of Romans, the church he intends to visit). Our sense is that Paul and the early Christians were quite willing to adopt and to adapt structures that seemed appropriate to their diverse and unique communities. We can guess that the differing structures and understanding of church leadership reflect the different natures of the communities, both the communities of faith and the cities in which they were found.

1. For the stress on conflict resolution as a clue to understanding leadership, I am indebted to Wayne A. Meeks, *The First Urban Christians: The Social World of the Apostle Paul* (New Haven: Yale Univ. Press, 1983), 111–31, and to Edward Schillebeeckx, *The Church with a Human Face: A New and Expanded Theology of Ministry,* trans. John Bowden (New York: Crossroad, 1985), 50–54.

2. Meeks, *First Urban Christians.*

3. Ibid., 73.

4. Ibid., 75–76.

In part, the structure and leadership of some church communities were closely related to the house churches, the church following the structure of the household itself. In part, it may be that Christian communities borrowed ideas for structure and even the names of officers from other associations in their town, though here the evidence is disappointingly sparse. One appealing possibility is that the term *episkopos* emerges especially from Hellenistic towns and temples and the term *presbyteros* from the synagogue. Paul uses the first term in his letters to Hellenistic churches, but not the second. Yet the evidence is ambiguous.[5]

In his article on the background of the term *episkopos* in the *Theological Dictionary of the New Testament,* for example, Hermann W. Beyer shows the variety of Greek and Hellenistic uses for that term. Sometimes the gods were understood as overseers, or *episkopoi.* Sometimes the title was given to officials of the state. Sometimes the term referred to a local official, in some cases a cultic official. There are also references to the function, if not the title, of overseer in the Septuagint, and there may be some correlation between the *episkopos* and the *mebaqqer* of the Qumran community who seemed to have both instructional and administrative responsibilities.[6]

The term *presbyteros* (elder) may have its particular background in the Jewish communities, but even here Günther Bornkamm notes that the term was used for civic leaders in Sparta.[7] I would guess that Pauline churches picked up something of their structure and their titles from the communities in which they lived, but the evidence is uncertain. What does seem constant, as we shall see, is the authority and importance of the apostle, as itinerant church founder but also as ongoing mentor and guide (and even dictator) for the church's practice.

When the Christian faith was new and when the tenure of the church

---

5. See Hans Lietzmann, "Zur altchristlichen Verfassungsgeschichte" (1914), in Karl Kertelge, ed., *Das Kirchliche Amt im Neuen Testament* (Darmstadt: Wissenschaftliche Buchgesellschaft, 1977), 93–143.

6. On *episkopos,* see Hermann W. Beyer, "Episkopos," in *TDNT* 2:608–22. On various titles for Christian leaders, see Lietzmann, "Zur altchristlichen Verfassungsgeschichte." I am grateful to John Donahue for his helpful survey in an unpublished paper for colleagues at the Jesuit School of Theology in Berkeley, California. Peter Lampe (*Die stadtrömischen Christen in den ersten beiden Jahrhunderten: Untersuchungen zur Sozialgeschichte* [Tübingen, J. C. B. Mohr, 1987], 336–40) notes some of the background of the term.

7. Günther Bornkamm, "Presbyteros," in *TDNT* (1968), 6:651–83.

on earth was assumed to be exceedingly brief, there was neither time nor purpose for setting up systems of ordination, listing qualifications for office, or determining the marks of ongoing legitimacy. Christians were gifted by the Spirit, and those gifts were a foretaste of the new age soon to be fulfilled. The need for the church was not to set up structures but to acknowledge the gifts and to allow, encourage, diversely gifted people to live together without chaos, boasting, or shame.

In order to do this only the most rudimentary organization seemed necessary. Heads of households where churches met probably carried some of their authority into the community of faith. Those who had been Paul's fellow workers were to be acknowledged as carrying the charism of leadership. Prophets were heard because in fact they could prophesy, and we would guess that administrators were heeded because in fact they knew how to balance the books. The churches were bound together by a common faith and by a common loyalty to the apostles, at least on their better days. While Paul does not yet refer to the church as the body of all faithful people in every place, there is a strong sense of interdependence not only within congregations and communities, but also among them.

Above all, in Paul there is devotion to the gospel. The churches exist for the sake of the gospel, and not the other way around. When Paul feels the gospel is threatened, all claims of mutuality, interdependence, and egalitarianism move to the side. He beseeches; then he commands. Whether it works or not, we do not know; but there can be no doubt that he claims special authority.

Ernst Käsemann, who has traced the development of the early church as a decline toward what he calls "early catholicism," argues that what was best in the history of the church consists of what was best in the Pauline communities—and that this inevitably, but nonetheless sadly, began to disappear as church history progressed.[8] In his disputes with the Corinthian enthusiasts, suggests Käsemann, Paul already had to

8. See Ernst Käsemann, "Paul and Early Catholicism," in *New Testament Questions of Today,* trans. W. J. Montague (Philadelphia: Fortress Press, 1969), 236–51; and idem, "Ministry and Community in the New Testament," in *Essays on New Testament Themes,* trans. W. J. Montague (London: SCM Press, 1964), 63–94. For a discussion of the insights and dangers connected with the designation of the development of the church as a decline into early catholicism, see Joachim Rogge and Gottfried Schille, eds., *Frühkatholizmus im ökumenischen Gespräch* (Berlin: Evangelische Verlagsanstalt, 1983), and Reginald H. Fuller, "Early Catholicism: An Anglican Reaction to a German Debate," in Ulrich Luz and Hans Weder, eds., *Die Mitte des Neuen Testaments: Ein-*

make some appeals to structure, order, and authority.[9] However, the "ideal" church, evident at the heart of the Pauline writings, is a church where gifts rather than offices mark the distinctions among Christians and where the Spirit of God binds Christians together under the lordship of Christ: "To put it pointedly, but without exaggeration, the Pauline church is composed of nothing but laymen, who nevertheless are all, within their possibilities, at the same time priests and officeholders, that is, instruments of the Spirit for the enactment of the Gospel in the everyday world."[10]

Käsemann also argues that this vision of charismatic ministry depends on the expectation of the imminent return of Jesus. As the church discovers that its history will go on and on, the hope fades for sustaining the community by the Spirit alone. Now charismata give way to offices. The presence of the Spirit gives way to official recognition by ordination. Community gives way to hierarchy. Christ is no longer Lord over the church, but head of the church: part of the ecclesiastical machinery.[11] While Käsemann may overstate his point and claim too much for the Protestant vision now and for its prototype in Paul, nonetheless his sketch of the situation of the Pauline churches remains helpful.

Beyond these general statements, of course, each Pauline epistle reflects its own historical circumstance and the particular relationship the apostle had to each church. We shall attend to these circumstances as we look at particular passages related to the church and its leadership.

PAUL'S UNDERSTANDING OF APOSTLESHIP

Paul thinks of himself above all as an apostle. He begins four indisputably genuine Pauline letters by designating himself an apostle (Rom. 1:1; 1 Cor. 1:1; 2 Cor. 1:1; and Gal. 1:1).

Unlike Paul, for the most part Luke does not identify Paul as one of the apostles. The books of Luke and Acts identify the apostles with the twelve disciples who followed Jesus (with Judas replaced by Matthias; Acts 1:26). In 1 Cor. 15:5-7, Paul, however, explicitly distinguishes the apostles from the twelve who followed Jesus in his Galilean ministry:

---

heit und Vielfalt neutestamentlicher Theologie (Göttingen: Vandenhoeck and Ruprecht, 1983), 34–41.

9. See Käsemann, "Ministry and Community," 83.

10. Käsemann, "Paul and Early Catholicism," 245.

11. Ibid., 245–47.

"[The risen Lord] appeared to Cephas, then to the twelve. Then he appeared to more than five hundred brothers and sisters.... Then he appeared to James, then to all the apostles." Here the group of apostles is larger than the twelve, though the twelve may be included. (Peter apparently is included among the apostles in 1 Cor. 9:5, though even here it is not clear.) At the end of the list of those who saw Jesus, Paul includes himself: "Last of all, as to one untimely born, he appeared also to me. For I am the least of the apostles, unfit to be called an apostle, because I persecuted the church of God" (1 Cor. 15:8-9).

Two features of Paul's understanding of apostleship are evident in this passage. First, the apostle is one who has seen the risen Lord (though not all who have seen the risen Lord are considered apostles). Paul also emphasizes this feature of his apostleship in 1 Cor. 9:1. Second, a major responsibility, if not the major responsibility, of the apostle is to preach: "Whether then it was I or [one of the other apostles], so we proclaim and so you have come to believe" (1 Cor. 15:11). The same stress on the preaching ministry of the apostle is evident in 1 Cor. 2:1-5 and appears again in Paul's defense of his apostleship against his critics in 2 Corinthians: "That is, in Christ God was reconciling the world to himself, not counting their trespasses against them, and entrusting the message of reconciliation to us. So we are ambassadors for Christ, since God is making his appeal through us" (2 Cor. 5:19-20; see also Philemon 9).

The stress on the apostle as ambassador, and therefore as preacher, may possibly be related to the rabbinic notion of the *shaliach,* the one who is sent. The *shaliach* carried both the message and the authority of the one who sent him.[12] Here there is some sense that the apostle carries Christ's authority, represents Christ (as does the minister in both *Lumen Gentium* and *Baptism, Eucharist, and Ministry*). In these passages, the authority consists in the message that the apostle bears. We find the same theme even more clearly in 2 Cor. 4:5: "For we do not proclaim ourselves; we proclaim Jesus Christ as Lord with ourselves as your slaves for Jesus' sake."

Jürgen Roloff provides cautionary notes on the connection between the rabbinic concept and New Testament apostleship. For one thing, clear references to the *shaliach* in rabbinic writings are later than the New Testament. For another, the rabbinic messenger carries special au-

---

12. See Karl H. Rengstorf, "Apostolos," in *TDNT* 1:407–46, esp. 414–18.

thority only for the duration of the specific mission. One is not called from the womb to be a *shaliach.* Roloff also points out, however, that the notion of the one sent may be older than the extant rabbinic literature, citing 2 Chron. 17:7-9; 1 Sam. 25:40; and 2 Sam. 10:1ff.[13]

The apostle clearly writes to the churches as one having particular authority over their faith and practice. One suspects that the repeated use of the title "apostle" as part of Paul's greeting is a not so subtle reminder to the churches that he has the right to speak to them and to expect their obedience. Interestingly, in Philippians, where Paul's authority seems to be already acknowledged, he does not call himself apostle in his salutation. (Nor in 1 Thessalonians, nor in Philemon, where his self-designation as "a prisoner for Christ Jesus" sets the mood for the appeal on behalf of Onesimus [Philemon 1].)

In part, Paul's apostolic authority derives from his call. The fullest statement of that call is found in Gal. 1:11-16:

> For I want you to know, brothers and sisters, that the gospel that was pro-claimed by me is not of human origin; for I did not receive it from a human source, nor was I taught it, but I received it through a revelation of Jesus Christ. . . . But when God, who had set me apart before I was born and called me through his grace, was pleased to reveal his Son to me, so that I might proclaim him among the Gentiles, I did not confer with any human being, nor did I go up to Jerusalem to those who were already apostles before me, but I went away at once into Arabia, and afterwards I returned to Damascus.

It is clear here that Paul sees his apostolic authority as being a direct gift (charism) from God. The gift does not derive from any designation on the part of other apostles. Its authority need not be checked out with the other apostles. Furthermore, the point of the call is to set Paul aside for the preaching of the gospel. The Greek for Gal. 1:16 can more appropriately be read: "[God] . . . was pleased to reveal his son *through* me," rather than "God . . . was pleased to reveal his son *to* me," and what Paul receives at the time of his call is not conversion to Christianity but the gospel to be proclaimed. The whole passage is clearly shaped by Paul's knowledge of the story of the call of Jeremiah in Jer. 1:5, and like the prophets, Paul sees himself as one who is commissioned of God to declare God's word. He is sent, an apostle.

---

13. See Jürgen Roloff, *Apostolat—Verkundigung—Kirche: Ursprung, Inhalt und Funktion des kirchlichen Apostelamtes nach Paulus, Lukas, und den Pastoralbriefen* (Gütersloh: Gütersloher Verlagshaus Gerd Mohn, 1965), 9–15.

In part, however, Paul's authority derives from the churches he has founded. Not only does he assert apostleship over them; he also claims the legitimacy of his apostleship from them: "Am I not free? Am I not an apostle? Have I not seen Jesus our Lord? Are you not my work in the Lord? If I am not an apostle to others, at least I am to you; for you are the seal of my apostleship in the Lord" (1 Cor. 9:1-2).

Again in 2 Corinthians, where Paul is most concerned to defend his apostleship, he derives his authority from the church itself. Apparently his opponents, the so-called super apostles, come complete with letters of recommendation from other churches.[14] "Surely we do not need, as some do, letters of recommendation to you or from you, do we? You yourselves are our letter, written on our hearts, to be known and read by all" (2 Cor. 3:1-2). The passage nicely shows the twofold nature of Paul's apostolic authority: on the one hand, it derives from Christ, from the Spirit of God; on the other hand, it is validated by the churches Paul has founded. The passage also shows that Paul cannot take acceptance of his apostolic authority for granted.[15]

There is a further feature of apostolic authority, made clear particularly in the work of John Howard Schütz. Schütz points out that in part Paul's authority derives from the fact that his life takes on the shape of the gospel he proclaims. He declares Christ whose power is made known in weakness, and as he describes his own life, it is clear that Paul finds his own power made perfect in weakness too. We can see this especially in 2 Cor. 4:8-11.[16]

To summarize: for Paul, the apostle is one who has seen the risen Lord and who is commissioned to preach the gospel. The apostle has

---

14. These letters may perhaps come from the Jerusalem apostles, or, as Victor Paul Furnish thinks more likely, from other Hellenistic churches, as apparently these opponents are apt also to ask for such letters from the Corinthian church (see 2 Cor. 3:1b). See Victor Paul Furnish, *II Corinthians,* AB (Garden City, N.Y.: Doubleday, 1984), 193.

15. Gerd Theissen suggests that three forms of legitimacy were at stake between Paul and some of his "apostolic" opponents: charismatic legitimacy (the call); traditional legitimacy (rootedness in Palestinian Judaism, or specific authorization by an established church); and functional legitimacy (the practical "workmanship" of the apostle). Paul, as my analysis would also suggest, was stronger in his charismatic and his functional legitimacy than in his "traditional" legitimacy, and he stresses the call and the fruits of his work. See Gerd Theissen, *The Social Setting of Pauline Christianity: Essays on Corinth,* trans. John H. Schütz (Philadelphia: Fortress Press, 1982), 48–54.

16. John Howard Schütz, *Paul and the Anatomy of Apostolic Authority,* SNTSMS 26 (Cambridge: Cambridge Univ. Press, 1975), 244–48.

the right to exercise authority over the churches he or she has founded.[17] This authority derives in part from the call of God that sets the apostle apart as apostle; it derives in part from the churches themselves and from the fact that they are the fruits of the apostle's labors. Paul's authority is further based in the fact that his life and ministry have taken on the shape of Christ's own life and ministry: humility (almost) to death; resurrection to new life. Paul's assertion of his apostolic authority does not disguise the fact that he does have to argue for that authority again and again.

CONFLICT RESOLUTION IN THE PAULINE CHURCHES

Paul's letters are full of the evidence of conflict and of his attempts to bring a resolution appropriate to his understanding of the gospel. From a multitude of instances, I select three that are particularly useful to our purposes.

1 COR. 1:10-17

Now I appeal to you, brothers and sisters, by the name of our Lord Jesus Christ, that all of you be in agreement and that there be no divisions among you, but that you be united in the same mind and the same purpose. For it has been reported to me by Chloe's people that there are quarrels among you, my brothers and sisters. What I mean is that each of you says, "I belong to Paul," or "I belong to Apollos," or "I belong to Cephas," or "I belong to Christ." Has Christ been divided? Was Paul crucified for you? Or were you baptized in the name of Paul? I thank God that I baptized none of you except Crispus and Gaius, so that no one can say that you were baptized in my name. (I did baptize also the household of Stephanas; beyond that, I do not know whether I baptized anyone else.) For Christ did not send me to baptize but to proclaim the gospel, and not with eloquent wisdom, so that the cross of Christ might not be emptied of its power.

While we have no way of knowing for sure what lies behind the Corinthian fuss about Paul and Apollos and Cephas, Nils Dahl suggests that what has raised the issue of apostolic authority may be precisely

---

17. See Rom. 16:7 and the reference, almost certainly, to Junia, a woman esteemed "among the apostles." In addition to raising the question of whether women were considered apostles, this passage suggests that perhaps sometimes Paul uses the term "apostle" of church delegates whether or not they were founders of congregations. Cf. 2 Cor. 8:23, and see Elisabeth Schüssler Fiorenza, *In Memory of Her: A Feminist Theological Reconstruction of Christian Origins* (New York: Crossroad, 1984), 47, 48, 172.

the letter, 1 Corinthians itself.[18] The Corinthians are arguing over a number of issues, and Stephanas and others have suggested that the congregation write Paul, asking his advice as the church's founding apostle. Other Corinthian Christians have suggested that the congregation should rather appeal to Apollos. (The evidence that Paul is responding to a letter asking his advice is found especially in 1 Cor. 7:1.)

We note that Paul assumes that the fundamental authority for solving this dispute is the authority of Jesus Christ. Paul appeals, beseeches, and begs, but here (at least) he does not give orders. He speaks "by the name of our Lord Jesus Christ," and he reminds the Corinthians that they were not baptized into (not just "in") the name of Paul but (by implication) into the name of Jesus Christ. (This may suggest another issue than that mentioned by Dahl. The Corinthians may be seeking their identity in the "names" of the persons who baptized them—especially Paul or Apollos. Paul insists that the name of the one who baptizes does not matter; what matters is the name into which one is baptized.)[19]

Nonetheless, in this passage and in the salutation that begins the letter ("Paul, called to be an apostle of Christ Jesus by the will of God...") there is, on the one hand, no doubt that Paul thinks he has the authority to answer the questions addressed to him. Indeed, if Dahl is correct, the rest of the letter represents Paul's exercise of that authority. On the other hand, there is certainly no sense of any hierarchical distinction among the key church leaders—here Paul, Apollos, and Cephas (Peter). Paul does not say, "You are under my jurisdiction, so pay no heed to Apollos and Cephas." Nor does he take the fact that he founded the Corinthian church as grounds for any unique authority on his part (see 1 Cor. 3:5-8).

From the side of the Corinthians, it is evident that some of them at least think Paul has sufficient authority—whether apostolic or personal—that they want to appeal for his help in their disputes. Indeed

18. See Nils A. Dahl, "Paul and the Church at Corinth," in *Studies in Paul* (Minneapolis: Augsburg, 1972), 40–61, esp. 51–52. Gerd Theissen suggests, not necessarily in contradiction to Dahl, that the dispute may be among the wealthier "patron" leaders within Corinth. Some (presumably including Stephanas) have served as host and sponsor to Paul when he was staying there; others have sponsored Apollos. Church leaders are loyal to the missionary to whom they were bound not only by affection but by material commitment. See Theissen, *Social Setting,* 54–55.

19. See Hans Conzelmann, *I Corinthians,* trans. James W. Leitch, Hermeneia (Philadelphia: Fortress Press, 1975), 35.

it may be that Paul insists that he and Apollos are only God's servants precisely because the Corinthians are apt to ascribe to them more authority than they can legitimately own.[20] There is also an implicit issue of authority and leadership among the Corinthians themselves. In 1 Cor. 1:16, Paul acknowledges that he baptized Stephanas and his household. Paul's disingenuousness in apparently forgetting the first persons he baptized in Corinth is probably strategic. Perhaps those who have been baptized by Apollos think Stephanas is trading on his special tie to Paul when he volunteers to carry the list of disputed questions to the apostle. By separating Stephanas's appeal from the fact that Paul baptized him, Paul may hope to be able to win more credence for Stephanas among those who were baptized by Apollos.

Then at the end of the letter, Paul returns to Stephanas again:

> Now, brothers and sisters, you know that members of the household of Stephanas were the first converts in Achaia, and they have devoted themselves to the service of the saints; I urge you to put yourselves at the service of such people [RSV: "be subject to such men"] and to every one who works and toils with them. I rejoice at the coming of Stephanas and Fortunatus and Achaicus, because they have made up for your absence; for they refreshed my spirit as well as yours. Give recognition to such persons. (1 Cor. 16:15-18)

If Dahl is right, the immediate issue is that the Corinthians should pay attention to the letter that Stephanas and his friends are taking back to Corinth, 1 Corinthians. By attending to Stephanas's authority they attend to Paul's authority as well. (In which case the RSV's "be subject to such men" captures the issue better than the vaguer "put yourselves at the service of such people.")

Antoinette Wire's fascinating reconstruction of the Corinthian community suggests other reasons that Paul may be concerned to reinstate his authority through Stephanas. Especially behind the Pauline injunctions of 1 Corinthians 12–14 Wire finds evidence of a group of Corinthian women prophets who take more seriously and radically than Paul the claims of equality in the Spirit. For this reason they share in participatory worship, not waiting on one another to speak, prophesying

---

20. Some scholars have suggested that the Corinthians see Paul and Apollos as mystagogues who initiate the Corinthians into a new spiritual "wisdom." The Corinthians are identifying strongly with these teachers rather than with Christ, whom they teach. See Conzelmann, *I Corinthians,* 33–36.

unashamedly with heads uncovered. Perhaps also as part of their equality they have taken on celibacy as a way of denying the subordinating claims of males. Wire suspects that Stephanas may well represent Paul's less radical view of Christian freedom, at least in the Corinthian situation, and that Paul's injunction to attend to Stephanas goes along with the concern for order and decorum evident throughout 1 Corinthians 12–14.[21]

In addition to trying to gain credibility for his letter, Paul also had three other possible grounds for suggesting that Stephanas should be given special recognition. Any or all of these may be implicit grounds for his leadership. Stephanas does have a special tie to Paul. Stephanas was (with his household) the first convert in Achaia. Stephanas may be the host of a church that meets in his house. (The references to "households" may suggest, not just family, but a household of family, slaves, and attendants all meeting together in one house under the leadership of the householder.)[22]

We also note that Paul does not imply any hierarchical or exclusive prestige or authority for Stephanas. When urging "subjection" or "service" to Stephanas and his companions, Paul goes on to urge the same deference "to every one who works and toils with them."

1 COR. 5:1-5

It is actually reported that there is sexual immorality among you, and of a kind that is not found even among pagans; for a man is living with his father's wife. And you are arrogant! Should you not rather have mourned, so that he who has done this would have been removed from among you?

For though absent in body, I am present in spirit; and as present[23] I have already pronounced judgment in the name of the Lord Jesus on the man who has done such a thing.[24] When you are assembled, and my spirit is present with the power of our Lord Jesus, you are to hand this man over to Satan for the destruction of the flesh, so that his spirit may be saved in the day of the Lord.

---

21. Antoinette Clark Wire, *The Corinthian Women Prophets: A Reconstruction through Paul's Rhetoric* (Minneapolis: Fortress Press, 1990), 179.

22. See Meeks, *First Urban Christians,* 75–76.

23. This is a better translation than the NRSV's "as if present," which misreads the conditional. See Meeks, *First Urban Christians,* 128.

24. The sentence should perhaps be translated, "I have already pronounced judgment on the man who has done such a thing in the name of the Lord Jesus." See NRSV margin. If this is correct, the incestuous man is living out of a disastrous misunderstanding of Christian freedom. See further my discussion of the article by Adela Collins, below.

Wayne Meeks reminds us that what we have here is not Quaker consensus or a free-church congregational meeting to vote on the appropriate discipline for the offender: "Paul's directive about the assembly is hardly a limitation of his apostolic authority in deference to a more democratic polity. It is more nearly the opposite. In the decision of the assembly, about which he allows no doubt, it will become apparent to the Corinthian doubters that the apostle's physical absence makes no difference."[25]

What we do have is again a balance among Christ's authority, the apostle's authority, and the role of the congregation. As in Paul's admonition to the Corinthians to be of one mind, so here he announces that the judgment he pronounces on the incestuous man is not based on his own authority but is pronounced "in the name of the Lord Jesus." And the sentence is to be carried out "with the power of our Lord Jesus."[26] It is also clear, however, that it is the apostle who pronounces Christ's sentence, and here Paul does not beseech, suggest, or plead. He gives orders. In his word and in the Spirit he will be present for the judgment. Even from a distance, he can still be Christ's ambassador. In a clearly subsidiary way, then, the congregation performs the judgment the apostle announces. There is no room here for advice and consent. There is room only for obedience. Many times Paul exhorts, begs, as a kind of elder brother in Christ. Here he commands as a stern father.[27]

I am persuaded by Adela Collins that the hope that Paul expresses is not hope for the redemption of the spirit of the believer but for the reign of the Spirit in the community. The possessive pronouns of the NRSV translation are not found in the Greek text. A more neutral translation of the passage helps explain the connection to the verses that follow:

> When you are assembled, and my spirit is present with the power of our Lord Jesus, you are to hand this man over to Satan for the destruction of the flesh, so that the Spirit might be saved in the day of the Lord. Your boasting

25. Meeks, *First Urban Christians,* 128. See also Conzelmann, *I Corinthians,* 97.

26. Whatever else the "sentence" may imply it certainly includes excommunication. See Luke T. Johnson, *Decision Making in the Church: A Biblical Model* (Philadelphia: Fortress Press, 1983), 40.

27. In the Letter to Philemon, Paul seeks to maintain a balance between request and command, the brotherly and the fatherly injunctions: "Accordingly, though I am bold enough in Christ to command you to do what is required, yet for love's sake I prefer to appeal to you..." (Philemon 8, 9).

is not a good thing! Do you not know that a little yeast leavens the whole batch of dough? Clean out the old yeast so that you may be a new batch, as you really are unleavened. (1 Cor. 5:4b-7a)[28]

Collins reminds us that the distinctions between "flesh" and "spirit" for Paul are not usually distinctions between the faculties of the individual but represent orientations of the whole person or the community. Paul's concern, as the reference to leaven makes clear, is not for the soul of the offender but for the sanctity of the church. If they "destroy the flesh" by removing the incestuous man with his "fleshly" behavior from their midst, by excommunication, the Spirit under which the church lives will preserve the community for the final judgment, when Christ returns.[29]

In Collins's reading it is not only the behavior of the incestuous man that Paul condemns, but also a false version of Christian freedom. Reading with the NRSV's margin notes, she argues that the offender is actually living incestuously "in the name of the Lord Jesus." And the congregation, also misunderstanding Christian freedom, cheers him on. Hence Paul's warning: "Your boasting is not a good thing!"[30]

The clear note in this passage, therefore, is the note of apostolic authority, authority exercised not so much for the sake of the individual as for the sanctity and unity of the churches. As we shall see, everything we want to say about shared gifts and diffuse authority in the Pauline churches needs to be qualified by the one indisputable "structure" that Paul assumes. He assumes his right to speak authoritatively on the issues that the churches raise.

GAL. 2:1-10

Then after fourteen years I went up again to Jerusalem with Barnabas, taking Titus along with me. I went up in response to a revelation. Then I laid before them (though only in a private meeting with the acknowledged leaders) the gospel that I proclaim among the Gentiles, in order to make sure that I was not running, or had not run, in vain. But even Titus, who was with me, was not compelled to be circumcised, though he was a Greek. But because of false believers secretly brought in, who slipped in to spy on the freedom

28. Adela Y. Collins, "The Function of 'Excommunication' in Paul," *HTR* 73 (1980): 251–67. On the mistaken use of possessive pronouns, see p. 259.

29. Ibid., 263.

30. See ibid., 253.

we have in Christ Jesus, so that they might enslave us—we did not submit to them even for a moment, so that the truth of the gospel might always remain with you. And from those who were supposed to be acknowledged leaders [RSV: "reputed to be something"] (what they actually were makes no difference to me; God shows no partiality)—those leaders [RSV: "who were of repute"] contributed nothing to me. On the contrary, when they saw that I had been entrusted with the gospel for the uncircumcised, just as Peter had been entrusted with the gospel for the circumcised (for he who worked through Peter making him an apostle to the circumcised worked through me in sending me to the Gentiles), and when James and Cephas and John, who were acknowledged pillars [RSV: "reputed to be pillars"], recognized the grace that had been given to me, they gave to Barnabas and me [Gk. and RSV: "to me and Barnabas"] the right hand of fellowship, agreeing that we should go to the Gentiles and they to the circumcised. They asked only one thing, that we remember the poor, which was actually what I was eager to do.[31]

Paul's opponents in Galatia are apparently Judaizers. They want gentile converts to Christianity to take on at least some of the obligations of the Jewish law. It may be that the Judaizers have appealed to the Jerusalem apostles—Peter, James, and John—as authorities for their view. This would explain why Paul seems to argue in two rather different ways. On the one hand, he insists that he has the approval of the Jerusalem "pillars" for his mission. On the other hand, he insists that he does not need their approval, anyway.[32]

Paul, of course, believes in a law-free, or at least a circumcision-free, gospel for gentile converts. In making this claim he wants to insist on his independent authority but is apparently not quite able to do so. In his rhetoric he is extremely reticent to attribute any special legitimacy to the Jerusalem leaders.[33] They are those who were "*reputed* to be pillars*" (Gal. 2:9; RSV, better than the NRSV's "acknowledged pillars"). In verse 2 Paul refers to these Jerusalem leaders as "acknowledged leaders" (or "those who were of repute"), but by verse 6 he has qualified that claim: "And from those who were reputed to

---

31. At various places the RSV preserves better than the NRSV both the irony and the word order of the Greek text. It is not clear that "those who were supposed to be acknowledged leaders" is an adequate revision of "those who were reputed to be something" in Gal. 2:6.

32. See Hans Dieter Betz, *Galatians,* Hermeneia (Philadelphia: Fortress Press, 1979), 96. Betz's discussion of the whole passage is most instructive.

33. For Luke, in Acts, these would include the Jerusalem "apostles," but Paul, at least here, avoids this designation.

be something (what they were makes no difference to me; God shows no partiality)—those, I say, who were of repute added nothing to me" (RSV).

However, despite Paul's claims for independence, there is clearly an acknowledgment of the interdependence of the churches. To the extent that interdependence implies that Paul needs approval from the Jerusalem authorities, he acknowledges it very grudgingly. To the extent that interdependence implies that gentile churches should help the "poor" in the Jerusalem church, Paul acknowledges it gladly.

Of course, at least from Paul's standpoint, any claim of the Jerusalem leaders to authority ends when the gospel is threatened. By Paul's description, Peter denied the validity of the gospel by refusing to share table fellowship with gentile Christians, apparently under pressure from other Jerusalem Christians (Gal. 2:11-14).[34] The church is therefore not without structure, but the structures are informal and depend on mutual consent. For Paul, at least, they are always subservient to the command of the Lord and the demands of the gospel.

Paul's accounts of these three disputes in his letters give a fairly clear sense of the way he understands the role of authority and leadership in situations of church conflict. The primary authority is that of God or Christ or the Spirit. The church finds its identity as God's people, Christ's body. Paul believes that Christ continues to act and speak in the church and that it is the obligation of believers to attend to that acting and speaking.

Derived from the authority of Christ is the authority of the apostle as Christian leader. Paul acknowledges his own authority and that of Apollos gladly. In Galatians he acknowledges the authority of the Jerusalem "pillars" more grudgingly, but acknowledge that authority he does. He seems to understand the authority of the apostles and pillars as being roughly equal. The individual congregations are to acknowledge the authority of the apostle precisely because that authority is grounded in the gospel. Sometimes Paul seeks to exercise his authority by persuasion:

---

34. For an extended discussion of the lines of power in the early church as evidenced in the dispute between Paul and the Jerusalem leaders, see Bengt Holmberg, *Paul and Power: The Structure of Authority in the Primitive Church as Reflected in the Pauline Epistles,* ConBNT 2 (Lund: CWK Gleerup, 1978), 11–39. Holmberg perhaps justifiably takes Paul's view of the outcome more skeptically than I and sees the Jerusalem circle as having an implicit central authoritative role for the development of the early church—including Paul's mission. For another reading, see Betz, *Galatians,* 105–12.

a brotherly beseeching. Sometimes Paul seeks to exercise that authority by command: a fatherly insistence.

In the discussion of Stephanas and his household in 1 Corinthians 1 and 1 Corinthians 16 we see that individual local leaders were also emerging in the churches. Paul suggests that their authority was not self-evident, as was the apostles', but he urges the Corinthians to acknowledge that authority. There is no clear sense, however, that this authority is somehow derived from appointment by Paul or the other apostles. In that sense it does not represent nascent or actual hierarchy. In the reference to the assembly called to judge the incestuous man (in 1 Corinthians 5), Paul also makes clear that the congregation has authority, though here it is not the authority to make a decision but the authority to carry it out—in the Spirit.

Perhaps most important, the very *fact* of Paul's letters indicates the reality of the congregation's authority. Paul does not appeal just to church leaders or primarily to church leaders to validate his claims for the gospel. His appeal is consistently to his "brethren" or "brothers and sisters"—to the whole congregation. It is their assent he seeks, their growth he seeks to nurture, their faith that helps to validate his own apostleship. His letters, his appeals, are to the whole people of God to stand with him—and he believes with the gospel—in the disputes he seeks to adjudicate.

OFFICES IN THE PAULINE CHURCHES

I begin with the central claim and then will elaborate. There is no consistency in the names and descriptions of "offices" in the churches to whom Paul writes. Different churches apparently have different structures.[35] Perhaps this is because of the different needs and interests of the various congregations. Perhaps it is because each church tends to borrow its understanding of office, title, and function from its own society, from other associations in its community.

Among those who have responsibility for the local churches are those whom E. A. Judge calls Paul's "retinue"—those who travel with him and go from him to the churches. These associates apparently carry some of his own apostolic authority.[36] These helpers of Paul assist him

---

35. See Karl Kertelge, *Gemeinde und Amt im Neuen Testament* (Munich: Kösel-Verlag, 1972), 117–18.
36. See Edwin A. Judge, "The Early Christians as a Scholastic Community," *JRH*

in the writing of his letters. For instance, Paul writes 1 Corinthians with "our brother Sosthenes" (1 Cor. 1:1) and Philippians with Timothy (see Phil. 1:1; see also 1 Thess. 1:1; 2 Cor. 1:1; Philemon 1). The exact function of these co-workers in the writing of the epistles is not clear. For instance, in 1 Thessalonians where the salutation lists Paul, Silvanus, and Timothy, the letter begins as if all were involved in its message: "We always give thanks to God for all of you" (1 Thess. 1:2). In Philemon where the greetings are from Paul and Timothy, the message is apparently from Paul: "When I remember you in my prayers I always thank my God. . . . I, Paul, do this as an old man, and now also as a prisoner of Christ Jesus. I am appealing to you for my child, Onesimus" (Philemon 4, 9-10). In either case there is at least the implicit claim that something of the authority of the apostle to give directions to the church also extends to Paul's colleagues.

Furthermore, Paul's associates sometimes serve as apostles from the apostle. He sends them to provide direction and sustenance in his stead. He sends them to bring back news of the churches. Timothy especially has this role of surrogate for the apostle: "I hope in the Lord Jesus to send Timothy to you soon, so that I may be cheered by news of you. I have no one like him, who will be genuinely concerned for your welfare. All of them are seeking their own interests, not those of Jesus Christ. But Timothy's worth you know, how like a son with a father he has served with me in the gospel" (Phil. 2:19-22). Here we note that Paul sends Timothy with his own authority but cannot simply assume that authority without arguing for it. Timothy is to be heeded, first, because he is a person of worth as the Philippians should themselves acknowledge. He is to be heeded, second, because of his special, filial relationship to Paul (see also 1 Thess. 3:1-2; and, on Epaphroditus, Phil. 2:25, 29-30).

In these passages we see clear evidence that Paul was accompanied by other Christians and that he hoped that some of his authority would also be theirs. Paul, however, does not simply assume that these leaders will be acknowledged by the churches but argues in each case for such acknowledgment. The claim that these leaders should be honored rests not only on the fact that they are Paul's fellow workers, but also on

---

1 (1960): 4–15, 125–37. "They [the retinue] remain under Paul's immediate control, and their authority in the enterprise is expressly derived from him" (p. 134). See also Meeks, *First Urban Christians,* 82.

their individual worth and the loyalty they have shown to the service of the gospel.

In addition to these companions of Paul who have some claim to authority and standing in the local congregations, it is clear that Paul acknowledges the role of local church leaders as well. In some cases the leaders Paul mentions are apparently the heads of households where house churches meet (or the heads of house churches that consist almost entirely of their own household). We have seen that Stephanas's claim to leadership in Corinth may rest not only on the fact that he and his household were the first converts in that area, but also on his role as the head of a household and quite possibly of a house church (see 1 Cor. 1:16; 16:15-18).[37] It is also noteworthy that his authority is apparently not self-evident to the Corinthians (even to those who meet in his house?) because Paul has to argue for it (1 Cor. 16:18).

In this same chapter of 1 Corinthians we see that Aquila and Prisca were apparently also considered church leaders, in part because the congregation gathered in their house (presumably in Ephesus; see 1 Cor. 16:8). We note that here at least no distinction is made between the male and female house church leader: "The churches of Asia send greetings. Aquila and Prisca, together with the church in their house, greet you warmly in the Lord" (1 Cor. 16:19). Assuming that Romans 16 is an original part of that epistle, then Prisca and Aquila have become hosts of a congregation in their house at Rome (Rom. 16:3-5a; similarly Philemon and Apphia in Philemon 1-2).

While the evidence is not conclusive, scholars suggest that it is likely that the Pauline churches, for all their equality in the Spirit, nonetheless reflected something of the social structure of their time. Heads of households and of house churches were quite likely those Christians who were wealthy enough to house and feed Paul or other missionaries on their visits to Hellenistic towns. Along with that patronage quite likely went a certain authority. And it would not be surprising if those who had positions of leadership in a household, a guild, or a community were acknowledged as having particular authority in the church as well.[38]

There are also obviously local church leaders whose authority does

---

37. See also Meeks, *First Urban Christians,* 78, 118, 119.

38. Judge, "Early Christians," 7; see also idem, *The Social Pattern of Christian Groups in the First Century: Some Prolegomena to the Study of New Testament Ideas of Social Obligation* (London: Tyndale Press, 1960), esp. chap. 5. For a somewhat different

not derive from their role as the head of households where house churches met. Wayne Meeks's comment, however, provides a proper cautionary note:

> Acts and the Pauline letters make no mention of formal offices in the early Pauline congregations. This fact is striking when we compare these groups with the typical Greek or Roman private association. The clubs' inscriptions show a positive exuberance in the awarding and holding of offices, which, as we saw earlier, commonly imitated those of city government. We find nothing comparable when leading roles in the Pauline congregations are mentioned.[39]

In 1 Thess. 5:12-13, Paul again exhorts the Christians to give proper credence to their leaders: "But we appeal to you, brothers and sisters, to respect those who labor among you, and have charge of you [perhaps, 'care for you'] in the Lord and admonish you; esteem them very highly in love because of their work. Be at peace among yourselves." Here quite clearly the participles ("labor," "have charge of" [or "care for"], "admonish") refer to the functions of the leaders rather than their titles. The functions are in part pastoral and in part supervisory. The participle *proistamenous,* which the NRSV translates "have charge of you," is used in the nominal form in Rom. 16:2, where Phoebe is a *prostatis.* The NRSV translates that term as "benefactor." Perhaps some combination of care and authority is suggested in 1 Thessalonians. Abraham Malherbe, however, reminds us how new the congregation is and suggests that it is diverse functions of caring within the community, not distinct offices, that Paul has in mind.[40]

My suspicion is that the next admonition is for the church leaders and further specifies their functional responsibilities: "And we urge you, brothers, to admonish the idlers, encourage the faint hearted, help the weak, be patient with all of them" (following the NRSV's marginal note) (1 Thess. 5:14). (Then the next verse includes leaders and followers alike: "See that *none of you* repays evil for evil.")[41]

---

analysis that still acknowledges the role of patronage, see Theissen, *Social Setting,* 54–57, 87–91.

39. Meeks, *First Urban Christians,* 134.

40. Abraham Malherbe, *Paul and the Thessalonians* (Philadelphia: Fortress Press, 1987), 88–89.

41. Malherbe (ibid., 89), however, thinks the references to "brothers" imply an address to the whole congregation.

In Phil. 1:1, however, uniquely in the indisputably Pauline letters, we have reference to "officers" if not to "office." "Paul and Timothy, servants of Christ Jesus, to all the saints in Christ Jesus who are at Philippi, with the bishops [or 'overseers,' *episkopoi*] and deacons [or 'ministers,' *diakonoi*]." Unfortunately the rest of Philippians gives us virtually no clues to the functions or authority of these leaders.

In Phil. 4:2-3, Paul states: "I entreat Euodia and I entreat Syntyche to agree in the Lord. And I ask you also, true yokefellow, help these women, for they have labored side by side with me in the gospel together with Clement and the rest of my fellow workers, whose names are in the book of life" (Phil. 4:2-3; RSV). Are the *episkopoi* and *diakonoi* represented in part by Euodia, Syntyche, the yokefellow, Clement, and the fellow workers? If so, their authority (like that of Timothy) seems to derive in part from the fact that they have been Paul's co-workers. But we have no evidence whether such "bishops and deacons" were elected by the congregation, appointed by the apostle, or chosen in some other way.[42] We also have no evidence that the terms "bishop" and "deacon" represent set offices, with particular requirements and hierarchical legitimacy. If 1 Thessalonians and the images in 1 Corinthians and Romans (see below) are any guide, we can guess that Paul still sees leadership functionally more than officially, but we cannot know this for sure.

Paul makes no further reference to *episkopos* (or *episkopē,* governance, oversight) in his epistles, but the term *diakonos* (deacon or minister) does occur frequently. In 2 Cor. 3:6, Paul says that he and others (his fellow true apostles?) acknowledge that "[God] has made us competent to be *diakonoi* of a new covenant, not of letter but of spirit; for the letter kills, but the Spirit gives life." In 1 Cor. 3:5, Paul and Apollos are *"diakonoi* through whom you came to believe, as the Lord assigned to each." In 2 Corinthians, Paul also contrasts true apostles, who are *diakonoi* of God, with false apostles, who are *diakonoi* of Satan—disguised as *diakonoi* of righteousness or of Christ (see 2 Cor. 6:4; 11:15, 23).

All these Pauline texts help support John N. Collins's argument

---

42. Raymond Brown guesses that such local officials were appointed by the apostle, but he acknowledges that this is a guess. See Raymond A. Brown, *"Episkopē* and *Episkopos,"* in *TS* 4, no. 2 (1980): 329.

that in the Hellenistic world the *diakonos* was not primarily a servant and certainly not primarily a servant at table. The *diakonos* was primarily an intermediary, one entrusted with a message or a commission by another. In 2 Corinthians, Paul explicitly applies the term to himself as a spokesperson for God and for the gospel.[43] By extension we can presume that "deacons" for Paul were also intermediaries, sometimes intermediaries for him and his authority, more often those who were entrusted with the gospel, its proclamation, and its responsibilities.

In 1 Cor. 16:15, Paul states that Stephanas and his household have "devoted themselves to the *diakonia* of the saints." This may mean that like Paul they are spokespersons for the gospel. Further, we have already suggested that Stephanas may serve as an emissary between Paul and the Corinthian congregation.[44] In Rom. 16:1-2, Phoebe is a *diakonos*—either a deacon or a minister. Again we are not sure what the title implies (if it is a title). Phoebe is commended for two things: helping others, and helping Paul. If John Collins is right, her ministry consists primarily in her role as an emissary.[45] It is also likely that Phoebe has been a patroness of the Christians as well as a helper and emissary, and perhaps also a benefactor of Paul. (The noun translated "helper" comes from the same root as the participle in 1 Thess. 5:12 where Paul exhorts the Thessalonians to honor those leaders who "help" them or perhaps "have charge of" them.)[46]

Returning to the "deacons" of Phil. 1:1, it seems likely that the term is used more regarding a function than an office. What is less clear is whether the deacons, like the apostles and like Phoebe, serve as subordinates and emissaries to the gospel or whether they are subordinates and emissaries, go-betweens, for the overseers. If the former is the case, then "bishops" and "deacons" may represent different functions—possibly administrators and proclaimers; possibly local leaders and visiting messengers. Those who serve those functions may also have roughly equal

---

43. John N. Collins, *Diakonia: Re-interpreting the Ancient Sources* (New York and Oxford: Oxford Univ. Press, 1990), 198. On the larger background, see esp. 78–79, 97–99, 335–37.

44. Ibid., 224.

45. Ibid., 224–25.

46. See Meeks, *First Urban Christians,* 60, and the material by Judge cited therein. On Phoebe as "minister," not "deaconess," see Schüssler Fiorenza, *In Memory of Her,* 47–48, 169–70.

authority. If the latter is the case, then the "deacons" are functionally subordinate to those "bishops" they represent.[47]

What seems evident is that it is impossible to assign any clear meaning to the term *episkopos* and that the term *diakonos* is used in diverse, interrelated ways. Sometimes the *diakonoi* are distinguished from the apostles, but sometimes the apostles are themselves deacons, servants, ministers; put another way, sometimes what makes deacons deacons is precisely that they are sent, like apostles, with a commission.

It is clear that other leaders beside the apostles had authority and provided service in the Pauline churches. However, there is scant evidence that these leaders could rightly be called officers and uncertain evidence that they even had titles. Their roles seemed to be largely functional: based on their leadership of the households where the churches met, or on their service to the members of the church, or on their relationship to Paul as fellow workers.

Nor do we know why Paul uses certain titles (or refers to certain functions) in his correspondence with one church and not with another. Why bishops only in Philippi? Why administrators (*kybernēseis*) only in Corinth (1 Cor. 12:28)? My guess would be that local churches derived the titles, or labels, for their leaders from other associations around them, but this plausible suggestion is by no means certain.[48] It is certain that Paul recognizes quite different structures for different congregations without any claim that one community should reorganize on the model of another.

What is not clear is how the authority of church leaders was legitimated. Were they appointed by the apostle? Were they chosen by the congregations? My sense in reading the material is that while Paul urges recognition of their authority, he does not claim the power to appoint these leaders. Rather he acknowledges their gifts and their service to the gospel, and he urges the church members to do the same.

---

47. Collins (*Diakonia*, 235–37) makes the latter interpretation, but it is not clear that his own book points most clearly in that direction.

48. See Judge, *Social Pattern*, 45, but see also Meeks, *First Urban Christians*, 79, for skepticism about our ability to make such connections. The most helpful list of references, especially on *episkopos*, may still be Lietzmann, "Zur altchristlichen Verfassungsgeschichte," esp. 96–101. His connections are all "pagan" rather than Jewish for *episkopos*.

IMAGES OF THE CHURCH IN PAUL

THE BODY OF CHRIST

Paul's images for the community, for the church, provide essential background for his understanding of leadership within the church. Certainly a predominant image is that of the church as the body of Christ. Paul develops this image in 1 Corinthians and in Romans.

1 Corinthians 12

The image is most fully developed in 1 Corinthians. The context for Paul's writing about the church as the body of Christ is the dispute over the issue of glossolalia. Some Corinthian Christians have received the gift of speaking in tongues, and it seems to Paul that they boast about that gift, setting themselves apart from their fellow Christians.[49] Paul does not deny the validity of the gift, but he does deny the appropriateness of the boasting.

In his argument against claiming tongue-speaking as a uniquely valid gift, Paul sandwiches his picture of the church as the body of Christ between two more general discussions of spiritual gifts in the church. In the first discussion the gifts seem to represent different functions within the community; in the second discussion they hint more at a development toward offices.

The pertinent discussion of spiritual gifts begins with 1 Cor. 12:4-11. In this passage Paul affirms the underlying unity of the church, but here it is the gift and presence of the Spirit rather than the image of the body that signify and cement that unity. Within the context of the discussion about speaking in tongues, Paul carefully concedes that speaking in tongues is a spiritual gift, but he puts it next to last on his list. Last, Paul mentions the interpretation of tongues. This follows logically after the mention of glossolalia and gives Paul a chance to suggest what he will later emphasize—that ecstatic speech needs to be interpreted if it is to be edifying. Not surprisingly the utterance of wisdom, the utterance of knowledge, and prophecy all appear earlier on the list than glossolalia. Wisdom, about which Paul shows considerable reticence in 1 Corinthians 1–2, is listed high among the gifts, but is still only *among* the gifts, not the ground of salvation.

---

49. Intriguingly, Antoinette Wire (*Corinthian Women Prophets,* 143) again attributes the glossolalia especially to women prophets; perhaps speaking in the tongues of angels is related to the angelic worship Paul seems to warn against in 1 Cor. 11:10.

The list of gifts here seems to be highly functional. People are designated by what they are empowered to do, not by any authority conferred either by the apostle, by any hierarchy, or by the congregation itself. There follows the image of the body itself:

> For just as the body is one and has many members, and all the members of the body, though many, are one body, so it is with Christ. For in the one Spirit we were all baptized into one body—Jews or Greeks, slaves or free—and all were made to drink of one Spirit.
>
> Indeed, the body does not consist of one member but of many. If the foot would say, "Because I am not a hand, I do not belong to the body," that would not make it any less a part of the body. And if the ear would say, "Because I am not an eye, I do not belong to the body," that would not make it any less a part of the body. If the whole body were an eye, where would the hearing be? If the whole body were hearing, where would the sense of smell be? But as it is, God arranged the members in the body, each one of them, as he chose. If all were a single member, where would the body be? As it is, there are many members, yet one body. The eye cannot say to the hand, "I have no need of you," nor again the head to the feet, "I have no need of you." On the contrary, the members of the body that seem to be weaker are indispensable, and those members of the body that we think less honorable we clothe with greater honor, and our less respectable members are treated with greater respect; whereas our more respectable members do not need this. But God has so arranged the body, giving the greater honor to the inferior member, that there may be no dissension within the body, but the members may have the same care for one another. If one member suffers, all suffer together with it; if one member is honored, all rejoice together with it.
>
> Now you are the body of Christ and individually members of it. (1 Cor. 12:12-27)

As he begins his discussion of the body of Christ, Paul links the image to two themes he has already presented. He links the unity in the body to the unity of the Spirit, and he links unity in Christ to his reminder in 1 Corinthians 1 that the Corinthians were baptized not into Apollos or Paul, but into Christ. "For in the one Spirit we were all baptized into one body" (1 Cor. 12:13a). Significantly, what Paul wants first of all to affirm is not the unity of the various gifts in Christ but the unity of all sorts and conditions of people: "we were all baptized into one body—Jews or Greeks, slaves or free." And then the tie to the Spirit again: "and all were made to drink of one Spirit" (1 Cor. 12:13b, 13c).

In verse 14, Paul goes on to insist on the unity of believers despite their different gifts, or because of their different gifts. All are part of

Christ's Body. Three essential claims are suggested by Paul's use of this image. First, Paul claims that the church lives only under and through the lordship of Christ. Here Christ is over against the church that is his body, unlike in Ephesians where Christ as the head of the church is very nearly identified with the community itself. In Corinthians, Christ is both in and over against the community of faith.[50] Second, Paul claims that the members of the church, with their various gifts, have no right to boast and no reason to be ashamed. All the different gifts are necessary to the body. Here Paul clearly attends to the danger that those who speak in tongues or those who claim special wisdom (see 1 Corinthians 1–2) will think that their gifts make them superior to their brothers and sisters, while those brothers and sisters will think of themselves as second-class Christians. Third, Paul claims that in the body of Christ, all Christians are interdependent. The exercise of one Christian's gifts depends on the gifts another Christian brings to the community. All church members, whatever their office or function, are servants of one another and ministers of Christ.

While the image of the body of Christ does not speak directly to the issue of leadership in the church, indirectly it is central to our understanding of Paul's thought. Rather than speaking of offices, appointments, or responsibilities, Paul speaks of gifts—given by the Spirit for the service of Christ and the sake of the body. While these gifts are distinguished by their function, they are not ranked either in value or in authority. In this image, at least, there is no sense that the church consists of its leaders, or that they are any more essential to its functioning than those whose gifts are quite different. To say that the image of the church is egalitarian would be perhaps to impose an anachronistic vision on Paul.[51] But for Paul the church is clearly interdependent, familial, and nonhierarchical. It lives by the Spirit for mutual service in the name of Christ.

Following the central image of the body of Christ, Paul turns to the

---

50. On this point see Ernst Käsemann, "The Theological Problem Presented by the Motif of the Body of Christ," in *Perspectives in Paul,* trans. Margaret Kohl (Philadelphia: Fortress Press, 1971), 102–21, and idem, "Das Interpretationsproblem des Epheserbriefes," in *Exegetische Versuche und Besinnungen* (Göttingen: Vandenhoeck and Ruprecht, 1964), 2:256–57.

51. Wire's book (*Corinthian Women Prophets*) in fact is an argument that Paul's "opponents," the Corinthian women prophets, are in many ways more "egalitarian" than he.

"outside" of his sandwich again, another list of the gifts or functions that the body of Christ includes:

> Now you are the body of Christ and individually members of it. And God has appointed in the church first apostles, second prophets, third teachers; then deeds of power, then gifts of healing, forms of assistance, forms of leadership, various kinds of tongues. Are all apostles? Are all prophets? Are all teachers? Do all work miracles? Do all possess gifts of healing? Do all speak in tongues? Do all interpret? (1 Cor. 12:27-30)

Hans von Campenhausen suggests that the first three gifts in this list (that is, those of being apostles, prophets, and teachers—the gifts indicated by the ordinals "first," "second," and "third") seem to be more "office-like," while the rest of the list is more "function-like." Granted that that distinction is more ours than Paul's, nonetheless the fact that these three are set apart may indicate that they were moving toward a more official, settled status than the rest.[52]

I have already discussed Paul's understanding of apostles. Prophets, in this context where Paul is discussing glossolalia, are clearly those who provide articulate speech for the worship of the community (see 1 Cor. 14:2-3). David Aune presents a helpful summary of "prophets" as we see them in Paul's writings:

> On the basis of 1 Cor. 12-14 it appears that prophets, or those who prophesied, were active only within the framework of Christian worship.... Although Paul conceptualizes those who prophesy at Corinth as "prophets" ...and regards prophets as holding a particular office in the church second only to apostles,...the view held by the Corinthians themselves is not clear. Undoubtedly Paul's conception of the prophetic role was primarily informed by OT models, though the same assumption cannot be made of the Corinthian Christians themselves. Paul regards "prophets" after apostles, as a divinely appointed role in the church.[53]

It is also clear that Paul saw the prophets' authority as being subservient to that of the apostles (especially his own). This is suggested

---

52. See Hans von Campenhausen, *Ecclesiastical Authority and Spiritual Power in the Church of the First Three Centuries,* trans. J. A. Baker (London: Adam and Charles Black, 1969), 60; Eduard Schweizer (*Church Order in the New Testament,* trans. Frank Clarke, SBT [Naperville, Ill.: Alec Allenson, 1961], 100) holds that the entire list is functional and charismatic, and downplays any distinction here between office and function.

53. David E. Aune, *Prophecy in Early Christianity and the Ancient Mediterranean World* (Grand Rapids, Mich.: Eerdmans, 1983), 196–97.

in the order of gifts in the list of 12:28: "God appointed first apostles, second prophets." This is made explicit at the end of 1 Corinthians 14 where Paul asserts that any true prophet will recognize Paul's own authority: "Anyone who claims to be a prophet, or to have spiritual powers, must acknowledge that what I am writing to you is a command of the Lord. Anyone who does not recognize this is not to be recognized" (1 Cor. 14:37-38).[54] What is not clear is whether the prophets received any official acknowledgment from the local church. (Were they designated as prophets or did they simply prophesy?) Nor is it clear whether these prophets were local figures or itinerant, like the apostles.

Teachers are mentioned only in this paragraph in Paul, so we really have no context by which to decide how he understood their function. (There may be a parallel in Rom. 12:7 where "the teacher" is to use that charism "in teaching.") A sheer guess would be that unlike the apostles (and prophets?), teachers were local leaders, and it *may* be that while the prophets spoke oracles, the teachers interpreted tradition. We simply do not know.

After these three offices comes the list of functions, which includes those who are *kybernēseis* (literally "helmsmen," probably "administrators"). Whether those with this gift are in any way related to the *episkopoi* (overseers or bishops) of Phil. 1:1 there is no way to know. Last, of course, are speakers in "various kinds of tongues" (1 Cor. 12:28).

Again what we see is a fairly fluid understanding of church leadership, marked by gifts as well as responsibilities. The line between office and function may be there, but if so it is fuzzy, and the distinctions are not easy to draw. Apostleship is the first gift listed, and the implication here as elsewhere is that special authority accrues to the apostle. Beyond that the relationship between gift or function and authority is far from clear. What follows in 1 Corinthians 13 suggests that all gifts, functions, and offices are qualified and motivated by *agapē,* or they are not properly Christian at all.

Romans 12

The image of the body of Christ is developed far less fully in Romans than in 1 Corinthians. The discussion comes toward the beginning of the parenetic chapters of this letter. In Romans, Paul introduces himself

54. See ibid., 205.

and his gospel to a congregation he did not found. In chapters 12 to 15, he writes of the implications of living out God's righteousness for faithful people, and in chapter 12 he writes especially about the faithfulness within the Christian community. It may also be that he writes for churches comprised of both gentile and Jewish Christians, and certainly for a church of mixed social background. Therefore, the issue of getting along with one another has daily implications:[55]

> For by the grace given to me I say to everyone among you not to think of yourself more highly than you ought to think, but to think with sober judgment, each according to the measure of faith that God has assigned. For as in one body we have many members, and not all the members have the same function, so we, who are many, are one body in Christ, and individually we are members one of another. We have gifts that differ according to the grace given to us: if prophecy, in proportion to faith; ministry, in ministering; the teacher, in teaching; the exhorter, in exhortation; the giver, in generosity; the leader, in diligence; the compassionate, in cheerfulness. (Rom. 12:3-7)

The lordship of Christ is less emphasized here than in 1 Corinthians, though the opening sentences are again a warning against boasting and perhaps implicitly a warning against self-deprecation.

What does seem clear is that the gifts are defined more in terms of function rather than in terms of office. Paul speaks of "prophecy," not prophets. "The one who teaches" (as in the RSV) is really a better translation of Paul's terms than "teachers." Serving, contributing, aiding, and showing mercy are gifts of the Spirit as much as prophecy and teaching.[56]

We can guess why the Corinthian interest in offices has here disappeared. Paul has not been to Rome, so he may have no clear understanding of the structure of that congregation. He did not found the Roman church; he is not their apostle as he is the apostle to the Corinthians; so to stress the importance of apostleship would perhaps be inappropriate. (Paul begins 1 and 2 Corinthians with the self-designation: "Paul, an apostle ... "; in Romans he begins: "Paul, a servant of Jesus Christ, called to be an apostle. ... ")

---

55. See Lampe, *Die stadtrömischen Christen,* 63–65.

56. On the whole the RSV captures better than the NRSV the fact that these descriptions are participial phrases, not titles of offices: "the one who teaches"; "the one who exhorts"; "the one who gives"; "the one who leads," or, as in the RSV, "he who gives aid."

However, though the gifts here are not really offices, they are not simply functions, either. They are more like "virtues" (giving aid with zeal, doing acts of mercy with cheerfulness), rather as the "higher gifts" in 1 Corinthians prove to be not even apostleship, but faith, hope, and especially love. Here even more than in 1 Corinthians the image of the church cuts against any authoritative or hierarchical picture of church leadership. The church is an interdependent community marked not by a variety of powers, but by a variety of gifts. The gifts are not so much diverse functions or abilities; they are marks of the diverse character of faithful Christian persons.

MINISTRY BY MERCY: 2 COR. 4:1-6

A different image appropriate to Paul's understanding of ministry emerges from 2 Corinthians. Here it is not the picture of the body but the contrast between darkness and light that is central:

> Therefore, since it is by God's mercy that we are engaged in this ministry, we do not lose heart. We have renounced the shameful things that one hides; we refuse to practice cunning or to falsify God's word, but by the open statement of the truth we would commend ourselves to the conscience of everyone in the sight of God. And even if our gospel is veiled, it is veiled to those who are perishing. In their case the god of this world has blinded the minds of the unbelievers, to keep them from seeing the light of the gospel of the glory of Christ, who is the image of God. For we do not proclaim ourselves; we proclaim Jesus Christ as Lord, and ourselves as your slaves for Jesus' sake. For it is the God who said, "Let light shine out of darkness," who has shone in our hearts to give the light of the knowledge of the glory of God in the face of Jesus Christ. (2 Cor. 4:1-6)

The *diakonia,* ministry, to which Paul here refers is his own apostleship, which he defends against the charges of his detractors. We shall ask farther on how far Paul's apostleship can be a model for other forms of ministry, including contemporary ministry.

What is striking in this passage is that what makes ministry possible is not Paul's gifts, not charisma or charismata, but mercy, the same reality that brought Paul to faith and to his mission in the first place. The closest parallel is not 1 Corinthians 12 or Romans 12 but Gal. 1:13-16, where Paul attributes his *call* to God's grace. In the passage from 2 Corinthians, because the apostle receives ministry out of mercy, even talk of spiritual gifts seems inappropriate. He knows the Corinthians are capable of boasting of their gifts, gifts though they be. One can take pride in being gifted and be praised as charismatic. But in God's mercy one dare not boast. In this context the responsibility of the apostle is to proclaim the mercy he has received clearly, directly, and truthfully.

The apostle is a servant, a *doulos,* in two ways. First, he is a servant of the mercy he has received. Second, he is a servant of the community to whom he declares that mercy: "For we do not proclaim ourselves; we proclaim Jesus Christ as Lord and ourselves as your slaves for Jesus' sake" (2 Cor. 4:5). Creation is renewed by the new creation. The light that shone at the beginning is outshone by the light of God in the face of Christ. This light brings the apostle—and those who hear the apostle—out of darkness. Although here Paul is not discussing the whole range of gifts within the congregation, it is clear that he understands apostleship not only as gift but as mercy. It is a redemptive sign of the new creation that God provides in Jesus Christ. To be a minister of that mercy is to be devoted to the service of God and to the service of God's people: a minister of light.

Again what emerges from our discussion of these central images of the church is that for Paul leadership is primarily a matter of God's mercy and secondarily a matter of the gifts God has given. Church members are distinguished more by their functions, and even by their virtues, than by their offices—though it is clear that apostleship carries "official" weight and that prophecy and teaching may do so as well. So, too, perhaps, the "bishops" and "deacons" of Phil. 1:1. Those who exercise the various gifts are not, apparently, appointed by the apostle or elected by the congregation. Their gifts are recognized as they are exercised.

While there are hints of priority in Paul's understanding of gifts (apostles first and speakers in tongues last), there is no sense of hierarchy or even superiority. What is stressed is the interdependence of all Christian people. Even apostles are appointed to be servants of other Christians; and all Christians are called to serve one another and to upbuild the community.

THE PAULINE CHURCHES AND MINISTRY TODAY

We are left with some impressions and some questions for further consideration:

1. Radical Lutherans like Käsemann and loyal Baptists like me often look back with longing to the charismatic, "lay," almost egalitarian

churches to which Paul wrote. And there can be no doubt that they lived under the Spirit with a freedom and flexibility that are both a challenge and a judgment on our more structured churches and ordered ministries today. Nonetheless, we need recall that the charismatic church functioned as well as it did (and how well was that?) not only because of the pressure of the eschaton but also because of the authority of the apostle. Within local church communities there was apparently considerable flexibility in terms of leadership and structure, but Paul at least assumed that the churches to whom he wrote needed to acknowledge some clear authority—namely his own. (Or in the case of Corinth, also that of Apollos.)

2. In Paul's letters, however, we do get a picture of the church that is quite different from that suggested by Acts, say, or the Pastorals, or most of our church structures today. Ministry was by charism rather than education or appointment. There was a strong stress on the interdependence of all Christians and the interrelatedness of all forms of "ministry." All forms of ministry, including apostleship, were seen above all as servant ministries, and all existed for the sake of the gospel and for the upbuilding of the church.

3. While there were both local and translocal leaders (apostles and perhaps prophets), it is not clear how these were related one to another, or how the local leaders were chosen. The apostles, at least in Paul's case, saw the risen Lord and were called to apostleship. Were the local officers appointed by the apostles? Chosen by the local congregation? Or were their gifts simply, informally, acknowledged? My guess is that the last option is closest, but it is also clear that Paul sometimes claimed authority for people who had been his fellow workers, and perhaps this association with the apostle counted toward leadership at the local level.

4. Clearly, in Paul's self-definition, there was particular stress on proclamation, preaching. While he distinguishes apostles from prophets in 1 Corinthians, his own self-understanding (see Galatians 1) seems derived in large measure from Old Testament prophets. We need to ask how the apostolic function of proclamation relates to other forms of *diakonia,* both in the first century and today.

5. While it is clear that Paul saw himself as an ambassador for Christ, the terms of his representation seem to be that he proclaimed the gospel. What is noticeably missing in Paul's self-designation and in his description of the churches to whom he wrote is any claim that the apostle or

any designated officer presides at the Lord's Supper. Even if there is a designated "president," the stress on the whole church as the body of Christ throws into doubt any claim that such an officer would somehow represent Christ over against (or to) the congregation. For Paul, Christ is both represented by—and over against—the whole community of faith, without exception.

Looking from Paul's day to our own we need to discern the times. Are we at a time in our history when the dangers of dissension, enthusiastic excesses, spiritual anarchy, or growing secularity call us to circle the ecclesiastical wagons? Or is this a different kind of crisis—if not the eschaton at least one of those eras when the church needs to be driven more by the call to mission than by the obsession with preservation? To put the question is to suggest our answer. In a time when the numbers and influence of mainline Catholic and Protestant ministry seem to be in decline, we are called not to consolidate, but to preach, teach, evangelize, and act with new passion and excitement. We need to ask what gifts the Spirit is calling forth to serve the church in our own era.

From a Pauline perspective, we will argue against any vision of ministry that sees ordained leadership as *the* constitutive mark of the church's life. Ministry lives for the service of the church as the church lives for the service of the gospel in the world. We start with the body and derive from that the functions of its members, not with official functionaries as if somehow the body derived its meaning from them.

We will call into question the claim that those who are ordained as priests or ministers should take to themselves the whole diversity of gifts that Paul thought belonged to the body of Christ. Why should any one person be expected or required to be equally adept at administration, preaching, pastoral care, spiritual healing, spiritual direction? More often the gift of leadership today lies in discerning and encouraging in each congregation the recognition and development of those gifts the Spirit distributes among us.

However, Paul recalls to us the centrality of proclamation in the mission and upbuilding of the church. When he puts apostleship first among the gifts, it is not the apostle as overseer or orderer he stresses, but the apostle as *diakonos,* intermediary between God and humankind, proclaimer of the word.

Under Paul's influence we will be wary of first- and second-class

Christian citizenship. If the table becomes a symbol of separation and not of unity, it is not the Lord's Supper that we eat—even if the separation is only between special Christians who can officiate at the sacraments and regular Christians who can only receive. If the pulpit lifts up the minister more than God's word, the minister is no longer mercied into ministry, but promoted. Such promotion is far from Paul's vision of his own ministry.

It is possible that the real slip toward Käsemann's "early catholicism" came not so much with ordination or official structure, but with the designation of a particular officer to preside at the Eucharist. May it not be here—with the sense that the mysteries are reserved for some Christians to officiate; or with the suspicion that some Christians represent Christ over against other Christians—that the church begins to lose something profound and essential in the Pauline vision of the body of Christ? At the least the gift of presiding at the table is a derivative gift, related to gifts of proclamation and direction. More radically, perhaps it is a gift given to all Christians to share in service at a meal where only Christ presides.

The question remains how we understand the apostolicity of ministry today in the light of Paul's apostleship—or whether the category is appropriate to our ministry at all. We shall see that Luke-Acts far more than Paul ponders the issue of the lines between the first apostles and later church leaders. Paul probably did not anticipate later church leaders, and when speaking of his contemporary fellow apostles his list is looser and different than that in Acts. If apostleship is service to the gospel and its proclamation, Paul surely opens the way for the continuation of apostolic ministry. If apostleship depends on the particular relationship to the risen Lord and the authority that went with it, then that structure did end with Paul's death or shortly thereafter.

If "apostolic" authority means that we clergy can take on ourselves the authority of the apostle to the Gentiles, as if our situation replicated his situation, our call his call, our zeal his zeal, our lives the cruciform shape of his life, then apostolic authority is dead and gone. If apostolic authority means, however, the authority of the gospel Paul received and declared and applied to the needs of churches, then such authority for our time inheres not in particular church leaders but in the body of Christ itself. Contemporary structures need to be found that will combine charisma with order, Spirit with structure. For our day as for Paul's, it is the Spirit we most need to affirm and pray.

Hearing Paul we will especially remember that the church serves the gospel and not the other way around. We are servants of a saving word for the sake of the world's redemption. When the church becomes the goal of God's grace and not the instrument of God's grace, we mistake the gospel and betray our call.

CHAPTER 3

Ministry in Matthew

THE CHURCHES BEHIND THE GOSPELS

The Gospels present special difficulties when we seek to understand the evangelists' visions of the church and its ministry and especially when we try to discern the nature of the actual churches for which the Gospels were written.

Following most students of the Gospels in recent decades, I presume that the Gospels were not written as Scripture for all time but as guides for particular first-century Christian communities with particular needs and concerns. However, because the Gospels provide that guidance by telling the story of Jesus and his first followers, we are left to infer from the telling of that story the circumstances of the churches for which the story is being told. My assumption is that what we find in the Gospels is there because it had meaning for the late first-century communities for which those Gospels were written. More than that, the stories and sayings of Jesus are shaped in such a way that they speak quite directly to the needs of late first-century churches. By seeing how the stories and sayings are shaped we can understand something of the practice, problems, and structure of those early churches. Yet our information comes always by indirection. Where and how is the evangelist shaping his story to fit the needs of the community he addresses?

An example helps to make the point. Both the Gospel of Luke and the Gospel of Matthew recount an occasion on which Jesus told the

parable of the Lost Sheep. In Luke 15:3-7, the story of the Lost Sheep
is a foretelling of the joy in heaven at the repentance of a sinner, and is
closely linked to the parables of the Lost Coin and the Lost (Prodigal)
Son. In Matt. 18:12-14, Jesus tells the same parable to the disciples as
part of their instruction to exercise loving pastoral care over Christians
who might go astray.[1] We can guess that the context in Luke (however
shaped by the evangelist) comes closer to Jesus' concern than does the
story in Matthew. Jesus was not particularly concerned with issues of
church discipline, but with the call to repentance and the proclamation
of God's mercy in his own ministry, as the kingdom drew near. Matthew, however, knew that the kingdom tarried and worried about how
the church could best reflect God's mercy and justice in the meantime.
Therefore, reading this parable in the context of Matthew's Gospel and
especially in the context of Matthew 18, we can draw inferences concerning the nature of the Matthean church and concerning Matthew's
fears and hopes for that community.

There is a further problem in seeking to discern the communities
behind the Gospels. Almost certainly each of the Gospels represents
the end product of a long and fairly complicated process. Jesus lived,
acted, preached, taught. After his death and in the light of his resurrection, Christians told stories about his ministry and recalled his teaching.
Because they believed that Jesus still lived, Christians reshaped the stories and the teachings in the light of the needs of their own time and
their own communities. Stories and teachings were collected and written down. Matthew, Luke, and John certainly had before them written
texts that they collated, edited, and shaped to show forth their own faith
and to speak to the perceived needs of their own congregations.

Each of the Gospels, therefore, contains layers of tradition that originated years or decades before the Gospels were written. In looking at
a given story or saying we wonder whether its special pertinence is for
the evangelist's community, or for some other community, or for some
earlier stage in a particular church's development. For instance, John 9
clearly speaks to the problem of Jewish Christians being excluded from
the synagogue. Is this still a problem for the community for which the
Gospel is shaped? In Matt. 10:6, Jesus sends the disciples only to "the
lost sheep of Israel," yet in Matt. 28:19 Jesus tells his followers to

---

1. On this see John R. Donahue, *The Gospel in Parable: Metaphor, Narrative, and
Theology in the Synoptic Gospels* (Philadelphia: Fortress Press, 1988), 17–18.

"make disciples of all nations," perhaps particularly "of all Gentiles." Does this represent a shift in the perspective of Matthew's community, as well as a shift from the perspective of Jesus' earthly ministry to his postresurrection lordship? We will need to attend to these questions as we look at those passages that suggest the vision and the reality of Matthew's and John's churches and at the reality of the churches for which Luke and Acts were written. At the same time we will assume, with good evidence, that John, Matthew, and Luke are skilled and careful editors and that they include what they include with good reason: that even kernels of older tradition not only show earlier aspects of the church's development but speak to the churches for which John, Matthew, and Luke write.

MINISTRY IN THE GOSPEL OF MATTHEW

I will examine Matthew's vision of ministry by raising for his Gospel the same questions I raised for Paul's letters. It will be immediately evident that the questions were raised particularly with Paul in mind, but by some reshaping of the categories we may be able to compare Matthew fruitfully with Paul.

1. What is the probable historical and social context out of which Matthew's Gospel arose?

2. What is Matthew's understanding of discipleship? (The appropriate substitute for our question about Paul and apostleship.)

3. How are conflicts settled (or how does Matthew wish they were settled) in the Matthean congregation?

4. What kinds of officers or leaders are discernible in the Matthean congregation? What are the grounds of their authority?

5. What images of the church predominate in Matthew?

MATTHEW'S HISTORICAL SITUATION

Among students of Matthew's Gospel, three major options are presented for Matthew's historical setting: (1) Matthew's church still sees itself as part of the Jewish community, an alternative synagogue with Jesus as Messiah. (2) Matthew's church has made a break with the Jewish synagogues, but the break is recent and the wounds still fresh. The Gospel is basically a Jewish-Christian document. (3) Matthew's Gospel was written for a church both of Jews and Gentiles; the break from the synagogue lies in the background of the Gospel, but it is old business.

The new business rests in the mission of a mixed church of Gentiles and Jews to spread the gospel—especially among the Gentiles.

Günther Bornkamm is among those who maintain that Matthew's Gospel reflects a discussion among Jewish alternatives. Matthew sees the church as a distinct option within Judaism, not as a break from Judaism:

> Only the most meagre beginnings of a real ecclesiology, centered in the Church as an independent, empirically circumscribed entity, are to be found in Matthew's Gospel. There is no similar number of ecclesiological concepts and words corresponding to the wealth of Christological titles and statements.... Also lacking are all signs of special offices, as they are to be found, for example, in an exactly graded hierarchical structure in the "rules for the sect" [i.e., for the Qumran community].... Matthew's Gospel confirms throughout that the congregation which he represented had not yet separated from Judaism. The Messiahship of Jesus and the validity of his teaching are therefore, as we have already seen, presented and defended throughout in the framework of Judaism, and in the saying in 23:34 ... the disciples are characterized only by Old Testament-Jewish expressions, as the prophets, wise men and scribes sent out by Jesus. The struggle with Israel is still a struggle within its own walls.[2]

Many of the essays in a collection edited by David Balch come to the same conclusion.[3] The authors use categories drawn from the social sciences to help place the Matthean community, but the conclusion most of them draw is not very different from Bornkamm's. Anthony J. Saldarini seems to write for the majority of the contributors:

> This study will look at the Matthean community and its spokesperson, the author of the Gospel of Matthew, as deviant Jews. They have been labeled deviant by the authorities and by many members of the Jewish community in their city or area. Sociologically the Matthean community is a fragile minority still identified with the Jewish community by others and still thinking of itself as Jews.[4]

2. Günther Bornkamm, "End Expectation and Church in Matthew," in Günther Bornkamm, G. Barth, and H. J. Held, eds., *Tradition and Interpretation in Matthew*, trans. Percy Scott, NTL (Philadelphia: Westminster Press, 1963), 39. Bornkamm does acknowledge in a footnote on that same page that "the congregation was not devoid of order and particular functionaries."

3. David Balch, ed., *Social History of the Matthean Community: Cross-Disciplinary Approaches* (Minneapolis: Fortress Press, 1991).

4. Anthony J. Saldarini, "The Gospel of Matthew and Jewish-Christian Conflict," in Balch, *Social History,* 38–67; the quotation is from 38.

What does come clear in some of these essays is that the assumption that Matthew's concern with a mission to the Gentiles could not have been shared by a messianic-Jewish congregation is much too facile. Alan F. Segal notes what any careful reader of Matthew must note: that Matthew, Matthew's Jesus, and presumably Matthew's community still hold Torah and Torah observance in very high regard. Segal further adduces evident enthusiasm for gentile converts among some first-century Jewish groups, arguing that Matthew's openness to the gentile mission does *not* contradict the possibility that Matthew and his community were still self-consciously Jewish.[5]

The second option is presented by O. Lamar Cope, who presents evidence both from his reading of individual texts and from his analysis of the "Jewish" way in which Matthew interprets Old Testament texts:

> Christians evidently were not members of Pharisaic synagogues, for Matthew seems to distinguish "their synagogues" as separate institutions. The separation is under way. Pharisaic Judaism has not won full sway over Judaism in Matthew's area. Thus Matthew must be placed in the context of the painful time of separation of the church from Judaism which is also reflected in John's gospel. Because the hostility is not unrelieved by some admiration of the Pharisees (see 23:2), it is possible that Matthew's situation is less close to full separation than that of John.[6]

Amy Jill Levine suggests that the distinctions we draw between Jewish Christians and Hellenistic or gentile Christians may not be as clear as we think.[7] Matthew's Gospel represents the movement from a preresurrection mission to Jews alone to a postresurrection mission to "all the Gentiles." The mission to the Gentiles does not negate the mission to the Jews but expands it. Those excluded from the kingdom are not defined ethnically but socially: it is hypocritical leaders, not the Jewish people, from whom God's vineyard is taken.[8] Implicitly Levine envisions a Matthean community that includes both Jews and Gentiles and that is distinguishable from the synagogue.[9]

5. See Alan F. Segal, "Matthew's Jewish Voice," in Balch, *Social History,* 3–37.

6. O. Lamar Cope, *Matthew: A Scribe Trained for the Kingdom of Heaven,* CBQMS 5 (Washington, D.C.: Catholic Biblical Association, 1976), 126–27.

7. Amy Jill Levine, *The Social and Ethnic Dimensions of Matthean Salvation History,* Studies in the Bible and Early Christianity 14 (Lewiston, N.Y.: Edward Mellen Press, 1988), esp. 28–29.

8. Ibid., esp. 186–87, 206–11.

9. See ibid., 271, 273.

The third option is represented by Jack Dean Kingsbury and by Wayne Meeks. In the background of Matthew's Gospel lies the separation from the synagogue, but the community itself is moving on. It is a mixed church of Jews and Gentiles, and it is intent on the mission to the Gentiles. Kingsbury puts the evidence this way: "If the real readers [of Matthew's Gospel] were living in close proximity to a strong Jewish community, they are not to be thought of as a 'splinter group' that was nevertheless a member of the Jewish league of synagogues. The place of the real readers was no longer within Judaism but outside it." Kingsbury then goes on to cite the "apartness" of the disciples from the Jewish community, the reference to "their" (the Jewish) synagogues, and "the apparent organizational autonomy of the community to which Matthew belonged."[10] Furthermore, Kingsbury argues that the evident support of Matthew for the mission to the Gentiles suggests that Matthew wrote for a church composed of Gentiles as well as Jews. The break is already made with Judaism, and the church is a new and self-consciously different community.[11]

Wayne A. Meeks would apparently also place the community at the time of the Gospel at some distance from its original very strong ties to the synagogue:

> Yet there are many indications in the First Gospel that the connections with organized Jewish communities cannot have been so close when the gospel was written. If the Matthean Christians once held such an optimistic view of their mission to the organized Jews in their town, they have long since become disillusioned. In a remark that betrays a distance quite as complete as John, they can speak of a story about the disciples' faking the Resurrection, a story "spread among the Jews until this day" (28:15). This gospel contains a rising theme, climaxing in the trial and passion narrative, of the alienation of "the whole people" from Jesus, their appointed Messiah.[12]

I would suggest that the evidence points to a situation for the Matthean community somewhere between option (2) and option (3). It is

10. Jack Dean Kingsbury, *Matthew as Story* (Philadelphia: Fortress Press, 1986), 127–28.

11. See ibid., 124.

12. Wayne A. Meeks, "Breaking Away: Three New Testament Pictures of Christianity's Separation from the Jewish Communities," in Jacob Neusner and Ernest S. Frerichs, eds., *To See Ourselves as Others See Us: Christians, Jews, "Others" in Late Antiquity* (Chico, Calif.: Scholars Press, 1985), 93–115; the quotation is from 112. See also Raymond E. Brown, *The Churches the Apostles Left Behind* (New York: Paulist Press, 1984), 129.

clear that Matthew's church is being opened to the mission to the Gentiles. That may be one reason Matthew writes his Gospel. It is not clear, however, that the stress on such a mission presupposes a major gentile component within the congregation itself. Furthermore, the very vehemence of the argument with the Jewish leaders (especially Matthew 23) suggests that while the separation is real it is also recent and painful. One does not argue so harshly against opponents nearly forgotten in the service of battles long ended. The polemic has all the power of a family feud.

I therefore suggest that Matthew's Gospel comes out of a Jewish-Christian context where the lines between the synagogue and the church are being drawn ever more sharply. Part of that distinction between church and synagogue may lie in the church's willingness, even obligation, to spread the true Torah, Jesus' Torah, to "all the nations," or "all the Gentiles," though we have learned from Alan Segal that an opening toward the Gentiles was also an option within Judaism.[13]

The shape of Matthew's church and of its leadership reflects both the church's background in the Jewish community and its attempts to differentiate itself from that community. It reflects the church's ties to Judaism and its increasing openness to Gentiles.

MATTHEW'S UNDERSTANDING OF DISCIPLESHIP

Concern with the nature and function of apostleship, a concern that is present in Paul, is missing in Matthew. The term "apostle" occurs only once, appropriately in a context where the twelve disciples are being "sent forth" on their mission. (Matthew apparently retains the root understanding of "apostle" in the verb *apostellō,* "I send.") "Then Jesus summoned his twelve disciples and gave them authority over unclean spirits, to cast them out, and to cure every disease and every sickness. These are the names of the twelve apostles . . . " (Matt. 10:1-2).

Central to Matthew's Gospel, however, is the term "disciple." As we read Matthew's Gospel, sometimes it seems quite clear that the disciples not only represent Jesus' earliest followers but are also "transparent" for Matthew's own church.[14] At other times the disciples seem rather to represent an earlier foundational time, now past. When the disciples do

13. Segal, "Matthew's Jewish Voice."

14. See Ulrich Luz, "The Disciples in the Gospel according to Matthew," in Graham Stanton, ed., *The Interpretation of Matthew* (Philadelphia: Fortress Press, 1983), 98–128.

seem to represent, point to, Matthew's own church members, it is not clear whether they are representatives of all Christians or of Christian leaders.[15]

The root meaning of the term "disciple," "one who learns," is surely significant for the use of this term in Matthew. In his classic essay on Matthew's Gospel, Günther Bornkamm shows how the concept of a "learner" in Matthew is like and unlike the disciples among the rabbis:

> Discipleship of Jesus does not arise on the basis of a free attachment to a teacher, but on the basis of a call to follow him which issues from Jesus. Jesus does not exercise authority over his disciples on account of his knowledge of the Torah, nor is he a means to the end of gaining a similar wisdom in the law. Further, the position of a *mathētēs* is not a preliminary stage, with the intention that the disciple himself shall become a *didaskalos* (teacher) (23:8ff.), but signifies a lasting relationship to Jesus.[16]

In his study of discipleship in Matthew, Michael J. Wilkins shows that up to the time of Jesus the Greek term *mathētēs* and the closely related Hebrew *talmidh* usually refer more loosely to an "adherent" or "follower" and not so narrowly to a "pupil." The nature of the discipleship depends on the qualities of the leader.[17] Two considerations, however, suggest that for Matthew the term "disciple" does carry particular connotations of "learner." First, as Wilkins suggests, after Jamnia the term "disciple" increasingly refers to the student of a rabbi, and it seems likely that Matthew is written in part in contrast to Jamnia or at least to the increasing strength of Pharisaism that Jamnia represents. Second, if it is true that the nature of discipleship, adherence, depends on the qualities of the leader, then in Matthew's Gospel above all others, Jesus *is* teacher, rabbi (see esp. Matt. 23:8).[18]

---

15. Paul Minear argues that usually the disciples represent the Christian leaders or scribes of Matthew's time. The crowds represent the larger group of Christian believers, and the Pharisees and scribes represent the leaders of those synagogues that competed with the Matthean communities. See Paul Minear, *Matthew: The Teacher's Gospel* (New York: Pilgrim Press, 1982), 11–12; see also idem, "The Disciples and the Crowds in the Gospel of Matthew," *ATR* Supplement Series 3 (1974): 28–44.

16. Bornkamm, "End Expectation," 40.

17. Michael J. Wilkins, *The Concept of Disciple in Matthew's Gospel: As Reflected in the Use of the Term "Mathētēs"* (Leiden: E. J. Brill, 1988), 11–125, summarized on 217.

18. Wilkins (ibid., 145–46) acknowledges the validity of Bornkamm's basic point about the distinction between Jesus' disciples and rabbinic disciples.

In seeking to understand Matthew's use of the term "disciple" it is helpful to contrast that with his use of terms like "little one" or "least of these" for believers and with his use of the term *ochlos* for the crowd or multitude. Sometimes the disciples are contrasted with the "little ones," as if the disciples represented Christian leaders overlooking their flock. Sometimes, however, the disciples are themselves the "little ones." In Matt. 18:1-6, Matthew apparently contrasts the disciples with the "little ones," who represent the community of faithful Christians. In Matt. 10:42, however, as Jesus sends out the twelve, he pronounces this blessing: "And whoever gives even a cup of cold water to one of these little ones in the name of a disciple—truly I tell you, none of these will lose their reward." It is the little one who is identified with a disciple in this passage, not the one who gives the water. Here those who are sent out are both disciples and little ones.[19]

Perhaps "little one" ("least of these"—see Matt. 25:40) is a term that can be used of all Christian believers. When a distinction is made between leaders and followers in the church, some believers are further designated as "disciples," that is as church leaders.[20]

There is again an apparent distinction between the disciples and the little ones in Matt. 18:10. Apparently referring to members of the community rather than its leaders, Jesus says to the disciples: "Take care that you do not despise one of these little ones; for, I tell you, in heaven their angels continually see the face of my Father in heaven." Here it seems evident that the disciples are those who have special responsibility for the larger community of little ones, almost as shepherds for a flock. The issue is further complicated by the Great Commission to the eleven, at the end of Matthew's Gospel:

> Now the eleven disciples went to Galilee, to the mountain to which Jesus had directed them. When they saw him they worshiped him; but some doubted. And Jesus came and said to them, "All authority in heaven and on earth has been given to me. Go therefore and make disciples of all nations, baptizing them in the name of the Father and of the Son and of the Holy Spirit, and

19. So Eduard Schweizer, "Matthew's Church," in Stanton, *Interpretation of Matthew,* 138, and with a slightly different approach, Günther Bornkamm, "The Authority to 'Bind' and 'Loose' in the Church in Matthew's Gospel: The Problem of Sources in Matthew's Gospel," in ibid., 89.

20. For a helpful (and compelling) discussion of "little ones" in Matt. 25:31-46, see O. Lamar Cope, "Matthew 25:31-46, 'The Sheep and the Goats' Reinterpreted," *NovT* 11 (1969): 32–44.

teaching them to observe all that I have commanded you. And remember, I am with you always, to the end of the age." (Matt. 28:16-20)

On the one hand, the term "disciple" is here clearly identified with the eleven, the twelve minus Judas, and not with the larger community of those who believed in Jesus. On the other hand, the eleven are told to go and "disciple" all nations, and this discipling apparently consists of baptizing and teaching believers to follow the commandments of Jesus.[21] Does the term "disciple" thus refer to the smaller circle of Jesus' followers, of church leaders, when it is used of the very earliest community, and does it then refer to all believers when Matthew speaks "transparently" of discipleship in his own time (cf. Matt. 13:52)?

The disciples are more consistently contrasted with the crowds or multitudes (*hoi ochloi*). It is not immediately clear whether the multitudes represent the larger community of believers or the community of potential believers, those to whom the gospel is to be proclaimed. The Sermon on the Mount provides a test case. Who are the disciples here, who are the crowds?

As the sermon begins, Matthew says of Jesus: "When Jesus saw the crowds, he went up the mountain, and after he sat down his disciples came to him. Then he began to speak, and taught them, saying..." (Matt. 5:1-2). We could interpret the text to mean either that the teachings of the Sermon on the Mount were intended for the disciples (either as all Christians or as Christian leaders) or that the teachings were intended for the disciples and the crowds as well.

As the sermon continues, in 5:19-20, there is the hint that Jesus' words may be intended especially for the disciples, and that the disciples represent Christian teachers of Matthew's own time: "Therefore, whoever breaks one of the least of these commandments, and teaches others to do the same, will be called least in the kingdom of heaven; but whoever does them and teaches them will be called great in the kingdom of heaven. For I tell you, unless your righteousness exceeds that of the scribes and Pharisees, you will never enter the kingdom of heaven."

Two phrases suggest that Jesus here addresses not just believers, but also believing teachers. For one thing the test is not only whether the listeners keep the commandments, but whether they keep them *and* teach them to others (see Matt. 28:20).[22] Furthermore, those who listen are

---

21. See Luz, "Disciples," 109.
22. However, Professor Werner Lemke pointed out to me that in Deut. 6:4ff. the

compared to the scribes and Pharisees, not just to faithful Jewish people but to the teachers, the leaders of those people. If like is compared to like, then the implication is: "Your righteousness as Christian leaders should exceed the righteousness of those Jewish leaders."

However, as the Sermon on the Mount ends, in Matt. 7:28, Matthew indicates that the crowds, not just the disciples, have been the (intended?) audience: "Now when Jesus had finished these things, the crowds were astounded at his teaching, for he taught them as one who had authority, and not as their scribes" (Matt. 7:28-29). Here the crowds are apparently Christian believers, or potential Christian believers, being called to separate from their (Jewish) scribes and to accept the authority of this new and greater teacher.

Though the evidence is diverse and somewhat ambiguous, I am inclined to see the "crowds" in Matthew's Gospel as distinguished both from disciples and from the "little ones." The crowds for the most part do not represent the Christian church and certainly do not represent its leaders. They represent those (largely Jewish) folk who show interest in the gospel and amazement at Jesus and who provide an opportunity for mission, explicitly in Jesus' time but implicitly in Matthew's time as well:

> Then Jesus went about all the cities and villages, teaching in their synagogues and preaching the good news of the kingdom, and curing every disease and every infirmity. When he saw the crowds he had compassion for them, because they were harassed and helpless, like sheep without a shepherd. Then he said to his disciples, "The harvest is plentiful, but the laborers are few; therefore ask the Lord of the harvest to send out laborers into his harvest." (Matt. 9:35-37)

Jesus then goes on to commission the twelve to go as apostles to spread the gospel—precisely, we should think, to these undecided "crowds" or "multitudes" (see also Matt. 20:31; 21:11).[23]

Counterevidence may perhaps be found in the accounts of the feedings in Matt. 14:19 and 15:33. In each case Jesus gives the bread and fish to the disciples, who then distribute them to the crowds. Whether

---

commandment to teach the law is given not just to leaders but to the whole people Israel. "And these words which I command you this day shall be upon your heart; and you shall teach them diligently to your children, and shall talk of them when you sit in your house" (Deut. 6:6-7; RSV).

23. Wilkins (*The Concept of Disciple,* 170) has very much the same interpretation of the role of the crowds in Matthew.

the scenes represent a foreshadowing of the Eucharist or an elaboration of the theme that Jesus is the great teacher who provides for the needs of the soul, there might be a hint here that the disciples represent those church leaders who share the meal with the flock, or the teachers who pass on the authoritative word to the believers who listen. It would again be possible, then, to see the crowds as those who wait to receive the words from the disciples, as sheep waiting for their shepherds.

So, too, in Matt. 23:1-12, the "crowds," who are addressed along with the "disciples," are perhaps included among those who are to call each other "brothers"—that is, they may represent the community of believers. Alternatively, the injunction in verses 1 to 3 to heed the words but not follow the deeds of the scribes and Pharisees may be addressed to the disciples and crowds—especially the crowds—while the disciples are particularly addressed in verses 8 to 12 with the reminder not to use or accept special titles.

Again confessing that our questions may not be Matthew's questions, we can now suggest this much: sometimes the term "disciple" refers to one of Jesus' original twelve or eleven companions, with a kind of historical interest, but more often it points ahead to Matthew's own day; sometimes "disciple" apparently becomes a term for all believers of Matthew's time; sometimes it seems to refer more narrowly to Christian leaders and teachers. "Little ones," "least of these," and other such phrases are used to connote Christian believers in Matthew's time; sometimes the disciples are included among such believers (leaders are after all church members as well); sometimes the disciples are distinguished from the little ones, as shepherds from a flock. "The crowds" or "multitudes" seem most often (but not exclusively) to represent potential believers—the folk who constitute a mission field, to be persuaded from their false scribes to the true Christian scribes.[24]

One further distinction in Matthew's description of the disciples may help us appreciate his understanding of the church and its leadership. Frequently, it seems, when Matthew wants to write specifically of Jesus' original followers, and through them to refer to church leaders of his own time, he refers to "the twelve disciples," not to "disciples" alone.

In Matthew 10, Jesus addresses the twelve disciples (here only also

---

24. For a discussion of the crowds and the disciples in Matthew 13, see J. Dupont, "Le point de vue de Matthieu dans le chapitre des parables," in M. Didier, ed., *L'Evangile selon Matthieu: Redaction et Theologie* (Gembloux: Editions J. Duculot, 1972), 221–60.

"apostles") as he sends them forth on their mission. The directions given may reflect some of the conditions of Jesus' time, but surely, too, Matthew 10 contains instructions for itinerant church leaders in Matthew's own time. Here the "twelve" disciples point ahead not to all Christian people, but specifically to a group of Christian leaders. (Matthew 10:1 and 11:1 frame this section, with their references to the "twelve disciples.")

In Matt. 19:28 the promise is that the disciples "will also sit on twelve thrones, judging the twelve tribes of Israel." Here clearly the reference is to a particular function of the smaller circle of disciples; it is contrasted with the more general promise to believers in 19:29. However, the reference to the twelve in these verses seems less transparent toward Matthew's own time. The twelve are here the original circle around Jesus, without the direct implications for later church leadership we find in Matt. 10:1—11:1. (See also the references in the passion narrative [26:14, 20, 47] and the passion prediction [20:17].) Matthew 20:24-28 and 28:16-20 are apparently directives for the activity of Christian leaders, not only of Jesus' time but of Matthew's time.

We can add to our study, therefore, the claim that when the disciples are designated as "twelve" or "eleven," the reference is not to the larger community of believers but to a smaller circle of leaders. Sometimes that smaller circle seems to include only the original circle around Jesus. Sometimes the references to the twelve seem to point toward church leaders in Matthew's own time. They are sent forth to proclaim the gospel, to baptize, and to teach. They are not to lord it over other folk but to be servants of all.

I have suggested that sometimes, at least, the disciples are distinguished from believers and from the multitude of those who need to hear the gospel. They are the shepherds Jesus would send to a flock; the teachers whose righteousness should exceed that of the scribes and Pharisees; the missionaries sent forth to make disciples of all nations. Sometimes the disciples represent Matthew's portrayal of the past; more often they are also transparent for leaders of his own time.

If this is the case, we can draw some preliminary conclusions about how Matthew saw church leadership. Such leadership includes "making disciples," which requires baptizing new believers and especially teaching Jesus' commandments to them. Leadership is often itinerant, supported by those among whom the gospel is preached. The goal of such leadership is often to bring those undecided for the gospel but interested (like the crowds of Matthew's Gospel) into the circle of faith. Those who engage in such leadership are not to be concerned with their own greatness but are to be servants of all, living in the light of Jesus' willingness to ransom his life for the sake of humankind.

We will test these hypotheses by looking at other aspects of church leadership as we find it adumbrated in the Gospel of Matthew.

RESOLVING CONFLICTS IN MATTHEW'S COMMUNITY

Matthew presents two central passages that suggest how disputes are to be resolved within the church of his time. The passages show striking resemblances in vocabulary but apparent differences in emphasis.

The first passage comes in Matt. 16:13-20, Matthew's version of the confession at Caesarea Philippi. Peter confesses that Jesus is "the Messiah, the Son of the living God" (Matt. 16:16).

> And Jesus answered him, "Blessed are you, Simon son of Jonah! For flesh and blood has not revealed this to you, but my Father in heaven. And I tell you, you are Peter, and on this rock I will build my church, and the gates of Hades will not prevail against it. I will give you the keys of the kingdom of heaven, and whatever you bind on earth will be bound in heaven, and whatever you loose on earth will be loosed in heaven." (Matt. 16:17-19).

Two questions arise: What are the implications of Peter's special status here? And what does it mean that what Peter binds and looses on earth is bound and loosed in heaven?

Along with many other commentators, Günther Bornkamm assumes that this passage represents a creation of Matthew or of the Christian community some time after Jesus' resurrection and probably after the death of Peter as well. Its concern is not primarily with the historical Peter (who did not obviously exercise any such authority in the early church) but with Peter as foreshadowing the role of church leaders in Matthew's own time. Peter may well be honored by the Matthean community, but he is honored as one who provides a model for contemporary church leadership. Here is how Bornkamm explains the passage:

> The authority bestowed on Peter, therefore, no longer refers simply to the Torah, but to the commandments and the teachings of Jesus, even though, as the one with "binding" and "loosing" authority, Peter is described as a kind of "supreme rabbi." From this we may conclude that the conferring on Peter of the authority to "bind" and to "loose" must be understood as an "ideal"

scene containing traces of the beginning of a special Christian *halakah* in which we see the founding of the Church on Peter as the guarantor and authorized interpreter of Jesus' teachings.[25]

Bornkamm therefore sees Peter as representative of later church leaders and the power to bind and loose as being the power to interpret the teachings of Jesus authoritatively.

In the same volume of essays, however, Ulrich Luz sees Peter in this passage as representing all church members of Matthew's time, and the authority to bind and loose as being the power of forgiveness that Christians provide for one another. In his reading, Luz draws on the close relationship between this passage and Matthew 18, which I shall discuss below.[26]

Peter in the New Testament, an ecumenical study edited by Raymond E. Brown, Karl P. Donfried, and John Reumann, admits that the relationship between the authority given Peter in Matthew 16 and that given the circle of disciples in Matthew 18 is puzzling:

> The reader will see how difficult it is to decide whether the power of the keys promised to Peter in Matt 16:19 is exactly the same as the power of binding and loosing promised to him in the same verse—and also whether the power of binding and loosing associated with Peter, the rock on whom the church was to be built, is in all aspects the same power to be exercised by the disciples in Matt 18:18, where the context is one of dealing with recalcitrant Christians.[27]

We can raise our two questions more explicitly. Does Peter in this passage foreshadow the church leaders of Matthew's time or does he foreshadow all members of the community? Is the power he is given the power to interpret Jesus' new Torah, or the power to forgive sins?

25. Bornkamm, "Authority," 94. Here see also F. W. Beare, *The Gospel according to St. Matthew* (San Francisco: Harper and Row, 1981), 354.

26. Luz, "Disciples," 108. In his Sprunt Lectures at Union Theological Seminary in Virginia in 1990, Luz seemed to shift to the claim that the word about Peter as the rock is a late logion that does provide particular legitimacy for Peter as one of the apostles (but hardly as a bishop) and that the function of the keys has more to do with teaching authority than with forgiveness. Luz was kind enough to share the typescript of his lectures with me; I hope they will soon be in print. Wilkins (*The Concept of Disciple,* 183) thinks that the episode with Peter reflects a situation in Jesus' ministry and that Matthew uses Peter also as an example for later Christians.

27. Raymond E. Brown, Karl P. Donfried, and John Reumann, eds., *Peter in the New Testament* (Minneapolis: Augsburg, 1973), 100.

The answer to the first question depends in part on how we read the function of Peter throughout Matthew's Gospel. I have suggested that sometimes the disciples seem to be "transparent" to later Christian leaders and sometimes transparent to the whole Christian community of Matthew's time. So, too, it would seem with Peter. On the one hand, Peter is clearly among those who are designated as "the twelve apostles" and sent out on the special mission of Matthew 10. Here he prefigures not all later Christians but those with special teaching and missionary responsibilities. On the other hand, when Jesus calls Peter to come to him across the water and Peter begins to sink, Jesus says to him: "You of little faith, why did you doubt?" (Matt. 14:31). Here Peter represents the sometimes failing faith of all believers, not just of Christian leaders.

In the particular context of the confession at Caesarea Philippi it would seem that Peter is being singled out by Matthew not only from the general company of believers but also from the smaller circle of the disciples. The affirmation "You are Peter [the rock], and on this rock I will build my church" (Matt. 16:18) is probably not the assertion of Petrine primacy in an official hierarchy, but it does suggest that Peter represents someone or something other than the church itself. Bornkamm's argument here seems more plausible than that of Luz. Peter points not to the church as a whole but to its leaders. Furthermore, for the Matthean church he remains, for all his wavering, first among equals—a representative, almost prototypical leader.[28]

The second question, the meaning of binding and loosing, may best be answered after we attend to the similar passage in Matthew 18, but here at least it is striking that we have some contrast to Matt. 16:19 in Matt. 23:13. "But woe to you, scribes and Pharisees, hypocrites! For you lock people out of the kingdom of heaven. For you do not go in yourselves, and when others are going in, you stop them."[29] In Matthew 23 the issue seems not to be who can forgive sins but who has correct teaching, who can interpret Torah. The scribes and Pharisees do not have the keys to the kingdom. They are locked out. Peter, who does have the keys to the kingdom, may represent those Christian scribes who interpret the law rightly—as Christ's law.[30] Furthermore,

28. See the carefully nuanced discussion in Brown, Donfried, and Reumann, *Peter in the New Testament,* 105–7.

29. See also Wilkins, *The Concept of Disciple,* 195.

30. See here Eduard Schweizer, *The Good News according to Matthew,* trans. David E.

insofar as we can find help from (later) Jewish material, references to "binding" and "loosing" in the rabbis seem most often to refer to determining which regulations are binding and which are not.[31] As Joel Marcus points out, in the pericope preceding the confession at Caesarea Philippi, Jesus is warning his disciples against the "leaven," the false teaching of the Pharisees and Sadducees.[32] It is to this that the true teaching and authority of Peter as representative disciple is contrasted.[33]

If Peter is a representative of later church leaders in this passage, it is all the more striking that in the next pericope it is Peter who entirely mistakes the meaning of Christ's ministry. When Peter denies that Christ should ever suffer, Jesus says to Peter: "Get behind me, Satan! You are a stumbling block to me; for you are setting your mind not on divine things but on human things" (Matt. 16:23). Whatever authority is given the leaders of Matthew's church is no guarantee against their failure to understand the things of God. Teachers are warned not to rest on their prerogatives.[34]

The second passage that helps us understand the resolution of disputes in Matthew's church is found in Matt. 18:15-20:

> If another member of the church [lit.: your brother] sins against you, go and point out the fault when the two of you are alone. If the member [brother] listens to you, you have retained that one. But if you are not listened to, take one or two others along with you, so that every word may be confirmed by the evidence of two or three witnesses. If the member [brother] refuses to

---

Green (Atlanta: John Knox Press, 1975). He sees Peter's authority here as representing that of the whole community (pp. 342–44).

31. There is considerable recent literature on this question, and the issue is complicated by the question of how far rabbinic material from later centuries can illumine first-century Christian documents, even documents like Matthew with strong "Jewish" interests. The summary and conclusions by Joel Marcus seem quite persuasive: "The halakic interpretation, which sees 'binding and loosing' as promulgation of the true, divinely revealed torah, fits best the context within chap. 16" ("The Gates of Hades and the Keys of the Kingdom [Matt. 16:18-19]," *CBQ* 50, no. 3 [1988]: 451). Hans von Campenhausen stresses the interpretive function of binding and loosing but suggests that the issue of forgiveness is not separable from that of teaching authority (*Ecclesiastical Authority and Spiritual Power: The Church in the First Three Centuries,* trans. J. A. Baker [London: Adam and Charles Black, 1969], 129–30).

32. Marcus, "Gates of Hades," 451–52.

33. Wilkins (*The Concept of Disciple,* 195, 198), on the other hand, thinks that Peter's power to bind and loose has to do with his preaching the gospel in Acts and thereby opening the doors of the kingdom. This seems to undervalue the context that Marcus examines and the contrast with the scribes and Pharisees of Matt. 23:13.

34. See Minear, *Matthew,* 97.

listen to them, tell it to the church; and if the offender [brother] refuses to listen even to the church, let such a one be to you as a Gentile and a tax collector. Truly, I tell you, whatever you bind on earth will be bound in heaven, and whatever you loose on earth will be loosed in heaven. Again, truly I tell you, if two of you agree on earth about anything you ask, it will be done for you by my Father in heaven. For where two or three are gathered in my name, I am there among them.

It is clear that here we have a word of the risen Lord to the Matthean church and not primarily a word of Jesus to the "historical" circle of his disciples. The passage assumes the existence of "the church" and the presence in the church of the risen Jesus ("I am there among them"). The presence of Jesus in the church is not so much to provide comfort as to pronounce judgment. The binding and loosing by the church are validated by the presence of the risen Lord. The passage clearly points ahead to the commission of Matt. 28:16-20: "All authority in heaven and on earth has been given to me. . . . And remember, I am with you always, to the end of the age."

Whereas in Matthew 28 (and in Matthew 16) the authority Jesus has and confers is primarily the authority of teaching, here in Matthew 18 the authority is evidently that of including people in the company of the faithful or of excluding them from that fellowship. It is the authority to forgive or to excommunicate.[35] Further, there is a clear procedure for disciplining offenders. The one wronged first tries to persuade his or her opponent; failing that, one or two other church members come as witnesses again to use the power of persuasion; failing that, the whole church hears the case and beseeches the offender, and only failing that is the sanction of excommunication invoked.

The passage is striking for the patience it prescribes. Three attempts at reform precede the final, harsh judgment. The passage is further striking in that it presupposes *congregational* discipline. There is no appeal to particular church leaders to solve the dispute or to render judgment. There is no indication that any particular subgroup within the church should serve as witnesses for the offended party; any Christian brother or sister has the authority to help in this matter. This egalitarian, congregational authority is further stressed in the concluding verses of the

35. For a slightly different reading of the role of "binding and loosing," based on a reading of Josephus, see J. Andrew Overman, *Matthew's Gospel and Formative Judaism: A Study of the Social World of the Matthean Community* (Philadelphia: Fortress Press, 1990), 104-6.

passage where Jesus declares that in this case of judgment, presumably as in other cases, the decision of *any* two or three faithful Christians is binding, not only on earth but (as in Matt. 16:19) in heaven.

The passages from Matthew 16 and Matthew 18 do not provide overwhelming evidence on the way in which disputes were solved in the Matthean community. Nonetheless, we can suggest on the basis of these two passages what the pattern seems to be. In matters of interpretation of the law, and particularly of that new Torah given through Jesus, authoritative teachers—represented by Peter and then by the other disciples—had leadership in the Matthean congregation and were to be heard deferentially.[36] In matters of discipline, where one Christian wronged another, each Christian brother or sister had equal right to begin the procedure of reform or sanction. Each believer could be asked to serve as a witness (and therefore as a judge and advocate). All believers, as a congregation, had the right to make the final plea to the offender and, should the plea fail, to pronounce the judgment.

As we seek to understand leadership in the Matthean congregation, therefore, these passages provide a mixed picture. There clearly was a place for leadership, especially for the leadership of teachers and interpreters of the law, "scribes of the kingdom." In essential matters of discipline, however, church members apparently had equal authority; Jesus promised to be present to any two or three Christians joined in deliberation, not just to congregational leaders.[37]

OFFICES IN THE MATTHEAN CHURCH

Most commentators would agree that Matthew's Gospel comes out of a Jewish-Christian context. It does seem clear that leadership in the Matthean church is still defined over against leadership and leaders in the synagogue. Whether this self-definition represents a still lively dispute or the remnants of an old debate, it is the definition that seems central to the titles and functions of leaders in Matthew's Gospel and presumably in Matthew's church.

---

36. Eduard Schweizer (*Church Order in the New Testament,* trans. Frank Clarke [Naperville, Ill.: Alec R. Allenson, 1961], 59) suggests, however, that the powers of interpretation and the power of banning or excommunication are closely related in both Matthew 16 and Matthew 18. What Matthew indicates is that the authority given to Peter now passes not to a single successor or to a hierarchy, but to the whole community.

37. See Schweizer, *Good News,* 371.

Matthew uses two titles that seem to reflect the nature and role of leaders in the Matthean church. The first title is "scribe." In Matthew 23, Jesus, clearly looking ahead to Matthew's time and Matthew's community, speaks to the *Jewish* scribes and Pharisees: "Woe to you, scribes and Pharisees, hypocrites!... You snakes, you brood of vipers! How can you escape being sentenced to hell? Therefore I send you prophets, sages [*sophoi*], and scribes [*grammateis*], some of whom you will kill and crucify, and some you will flog in your synagogues and pursue from town to town" (Matt. 23:29-34). What is clear here is that the leaders of Matthew's community are seen to be in continuity with the ancient prophets and are seen in contrast with the scribes of the synagogue. For Matthew both Christian "scribes" and "prophets" are those "sent" as the ancient prophets were sent, and like the prophets of old they face the hostility of the Jewish leaders (and of the Jewish people, "Jerusalem").

The passage calls us back to Matthew 10. In 23:34 Jesus says: "Therefore I *send* [*apostellō*] you prophets, sages, and scribes." And in 23:37 he speaks of Jerusalem killing the prophets and "stoning those who are *sent* [again from *apostellō*] to you!" Christian scribes, prophets, and sages are sent by Jesus as the prophets of old were sent by God. In Matt. 10:2 the twelve are referred to as the "apostles"—those sent; and in Matt. 10:5, "These twelve Jesus *sent* [*apostellō*] out, with the following instructions...." So, too, in Matt. 5:11-12, the disciples are compared to the ancient prophets.

The prophets, wise men, and scribes of Matthew 23 are therefore foreshadowed in the twelve disciples/apostles of Matthew 10 and Matt. 5:11-12. Both passages give clues to the leadership of the Matthean community that included those who were sent to represent God and God's Son among the Jewish people, who stood in contrast to the Jewish leaders, and who risked persecution for their faith. Because they are "sent," are persecuted, and are successors of the prophets of old, scribes and prophets are much alike in Matthew's community. What more can we say of these Christian scribes?

In Matt. 13:51-52 Jesus is discussing with his disciples the series of parables he has just told: " 'Have you understood all this?' They answered, 'Yes.' And he said to them, 'Therefore every scribe who has been trained for the kingdom of heaven is like the master of a household who brings out of his treasure what is new and what is old.' " In the light of Matt. 23:34 we can assume that such a scribe is a church leader, one sent by Jesus. As a scribe trained for the kingdom of heaven he stands in contrast to the Jewish scribes. As one who brings forth from his treasure what is both old and new, his job is to be a true interpreter of the law in the light of the stories about Jesus and in the light of Jesus' teaching. The Christian scribe therefore stands over against (though not always in contradiction to) the Jewish "scribes and Pharisees [who] sit on Moses' seat" (Matt. 23:2).[38]

The Christian scribe recalls Peter, who in Matt. 16:19 is given the power to "bind and loose," that is, the authority to interpret Torah for the Christian community, presumably by bringing forth both what is old and what is new.[39] (In Matt. 9:17 Jesus says that when new wine is put in new wineskins rather than old, "both"—the new and old wine—are preserved; cf. Mark 2:22 and Luke 5:38.)[40]

I have further suggested that in Matt. 23:13 when Matthew's Jesus condemns the Jewish scribes and Pharisees ("For you lock people out of the kingdom of heaven. For you do not go in yourselves, and when others are going in, you stop them"), Matthew may imply that, like Peter, the true Christian scribes possess the keys that open the kingdom to others. They bind and loose.

With some reason, Günther Bornkamm maintains that the scribe of Matt. 13:52 is also the evangelist's self-designation. The Gospel of Matthew does bring forth from the treasure of faith what is old (the Old Testament) and what is new (the story of Jesus).[41] If Matthew's Gospel is therefore the work of a Christian scribe, then we can suspect that for Matthew such scribes are those who take the place of the Jewish scribes by interpreting the law for the Christian community—the law as interpreted and fulfilled in Jesus Christ.

The second title Matthew apparently uses to refer to Christian leaders of his own time is "prophet." As I noted above, Christian prophets, like Christian scribes and "sages," are sent out by Jesus and face hostility in an unbelieving (Jewish?) world (see Matt. 23:34).

In Matt. 10:41 the twelve who have been sent out are explicitly seen to foreshadow the later Christian prophets who will go out in Jesus'

---

38. For a similar reading see Overman, *Matthew's Gospel*, 116–17.

39. See Schweizer, "Matthew's Church," 134.

40. See Donald A. Hagner, "The *Sitz im Leben* of the Gospel of Matthew," in SBLASP (Atlanta: Scholars Press, 1985), 268.

41. See Bornkamm, "End Expectation," 49. See also Beare, *Gospel according to St. Matthew,* 317–18.

name: "Whoever welcomes a prophet in the name of a prophet will receive a prophet's reward; and whoever welcomes a righteous person in the name of a righteous person will receive the reward of the righteous." (Here, as opposed to Matthew 23, it is prophets and righteous persons, not prophets, scribes, and wise persons, who are sent forth on Jesus' mission. The prophets are also associated with—identified with?—the righteous in Matt. 23:29; see Matt. 23:35.)

While it may not be possible to determine the distinctions between prophets and scribes in Matthew's community, there are some hints in Matthew's Gospel that may help. For one thing, we may guess that the prophets Jesus sends forth are to be contrasted to the false prophets Matthew's Jesus warns against in Matt. 7:15-16, 21-23. In this context it is clear that the false prophets are also "Christians" (as opposed to the false scribes of Matthew 23, who are Jewish leaders). The false prophets are criticized because though they call Jesus "Lord," they do not bear the fruit of faithful services. This may be to say that though they hear the gospel, they do not obey the new Torah that Jesus declares: they do not build upon the rock. In this way the false Christian prophets are rather like the false Jewish scribes who talk a good Torah but do not live it out (Matt. 23:3).

In Matthew 24, Jesus predicts the appearance of false prophets in the last days. In apocalyptic literature like Matthew 24 such predictions are often used to pronounce judgment on the *present* time of the author and the author's audience. We can guess that the false prophets Jesus predicts are the false prophets Matthew sees.

In Matt. 24:24, Matthew borrows his material quite directly from Mark (13:22) and warns of false Christs and false prophets who will "produce great signs and omens, to lead astray, if possible, even the elect." In Matt. 24:11, his own material, Matthew says: "And many false prophets will arise and lead many astray." In each case the issue seems not to be the miracle working in itself so much as the danger that false prophets will mislead the elect. True prophets, we should think, are those who teach truly—not so different from true scribes.[42]

Perhaps prophets are more associated with signs and wonders, and scribes are more associated with the interpretation of books. Even more

---

42. On the whole issue of "false prophets" in Matthew see the excellent discussion by David Aune in his *Prophecy in Early Christianity and the Mediterranean World* (Grand Rapids, Mich.: Eerdmans, 1983), 222–24.

tenuously, perhaps prophets wander, and scribes have communities where they stay. But here the evidence grows slim indeed.[43]

In addition to his use of the "titles" of scribe and prophet, Matthew gives us another clue to the role of leaders in the Matthean community in Matt. 23:6-12. Here Jesus says that the scribes and Pharisees

> love to have the place of honor at banquets and the best seats in the synagogues, and to be greeted with respect in the marketplaces, and to have people call them rabbi. But you are not to be called rabbi, for you have one teacher, and you are all students [Gk.: brothers]. And call no one your father on earth, for you have one Father—the one in heaven. Nor are you to be called instructors, for you have one instructor, the Messiah. The greatest among you will be your servant. All who exalt themselves will be humbled, and all who humble themselves will be exalted.

This passage suggests that there must have been places of leadership in the Matthean community or there would be no issue concerning what to call the leaders.[44] Not only the logic of the specific text but all the evidence we have looked at in Matthew leads us to conclude that some Christians did have positions of leadership, most particularly of teaching leadership. The issue is not whether there should be such leaders, but what dignity should be accorded them and, more specifically, what title, if any, they should receive.

Nonetheless, the warning against titles indicates that in Matthew's community the "scribes" or "prophets" were seen above all to be "brothers" of other Christians—not only disciples but little ones as well. The tension between the keys given to Peter in Matthew 16 and the keys given to all the faithful in Matthew 18 recurs here in the warning to the Christian community: the community will have scribes and prophets to interpret God's law, but these persons are not to have the "place of honor." The only real authority is that of God and of God's Son: true teacher and Lord.[45]

---

43. See ibid., 214–15.

44. See, for instance, Karl Kertelge, *Gemeinde und Amt im Neuen Testament* (Munich: Kösel-Verlag, 1972), 123, and Schweizer, "Matthew's Church," 139.

45. For a helpful discussion of "prophets" and "scribes/teachers" in Matthew's community, see Kingsbury, *Matthew as Story,* 129–31. For the relationship between these leaders and the "brotherhood" of the entire community, see Edgar Krentz, "Community and Character: Matthew's Vision of the Church," in SBLASP (Atlanta: Scholars Press, 1987), 571–72.

Two other passages in Matthew's Gospel may help us understand the "offices," or leadership functions in the Matthean community.

Matthew 18 is that section of the Gospel apparently devoted to church discipline, and we have already seen that the disciples whom Jesus here addresses function in some passages as forerunners if not as stand-ins for the church leaders of Matthew's day. Matthew 18:10-14 seems to use the disciples in such a transparent way when Jesus uses the parable of the Lost Sheep to stress the disciples' responsibility for "these little ones." We have seen that the "little ones" for Matthew are typically the Christian believers. This passage assumes therefore that there are leaders in the church, and that such leaders need always to avoid the danger of despising the Christians whom they lead. More than that, in the parable there may be a hint that these leaders exercise a kind of shepherdly overseeing role over their flock. The direct point of the parable is in the rejoicing over that which is lost, but indirectly the parable does suggest the image of shepherd or pastor for those church leaders the disciples represent.[46]

We find one final hint of the nature of office or leadership function in Matthew's community in Matt. 24:45-51. In the midst of his apocalyptic discourse, after the predictions of Matthew 24 and before coming to the eschatological parables of Matthew 25, Jesus draws this comparison:

> Who then is the faithful and wise slave, whom his master has put in charge of his household, to give the other slaves their allowance of food at the proper time? Blessed is that slave whom his master will find at work when he arrives. Truly I tell you, he will put that one in charge of all his possessions. But if that wicked slave says to himself, "My master is delayed," and begins to beat his fellow slaves, and eats and drinks with drunkards, the master of that slave will come on a day when he does not expect him and at an hour that he does not know. He will cut him in pieces and put him with the hypocrites where there will be weeping and gnashing of teeth.

The "hypocrites," we have seen from Matthew 23, are the scribes and Pharisees, the false leaders of the Jewish people. The "servants" point to the Christian scribes and leaders who have leadership in the household of God, and whose job is to give to that household "food at the proper time." Perhaps there is a hint of the eucharistic role of church leaders

---

46. See John P. Meier, *The Vision of Matthew: Christ, Church, and Morality in the First Gospel* (New York: Paulist Press, 1979), 130, and Wolfgang Trilling, *Das wahre Israel: Studien zur Theologie des Matthäusevangeliums* (Munich: Kösel-Verlag, 1964), 108–9.

here, but more likely and certainly more prominent is the suggestion that, like the scribes and Pharisees, Christian leaders are teachers who provide the food of right interpretation of God's Torah. Moreover, as with the scribes and Pharisees, the Christian teachers are to be judged not only by what they teach but by what they practice. They need to be wary lest, like the hypocrites, they declare God's law but act against it.

We do not have all the evidence we wish we had. What evidence we do have suggests this: while Matthew's congregation was in many ways egalitarian, especially in the matter of church discipline (see Matt. 18:15-20), there were also church leaders. These leaders are sometimes foreshadowed by the twelve or the disciples in Matthew's Gospel. Though we do not know if they had official titles, Matthew points to such leaders by his use of the terms "prophet" and "scribe" ("sage" may also be such a term, though the evidence here is exceedingly slim).

The Christian prophets and scribes are differentiated from Jewish scribes and Pharisees. Christian leaders have the true law to interpret (both old and new gifts pour forth from their treasury), and they are called to live out the law they teach, to separate themselves from the hypocrisy of the Jewish teachers. Like Jewish leaders, however, their primary task is to interpret God's Torah.

There may be a hint in the stories of the feedings that Matthean church leaders (represented by the disciples) had a servant role at the Lord's Supper. Along with any sacramental connotations, it seems also that those stories represent the same kind of "feeding" we find in Matt. 24:45—the food of true teaching. The one true rabbi has already said that "one does not live by bread alone but by every word that comes from the mouth of God" (Matt. 4:4). Perhaps further clarification on the role of leaders in the Matthean church will emerge as we study the images for the church in this Gospel.

IMAGES OF THE CHURCH IN MATTHEW

What Paul does by direction Matthew does indirectly. There are no direct discussions in Matthew of the nature of the church and no extended images (like that of the body of Christ) to describe Matthew's vision of the Christian community. The images emerge as part of the narrative and may help us glimpse Matthew's understanding of the church.

The Community of Disciples

I have already suggested that sometimes the disciples in Matthew's Gospel seem to be transparent, to point ahead to the church leaders of Matthew's time; at other times the reference to disciples seems to be more narrowly historical—to the circle around Jesus in his ministry. At yet other times "disciple" seems to be an image for all the believers of Matthew's time. Matthew 5–7, the Sermon on the Mount, for instance, is addressed to the disciples in the presence of the crowds, and the words to the disciples seem to be instruction for all Christian believers.[47] At the end of the Gospel, the commission to "make disciples" of all nations or all Gentiles and to teach them "to obey everything that I have commanded you" (Matt. 28:19-20) is not a commission to make church leaders but to call church members.

We have seen that Günther Bornkamm points out that while Matthew (like the rest of the early Christian community) apparently derives the term "disciple" from the Jewish community, the "disciples" in Matthew's Gospel and therefore presumably the Christians of Matthew's time do not function precisely as did disciples of the rabbis. For one thing the basis of their discipleship is not the truth of Jesus' teaching but his call to follow. It is after the decision to follow that they receive his instruction. For another thing the disciples are not on the way to becoming teachers themselves. They remain disciples for a lifetime.[48] Though I have suggested that some such "disciples" do have the teaching function of the Christian scribe, none is to be "rabbi" or "the teacher" (Matt. 23:8; 10:24-25).

The fact that the image of discipleship sometimes functions for all Christians, little ones and leaders alike, suggests that Matthew does stress equality and community in his understanding of the church. Furthermore, the use of the image reminds us that all church members, scribes and little ones alike, stand under the authority of the one true interpreter of God's Torah, Jesus. In that sense, as I have already suggested, scribes and prophets and other church leaders are quite seriously seen as first among equals in Matthew's community.

---

47. See Bornkamm, "End Expectation," 16. See, however, Matt. 5:11-12 and the discussion of the relationship to "prophets" above.
48. See Bornkamm, "End Expectation," 40–41.

The Church as Family

Wolfgang Trilling notes those instances where Matthew refers to the church as a community or fellowship of "brothers."[49] Trilling takes the familial image as constitutive of a major theme within the Gospel. God is the Father both of Jesus and of the community; Jesus is not only Lord and Son of God, but brother to his fellow Christians. The most obvious text is Matt. 25:40: "Truly I tell you, just as you did it to one of the least of these who are members of my family [Gk.: my brothers], you did it to me" (see also 25:45). This reading of the text assumes, as I also do, that the "brothers" of Jesus in Matthew 25 are not the needy in general but needy Christians, whose reception among the nations Jesus will judge.[50]

Trilling's stress on the image of brotherhood for the church is further confirmed by a passage that deals more directly with issues of church leadership, Matt. 23:8-10, where the "familial" hierarchy is described in slightly different imagery: "But you are not to be called rabbi, for you have one teacher, and you are all brothers [RSV; NRSV has 'students']. And call no man your father on earth, for you have one Father—the one in heaven. Nor are you to be called instructors, for you have one instructor, the Messiah."

In Matt. 12:49-50, in material fairly close to that in Mark we have the scene where Jesus' mother and brothers come asking to speak to him: "And pointing to his disciples, he said, 'Here are my mother and my brothers! For whoever does the will of my Father in heaven is my brother and sister and mother.'" In two ways Matthew's material differs from his source in Mark. First, those around Jesus are explicitly identified as disciples. Disciples *are* brothers, sisters, mother. Here, at least, disciples represent not only church leaders but all faithful folk. Second, where Jesus in Mark refers to "God" (Mark 3:35), here he refers to "my Father in heaven." This suggests that Trilling is correct in seeing a familial pattern underlying Matthew's understanding of the church and its relationship to God and to Christ (see also Matt. 18:15-20; 28:10).

The image of Christian believers as "little ones" (or "least of these my brothers," as in Matt. 25:40) seems also to fit here as representing a familial understanding of the church. At some points (especially 18:10-14) there may be the implication that some Christians represent the

49. See Trilling, *Das Wahre Israel*, 155, 212–13.
50. See my discussion and note 20 above.

"older" brothers and sisters with special pastoral responsibility for these "little ones."

In Matthew's community there are no doubt leaders who interpret Jesus' Torah and who, as prophets, both take the message and do miracles on their travels. Some may also serve a pastoral function in relationship to straying "sheep." But within the community Christians are seen as members of one family—as equal to one another, under the fatherhood of God and the leadership of Christ, God's Son.[51]

This discussion of the images of church in Matthew's Gospel serves to confirm the suggestions I have made about the nature of leadership in the Matthean community. The term "disciple" can be used not only for church leaders but for church members. This suggests that leaders and members are joined together in their obedience to Jesus and in their trust in his presence among them. The term stresses the unity among Christians at least as much as it does the different functions among them.

This unity among Christians is further underlined by the prevalence of language drawn from the family in Matthew, especially the use of the term "brothers." What emerges is the picture of a church united under the fatherhood of God in obedience to the Torah of Jesus. Some within that church have a special role as interpreters of Jesus' Torah, others as missionaries; and some (others?) perhaps have some particular pastoral responsibilities (see Matt. 18:10-14). What is more striking than the distinctions among Christians, however, is the unity between leaders and people, the strong stress on servant leadership, and the claim that all who follow Christ are brothers and sisters bound in love to him and to one another.

MATTHEW'S CHURCH AND MINISTRY TODAY

As we have learned, Matthew sees his church as a community of disciples. Like the disciples of the rabbis, they are to learn from their one rabbi, Jesus. Unlike the disciples of the rabbis, however, Christian disciples remain disciples forever—they do not become rabbis. There is only one rabbi for the Christian community.

Within this community of disciples there is a group of interpreters

---

51. The images of the community of faith as "disciples" and as "brothers" are nicely brought together in Kingsbury, *Matthew as Story,* 104–5.

of Jesus' Torah. Sometimes the twelve disciples of Jesus' ministry (and perhaps especially Peter) seem to be prototypes of these interpreters. Sometimes these interpreters are described as Christian "scribes." Again they are both like and unlike the scribes of the synagogue. Like the scribes of the synagogue, their job is to "bind and to loose," to interpret Torah for the life of their congregation. However, unlike the Jewish scribes, Christian scribes know that the key to true Torah is found in the life and teaching of Jesus. Further, Matthew would argue, unlike the Jewish scribes, who suffer from terminal hypocrisy, Christian scribes are expected to live out the higher righteousness they teach.

Matthew's community also acknowledges the place of Christian prophets. Like the prophets of old, these are leaders "sent" by divine command (and are therefore perhaps foreshadowed by the apostles of Matt. 10:2). Whereas the prophets of old were sent by the word of God, these prophets are sent by the call and command of Jesus. Like the prophets of old, Christian prophets run the risk of persecution by the people of Israel to whom they are sent. True Christian prophets must be distinguished from false Christian prophets who lead Christians astray by (undefined) wrong teaching. Certainly the false prophets engage in miraculous works, but it may be that the true prophets work miracles as well.

Matthew's church, as it emerges from the synagogue, also defines itself as a family. (In this sense it has a more "sectarian" understanding of the community of faith than did perhaps the established Jewish community from which it separates.) Christians are called "brothers" to each other and "brothers and sisters" to Jesus. Even those who have positions of leadership are not to use this leadership to lord it over their fellow Christians. They are to avoid titles like "Rabbi" or "Master" or "Father," which might lead them and their fellow Christians to confuse their servant ministry with a ministry of particular honor. All Christians are God's little ones: Jesus' "least" brothers and sisters. All Christians share responsibility for discipline when one "brother" wrongs another. Those who have special responsibility have only special responsibility—to teach Christ's Torah—not special privilege.

What we see is what we would expect to see (in this somewhat circular discussion of setting and text). We see a community in continuity and contrast to the synagogue. Both titles and functions reflect the understanding of leaders as prophets or interpreters of Torah, but over against the perceived shortcomings of the synagogue and the real needs of the emerging church, the community is also a community of equals. Christians are bound together as God's children and as Jesus' sisters and brothers, and they find their identity in the promise that the risen Christ is with them, always.

Again we come not so much to conclusions as to issues for further reflection.

1. The continuity between Matthew's church and the synagogue provides one possible model for contemporary ministry—that of the rabbi. While both the rabbinate and the ministry have evolved in striking, and strikingly different, ways since the first century, the model of religious leader as interpreter of Torah is one that deserves careful consideration.

On the one hand, the "scribe who has been discipled for the kingdom" is an interpreter of the sacred traditions. For Matthew these traditions include Scripture (the Old Testament) and the sayings and stories of Jesus. This is to say that the religious leader not only preaches the gospel but interprets the range of the canon for faithful people.

On the other hand, if Peter is a prototype of later Christian leaders in this Gospel, then the religious leader is given those keys that "bind and loose"—that is, the Christian scribe helps the community of faith determine which regulations are binding and which are not. Shifted to our time, this suggests that the Christian minister might consider the obligation to take more seriously her or his role as moral guide for the community of faith, a role often denigrated in our worry about "moralism."

2. Matthew's Gospel provides the opportunity for us to consider once again the relationship between community and authority in the church. The ambiguity of Matthew's use of the term "disciple" and the shift between the notion of authority given to Peter in chapter 16 and that given to the whole church in chapter 18 suggest either a healthy tension or an unhelpful confusion. Matthew, in his own quite different way, wants to hold together what Paul wants to hold together: a diversity of gifts and equality of grace. Christians are brothers and sisters to one another and to Christ. They are children of the heavenly Father. In that sense all are one. However, some among us do have the particular roles of scribes, prophets, and perhaps shepherds. These particular roles do not give special weight to our faithfulness. The scribes are not more in the kingdom than the little ones. They simply have a different responsibility.

This stress on different functions within a shared community is particularly evident in Matthew's reluctance to assign titles to Christian leaders. They are not to be called "Rabbi" or "Father," which raises questions about some of the ways in which we address clergy today. Matthew presumably would not affirm hierarchical structures where some Christians are called "Father"; and, as Raymond Brown points out, Matthew presumably would not be pleased at having some Christians called "Doctor," either.[52] It is, of course, not just the titles that are at stake here. It is the issue of status within the community. Are religious leaders super-Christians, closer to God and Christ than the rest of God's people? Or are they simply "little ones," like every other Christian, but little ones who have particular jobs within the community?

3. What is not clear in Matthew's Gospel is whether there is any sacramental role for church leaders. It may be that the stories of the feedings hint at a role for "disciples" as those who distribute the sacramental elements to the Christians. If so, the disciples are not surrogates for Christ. They do not preside at the meal. They are servants of the meal at which he alone is host. Along with, or instead of, the sacramental overtones, these stories also point beyond themselves to signify the teaching ministry of leaders. If there is a sacramental role it is subsidiary to and perhaps even derivative from the role of disciple as learner and interpreter. Matthew does not provide any clear grounds for drawing the line between clergy and laity at the table. What is essential to Matthew's vision has more to do with interpreting Christ's Torah than with serving at the Eucharist. Is this a more modest role? Does it help the clergyperson remember that he or she is a servant of all, as well as a servant of the word?

---

52. See Brown, *Churches,* 128–29. Nor would "Reverend" fare any better, to say nothing of "very" or "most" Reverend.

CHAPTER 4

Ministry in the
Johannine Literature

THE GOSPEL OF JOHN

John's Gospel is strikingly different from the Synoptic Gospels—
Matthew, Mark, and Luke. It follows a different outline of the events
of Jesus' life. Its prologue sets Jesus' story within the context of the
creation of the cosmos. Jesus' miracles serve largely as the occasion for
sermons on their deeper meaning. Jesus' discourses in John's Gospel are
very different both in style and in content from the sayings, sermons,
and parables of the Synoptics.

Unlike Matthew and Paul, John tells us nothing directly of his understanding of the church and its leadership. Nonetheless, we can detect in
John's narrative clues concerning the structure of the church for which
he wrote and clues concerning leadership in that church.

Again we look at our five questions:

1. What is the probable historical and social context out of which
John's Gospel arose?

2. What is John's understanding of apostleship, or, more appropriately, discipleship?

3. How are conflicts settled (or how does the evangelist wish they
were settled) in the Johannine congregation?

4. What kinds of officers or leaders are discernible in the Johannine
congregation? What are the grounds of their authority?

5. What images of the church predominate in John's Gospel?

THE HISTORICAL BACKGROUND OF THE JOHANNINE WRITINGS

As I suggested in the chapter on Matthew's Gospel, the Gospels in the New Testament do not give direct information on their historical setting—their author, their audience, the community from which and for which they were written. We infer the nature of that community from the nature of the book. Not surprisingly we posit a community whose shape and structure will fit our analysis of the images of community and office in the Gospel itself.

An understanding of the community behind the Fourth Gospel is complicated by the fact that numerous scholars have seen reflected in that Gospel the signs of a long and complex history of development. Rudolf Bultmann posits the work of an evangelist who uses and revises several preexistent (and sometimes even pre-Christian) sources and whose work is itself edited by an "ecclesiastical redactor."[1] Raymond Brown traces the development of a community and its faith as various new groups are assimilated into the Johannine church.[2] Working with models derived from Mary Douglas and expanding on an article by Wayne Meeks, Jerome Neyrey posits three stages of development in the Johannine community, each of which left its traces in the material of the Gospel itself.[3]

I shall provide suggestions about the community for which the present Gospel was written, though we need to acknowledge the likelihood of development both within that community and within the gospel tradition.

Though the term may be anachronistic, the evidence of John's Gospel suggests that the community of the Fourth Gospel was self-consciously

---

1. On this see Rudolf Bultmann, *The Gospel of John: A Commentary,* trans. G. R. Beasley-Murray, R. W. N. Hoare, and J. K. Riches (Philadelphia: Westminster Press, 1971), 6–7, 10–12, and throughout the commentary. A helpful study by D. Moody Smith (*The Composition and Order of the Fourth Gospel* [New Haven: Yale Univ. Press, 1965]) interprets Bultmann's results.

2. See Raymond Brown, *The Gospel according to John,* AB (Garden City, N.Y.: Doubleday, 1966), 1:lxvii–lxxix; and especially idem, *The Community of the Beloved Disciple: The Life, Loves, and Hates of an Individual Church in New Testament Times* (New York: Paulist Press, 1979), 13–91, 166–67.

3. See Jerome A. Neyrey, *An Ideology of Revolt: John's Christology in Social-Science Perspective* (Philadelphia: Fortress Press, 1988). Not surprisingly the three scholars do not entirely agree on the direction of the development, nor in what belongs to which layer of tradition. For instance, Bultmann sees the sacramental theology in John as the very latest stage of development; Neyrey puts it at his "stage two." See Bultmann, *Gospel of John,* 234–37; Neyrey, *Ideology of Revolt,* 130–32, 137–39.

more "sectarian" than the community of Matthew's Gospel or the other Synoptics. It was what Ernst Käsemann called a "conventicle."[4] By calling this community sectarian I mean to suggest that it defined itself over against the world around it. Rather than understanding the faithful life as one of interaction with the world, it understood that life as separation from the world and loyal support of those in the believing community.[5] Even if the Johannine community was not narrowly speaking a "sect," we can at least see the separateness of the Johannine community in its distinction from three other groups.

First, the Johannine church is self-consciously separate from the synagogue. John 9 uses an incident in the ministry of Jesus to present a paradigm of the division between Jewish Christians who composed part of John's community and those Jews who remained in the synagogue. The Jewish Christians were excommunicated for their faith.[6]

There is considerable difference among scholars concerning how far

4. See Ernst Käsemann, *The Testament of Jesus* (Philadelphia: Fortress Press, 1968), 32–33. Raymond Brown, who offers perhaps the most detailed suggestions concerning the development of the Johannine community, argues that in many ways the church was "sect-like," but had not broken from the "apostolic church" and so was not, strictly speaking, a sect (*Community*, 88–91).

5. The term is anachronistic in part because the distinction between church and sect grew out of sociological studies of later Christian communities. No first-century community was a "church" in the sense that later sociologists would define that term. Most first-century communities would have practiced believers' baptism, regularly if not exclusively—and would therefore fit one qualification for most later "sects." I am trying to get at an understanding of community in Johannine churches different from that evidenced in the other sources. As usual my argument is circular: from text to hypothetical community to text again. For an excellent essay on the use of the term "sect" and its roots in Weber and Troeltsch, see Michael Hill, "Sect," in Mircea Eliade et al., eds., *The Encyclopedia of Religion* (New York: Macmillan, 1987), 13:154–58.

6. On the relationship between Johannine Christians and the synagogue as exemplified in John 9, see especially J. Louis Martyn, *History and Theology in the Fourth Gospel*, rev. ed. (Nashville: Abingdon, 1979). The difficult issue is how this break is related to the account of the "curse" against heretics in the Babylonian Talmud, *Ber.* 28b. Martyn presents his argument of a close relationship along with criticism by Wayne Meeks and Morton Smith in the notes on pp. 54–57. In his essay on Matthew, Alan Segal argues that we may know more about first-century Judaism from the Gospels than we do from the Talmud ("Matthew's Jewish Voice," in David Balch, ed., *Social History of the Matthean Community: Cross-Disciplinary Approaches* [Minneapolis: Fortress Press, 1991]). If so, John provides primary evidence for some kind of synagogue expulsion in the first century, whether it derives from Gamaliel and Jamnia or not. There is a lucid discussion of all this by D. Moody Smith in his article "The Contribution of J. Louis Martyn to the Understanding of the Gospel of John," in Robert T. Fortna and Beverly R. Gaventa, eds., *The Conversation Continues: Studies in Paul and John, in Honor of J. Louis Martyn* (Nashville, Abingdon: 1990), 275–94; Steven T. Katz ("Issues in the Separation of Judaism and Christianity after 70 C.E.: A Reconsideration,"

into the background this separation from the synagogue has receded by the time of the writing of the Fourth Gospel. Jerome Neyrey sees the expulsion as a recent development, fresh in the experience of the evangelist. J. Louis Martyn places the expulsion at the second stage of the Gospel's development, toward the end of the first century C.E. Raymond Brown acknowledges the importance of the experience of expulsion but locates it at an earlier date, though also prior to the writing of the Gospel.[7] Furthermore, Brown suggests that the emergence within the community of a higher Christology, imported as new converts joined, was in part responsible for the increasing separation from the synagogue. Neyrey tends to argue in the other direction (though he admits the reciprocity of cause and effect). As Johannine Christians were expelled from the synagogue, they rationalized their separateness from this familiar "world" by claiming otherworldliness for their Lord and for themselves.[8]

Wayne A. Meeks emphasizes not only the separation of the Johannine believers from the synagogue but the evangelist's claim regarding the requisite next step for the believers: "Mere belief without joining the Johannine community, without making the decisive break with 'the world,' particularly the world of Judaism, is a diabolic 'lie.' "[9]

Second, the Johannine community is self-consciously separate from the emerging "apostolic church." My discussion of the contrast between Peter and the beloved disciple and of the late reconciliation between the two figures (and their respective communities) in John 21 will suggest a deliberate sense within the Johannine community that their witness and their practice represented a distinct and better way. The reference in the discourse on the good shepherd to other sheep not of this fold suggests an awareness of divisions within the larger Christian community and the

---

JBL 103, no. 1 [1984]: 43–76) offers a judicious rejection of the assumption that the decisions at Jamnia led to expulsion of Christians from synagogues.

7. See Martyn, *History and Theology,* 54–62. Martyn also tends to place the exclusion and the Gospel early in the chief rabbinate of Gamaliel, which began in 80 C.E. He does not rule out the possibility of further editing before the Gospel as we have it came together; see his *The Gospel of John in Christian History: Essays for Interpreters* (New York: Paulist Press, 1978), 90–121; Neyrey, *Ideology of Revolt,* 171; Brown, *Community,* 42; see also Smith, "Contribution," 286.

8. See Brown, *Community,* 63–64. He includes opposition Gentiles in "the world"; see also Neyrey, *Ideology of Revolt,* 211.

9. Wayne A. Meeks, "The Man from Heaven in Johannine Sectarianism," *JBL* 91, no. 1 (1972): 44–72; the quotation is from p. 69.

hope that the Johannine community will represent the eventual model for reconciling those differences: "I have other sheep that do not belong to this fold. I must bring them also, and they will listen to my voice. So there will be one flock, one shepherd" (John 10:16).[10]

Third, the Johannine community is self-consciously separate from "the world." This is most evident in the High Priestly Prayer of John 17 where Jesus says: "I have given them your word, and the world has hated them because they do not belong to the world, just as I do not belong to the world" (John 17:14). While every early Christian community to some extent defined itself over against the world, it is clear that Paul's vision for the Roman church or Luke's vision for his communities included a more positive interaction between the faithful and the larger society. The communities they envision are more churchlike; the community John envisions is more sectlike. The "world" certainly includes the synagogue and may include other apostolic Christian churches—but the term is also adumbrated to include everything outside the community itself. John's church sees itself as self-contained, or as related only to Jesus and the Father he reveals.

Wayne Meeks helpfully suggests that the cryptic mythology of the Gospel itself serves to reinforce the separate identity of its community of readers: "One of the primary functions of the book, therefore, must have been to provide a reinforcement for the community's social identity, which appears to have been largely negative. It provided a symbolic universe which gave religious legitimacy, a theodicy, to the group's actual isolation from the larger society."[11]

Jerome Neyrey, in his book *An Ideology of Revolt: John's Christology in Social-Science Perspective,* is especially provocative in tracing the relationship between Johannine Christology and the community's sectarian sense of separation from the Jewish world and from other Christians. Expanding on earlier work by Wayne Meeks,[12] Neyrey argues that we can see in various layers of the Fourth Gospel a progressive movement away from the synagogue and, by the end, an embattled sense of the community's separation from its society.

---

10. Martyn (*Gospel of John,* 119) seems to see the division as being primarily among Jewish Christians; Brown (*Community,* 90, 174) thinks the other sheep include especially the "apostolic" church. On p. 90 Brown cites another reference to Martyn as agreeing with him.

11. Meeks, "Man from Heaven," 70.

12. Ibid., 44–72.

What is both striking and problematic about Neyrey's approach is the attempt to locate layers of development in the pre-Gospel tradition. The method is archaeological or geological, finding the explanation for the text in the pretextual strata. Meeks's article, rather than presenting a social-scientific analysis of the layers of tradition, acknowledges an ongoing dialectic between social situation and developing theology but finally provides a sociologically informed reading of the text as we have it:

> So long as we approach the Johannine literature as a chapter in the history of *ideas,* it will defy our understanding. Its metaphors are irrational, disorganized, and incomplete. But if we pose our questions in the form, What functions did this particular system of metaphors have for the group that developed it? then even its self-contradictions and disjunctures may be seen to be *means of communication.*[13]

Neyrey's conversation with the work of Mary Douglas is highly suggestive, but one has to ask whether Douglas provides the clues to solve the Johannine puzzles, or whether Neyrey decides to identify the puzzles in the light of Douglas's clues. At any rate, a difficult question remains: Why is this text the text it is? If it includes earlier shards and strata, why does this artful evangelist hold on to the old while including the new? Do the text's tensions look like contradictions only because we have misunderstood his issues? For instance, is the distinction between high and low Christology our distinction or the Gospel's?[14]

Raymond Brown sees this sense of separation from other Christians as being a development that emerges after the exclusion from the synagogue. Neyrey sees the self-conscious separation—from Jews and from other Christians—as occurring in the same stage of the community's development, just about as the Gospel is written.[15] In either case, it is not surprising that the ethic and ethos of the community seem to be

---

13. Ibid., 68; see also 48–50.

14. Nils A. Dahl provides a possible model in his discussion of eschatology in John 5:28-29. Perhaps the conflict between realized and future eschatology represents our problem, not the problem of a first-century Christian community emerging from Judaism (Nils A. Dahl, " 'Do Not Wonder!' John 5:28-29 and Johannine Eschatology Once More," in Fortna and Gaventa, *Conversation,* 322–36). The editors, in n. 2, p. 335, see the implications for Neyrey's work. See also Wayne Meeks's cautionary note regarding Bultmann: "We have not yet learned to let the symbolic language of Johannine literature speak in its own way" ("Man from Heaven," 47).

15. See Brown, *Community,* 165–66, and Neyrey, *Ideology of Revolt,* 141–42.

relatively sectarian. That is, the Johannine community looks something like our contemporary communities that stress their over-againstness in relation to other denominations, churches, faiths—and to the larger society. Faithfulness is described not so much in terms of one's action in the world but in terms of a personal relationship to Jesus. This is evident both in the image of vine and branches in John 15 and in the claim that the believer's relationship to Jesus replicates Jesus' relationship to the Father, as sketched in John 17:21 and 14:20.[16]

Christian ethical behavior is not described in terms of faithful response to the world but in terms of the love between and among Christians within the community. As is often the case in more sectarian movements, the preservation and upbuilding of the community—which functions more like a family than like a social institution—are central to the strategies of Christian life: "I give you a new commandment, that you love one another. Just as I have loved you, you also should love one another. By this everyone will know that you are my disciples, if you have love for one another" (John 13:34-35).

It may not be coincidental that to this day more sectarian Christian groups feel a special affinity for the Fourth Gospel and often distribute copies of that Gospel to attract converts. Such Christian groups may intuitively recognize in the community for which the Gospel was intended a kinship to their own sense of identity. If Meeks is right, however, that the Gospel serves rather to reinforce community identity than to open its world to converts, these Christians may be using the wrong literature to provide their invitation.

For John, the Paraclete, the Spirit, becomes the bond that unites the community with Jesus (both with the teachings of the "earthly" Jesus and with the presence of the risen Lord) and the bond that unites community members with one another as they obey the commandment to love one another (John 14:15-17, 26; 16:13-15).

JOHN'S UNDERSTANDING OF APOSTLESHIP

The word "apostle" as a designation for followers of Jesus, or for church leaders, is entirely absent from the Fourth Gospel. In the one case where the Greek term *apostolos* is used, it seems not to have a technical meaning. Jesus is explaining why the disciples ought to follow

---

16. Brown rightly shows, however, that this "sectarian" consciousness did not include condemnation of the apostolic church (*Community*, 88–90).

his example and wash one another's feet: "For I have set you an example, that you also should do as I have done to you. Very truly, I tell you, servants are not greater than their master, nor are messengers [*aposto-los*, lit.: 'a messenger'] greater than the one who sent them [him]" (John 13:15-16).[17] The verb, *apostellō*, "I send," however, is frequently used by John. While its uses vary, most often Jesus is designated as the one whom God has sent: "Jesus answered them, 'This is the work of God, that you believe in him whom he has sent' " (John 6:29).[18]

However, John's Gospel further claims that as Jesus is sent by the Father, so Jesus' followers are sent forth by Jesus. The claim is explicit in John 17:18, in Jesus' High Priestly Prayer: "As you have sent me into the world, so have I sent them into the world."[19] In a passage I shall discuss further, below, Jesus breathes the Holy Spirit on "the disciples." Just before giving them the gift of the Spirit, he says: "Peace be with you. As the Father has sent me [*apostellō*] so I send [*pempō*] you" (John 20:21). Another passage makes a similar claim, that the life of the Son with the Father is reflected in the life of the disciples with the Son: "Just as the living Father sent me, and I live because of the Father, so whoever eats me will live because of me" (John 6:57). Here, of course, the reference is eucharistic, but the idea of a kind of hierarchical correspondence remains. The Father gives life to the Son whom he sends; the Son gives life to the disciples who partake of the eucharistic meal.[20]

While John at no point directly calls Jesus' disciples "apostles," he does indicate that just as God has sent Jesus, so Jesus sends the disciples. As Jesus bears testimony to God, the disciples bear testimony to Jesus. Like Jesus, they are ambassadors. In order to understand further

17. Raymond Brown confirms the translation of *apostolos* here as messenger, but adds: "It is not impossible that John is thinking of the disciples as 'apostles,' i.e., those sent to preach the resurrection" (*Gospel*, 553).

18. See also John 3:17, 34; 5:36, 38 [cf. 5:37]; 6:57; 7:29; 8:42; 10:36; 11:42; 17:3, 8, 18, 23, 25; 20:21.

19. Karl Kertelge points to the balance in John's Gospel between the emphasis on the disciples as those who "abide with" or "in" Jesus and these passages that refer to Jesus' "sending" of the disciples (*Gemeinde und Amt im Neuen Testament* [Munich: Kösel-Verlag, 1972], 35).

20. I am deliberately hedging on the question whether this eucharistic passage represents the work of a relatively late redactor, as Bultmann would argue; see Bultmann, *Gospel of John*, 234–37. Whatever the case with the eucharistic theology, the sense here of the relationship between Father, Son, and disciples is consistent with the main thrust of the Gospel's theology.

how these "sent" disciples function in John's Gospel, I shall need to look at the images of discipleship in my succeeding discussion of titles and officers in the Johannine church.

While there is no evident order of "apostle" corresponding to the particular authority of Paul in relation to his churches, there is attention to the role of the "beloved disciple," who apparently is seen by John's community as particularly authoritative. The authority of this disciple derives from the fact that he is a witness. It is he who bears some of the testimony that is central to the Gospel. It is this beloved disciple who first believes in Jesus' resurrection (John 20:8). It is presumably he who witnesses the crucifixion: "He who saw this has testified so that you also may believe. His testimony is true, and he knows that he tells the truth. These things occurred so that the scripture might be fulfilled" (John 19:35-36). The beloved disciple's role as exemplar may derive from his ability to love and follow Jesus, but his role as authority derives from his witness to the traditions about Jesus.

Jerome Neyrey has a further elaboration of the role of the beloved disciple and of the ways in which the Fourth Gospel contrasts him with Peter:

> It would seem safe to remark that "Peter" functions as a type of apostolic leadership based on eyewitness contact with the earthly Jesus and legitimated primarily in a commissioning of him by the same earthly Jesus—all fleshly and material criteria. The beloved disciple, however, represents a different type of leadership. It is more charismatic and dependent on performance and achievement for its legitimacy—criteria that appeal to spiritual or heavenly phenomena.[21]

In the developments that lead to the writing of the Gospel the Johannine community has had to distinguish itself from all worldly standards and leadership, including finally the leadership of Peter and the apostolic church, validated by the earthly Jesus and by fleshly, historical standards. By the time the Gospel is written (certainly by the final editing; see John 21:23) it is clear that the beloved disciple has died, so that he does not represent a living leader for the congregation but a revered reminder of its past.

Overall, then, the notion of "being sent" in John's Gospel suggests that the disciples are related to Jesus as Jesus is related to his Father.

21. Neyrey, *Ideology of Revolt*, 165.

One disciple, the beloved disciple, seems to represent an authoritative figure in the community. His authority derives in part from his privileged access to traditions about Jesus. What remains to be seen is whether the disciples are generally seen to foreshadow church leaders in the community of the Fourth Gospel or whether they represent the entire community.

RESOLVING CONFLICTS IN JOHN'S COMMUNITY

There are no passages in the Fourth Gospel that relate as directly to the solving of disputes in the community as Matthew 16 and 18 seem to do in that Gospel. However, that passage where Jesus breathes the Holy Spirit on his disciples, after the resurrection, recalls both Matt. 16:18-19 and Matt. 18:18:

> When it was evening on that day, the first day of the week, and the doors of the house where the disciples had met were locked for fear of the Jews, Jesus came and stood among them and said, "Peace be with you." After he said this, he showed them his hands and his side. Then the disciples rejoiced when they saw the Lord. Jesus said to them again, "Peace be with you. As the Father has sent me, so I send you." When he had said this, he breathed on them, and said to them, "Receive the Holy Spirit. If you forgive the sins of any, they are forgiven them; if you retain the sins of any, they are retained." (John 20:19-23)[22]

Here it is not the keys that provide authority for the disciples, but the gift of the Spirit. As with Matt. 18:18, the authority provided is clearly not primarily the authority to interpret God's will but the authority to forgive sins. The terms are reminiscent of the claims in Matthew 16 and 18 that Peter, or the disciples as a community, are given the power to "loose" and to "bind."

The sins that are to be forgiven or retained are surely to be forgiven or retained by God, so Jesus here gives to his disciples the authority to pronounce or deny forgiveness in God's own name and with God's

---

22. Hans von Campenhausen points out that this passage reverses the order of the Matthean (traditional?) pericope: "The inversion which John has made in his traditional material is significant. In both versions in Matthew the 'binding' of sin comes before the 'loosing.' The effect of this is to emphasise the disciplinary aspect of church authority, that which is concerned with protecting the community against the sinner. By contrast John puts the right of forgiveness first, and the retaining of sin remains in undiminished force only as, so to speak, the reverse of this" (*Ecclesiastical Authority and Spiritual Power in the Church of the First Three Centuries,* trans. J. A. Baker [London: Adam and Charles Black, 1969], 139).

own power. What seems clear, therefore, is that in any dispute over the forgiveness of sins, the disciples are given authority to adjudicate: to forgive or to retain. What is not clear is whether the "disciples" in this passage—or throughout John's Gospel—represent leaders of the community or the community as a whole.[23]

LEADERS IN THE COMMUNITY OF THE FOURTH GOSPEL

I have suggested that the beloved disciple represents a figure of authority for the Johannine community. However, his authority seems not to be that of a living leader but that of a revered witness to the traditions behind the Gospel. Further, as Neyrey suggests, he may represent a spiritual, Paraclete-guided model of leadership to be emulated by the evangelist's community. What is less clear is whether the circle of disciples in John's Gospel is "transparent" (Ulrich Luz's term for Matthew's "disciples")[24] to the whole Johannine community or only to the designated leaders of that community.

It does seem clear that the disciples *are* transparent. The Gospel's interest in them is not strictly historical. They not only represent the original circle around Jesus; they also point ahead to the time of the Gospel and to the Gospel's community. The connection between Jesus' disciples and John's community is most evident in the High Priestly Prayer of John 17. Here Jesus prays for his disciples, lifting concerns that surely are appropriate to the community at the time the Gospel was written. Lest the readers miss the connection, Jesus makes it explicit: "I ask not only on behalf of these, but also on behalf of those who will believe in me through their word" (17:20). In this passage, at least, the disciples are surrogates or forerunners, not just of Johannine church leaders but of the whole community of believers. This is true also in John 13 where Jesus explains the footwashing to the disciples; his instructions seem appropriate not just to a circle of leaders but to the whole community of faith:

> Do you know what I have done to you? You call me Teacher and Lord—and you are right, for that is what I am. So if I, your Lord and Teacher, have washed your feet, you also ought to wash one another's feet. For I have set

23. Campenhausen argues that the authority is here clearly given to the congregation as a whole (ibid., 140).

24. See Ulrich Luz, "The Disciples according to Matthew," in Graham Stanton, ed., *The Interpretation of Matthew* (Philadelphia: Fortress Press, 1983), 98–128, and chap. 3, above.

you an example, that you also should do as I have done to you. Very truly, I tell you, servants are not greater than their master, nor are messengers greater than the one who sent them. (John 13:12b-16)[25]

Raymond Brown further suggests that the ongoing distinction between the beloved disciple and Peter in the Fourth Gospel represents in part the Gospel's claim that it is not the apostolic authorities, signified by Peter, who are especially faithful to Jesus. It is all believers who love Jesus—and the beloved disciple becomes an idealized representation of all Christians who are loyal to Christ. Brown writes: "All Christians are disciples and among them greatness is determined by a loving relationship to Jesus, not by function or office."[26] To put the point in other terms: even the beloved disciple represents a faithful witness rather than an official, authoritative teacher. He serves also as a model for later Christians by his loyalty to Jesus. (I discuss the relationship of the beloved disciple to Peter in John 21 in an excursus below. I follow many commentators in thinking John 21 to be a later addition to the Gospel, somewhat shifting the evangelist's view of office and leadership in the church.)

All the evidence, therefore, seems to point to the claim that the disciples of John's Gospel are transparent, not to later church leaders, but to the whole community of believers. This implies, at least, that in essential matters John's Gospel envisions an equality among believers with little or no concern for special charisms, offices, or hierarchical authority.

This suggestion is further confirmed by the fact that in the Fourth Gospel the language used for the disciples is not the language of authority or even function, but is familial and by implication collegial. In John 15:8-9 the language is explicitly familial: "My Father is glorified by this, that you bear much fruit and become my disciples. As the Father has loved me, so I have loved you; abide in my love." In John 15:12-15 the imagery shifts to that of friendship, but again it implies collegiality among believers, not hierarchical distinction:

This is my commandment, that you love one another as I have loved you. No one has greater love than this, to lay down one's life for one's friends. You

---

25. Raymond Brown implies that this command was understood from the start in the Johannine community to apply to all Christians (*The Churches the Apostles Left Behind* [New York: Paulist Press, 1984], 88 n. 128).

26. Ibid., 93. The whole discussion is on pp. 91–93.

are my friends if you do what I command you. I do not call you servants any longer, for the servant does not know what the master is doing; but I have called you friends, because I have made known to you everything that I have heard from my Father.

The prayer that all believers should be one (John 17:20-23) again moves away from any image of hierarchical or official distinction. The unity among Christians is to mirror the unity of Father and Son. United to God through Jesus, believers are also united—in equality?—to one another.

This cluster of family or friendship images for the church is not coincidental. We get the sense that in this community, authority and power are relational and egalitarian rather than official and hierarchical. This is not a surprising development in a smaller, more sectarian community holding together against threats from outside the church and against a more established church as well.

IMAGES FOR THE CHURCH IN THE FOURTH GOSPEL

The major images for the community of faith in the Fourth Gospel do not suggest any hierarchical relationship between Christians. More strikingly, unlike Paul's image of the body of Christ with its emphasis on different gifts and on the interdependence of the believers, the Johannine images stress the dependence of each believer directly on Christ and by implication suggest an equality not only of status, but of function, among believers.

In John 10 the image is of the church as a flock of sheep and of Jesus—alone!—as the good shepherd: "I am the good shepherd. I know my own and my own know me, just as the Father knows me and I know the Father. And I lay down my life for the sheep. I have other sheep that do not belong to this fold; I must bring them also, and they will listen to my voice. So there will be one flock, one shepherd" (John 10:14-16).[27]

Even more striking is the image of John 15. Here the relationship is not of Christian to Christian (of branch to branch) but of each Christian directly and equally to Jesus, the vine: "I am the vine, you are the branches. Those who abide in me and I in them bear much fruit, because apart from me you can do nothing" (John 15:5). The Pauline stress on interdependence would not work for this use of the vine image. Raymond Brown elaborates on this point:

---

27. I shall note the expansion of this theme in John 21 in the excursus below.

The Johannine vine is also an image capable of [Pauline] interpretation. Stalk, branches, stems, leaves, and fruit could have been used to illustrate diverse charisms of service as easily as members of the body. But John writes only about the vine [Jesus] and the branches [Christians]. The gospel shows no interest in diverse charisms that distinguish Christians: it is interested in a basic, life-receiving status enjoyed by all.[28]

A brief narrative touch in John's story of the feeding of the five thousand confirms this vision of the church as consisting of believers equally and directly related to Christ. In Matthew, Mark, and Luke, when Jesus feeds the five thousand he distributes the food to the disciples, who then distribute it to the crowds. Not so in John's Gospel: "Then Jesus took the loaves, and when he had given thanks, he distributed them to those who were seated; so also the fish, as much as they wanted" (John 6:11; cf. Matt. 14:19; Mark 6:41; Luke 9:16).

My discussion of the images for church in John seems to confirm a picture of the Johannine community. In that church there was little or no stress on church leaders set aside either for special authority or for particular function. John's portrayal of the disciples makes them transparent not for any special group of church leaders, but for the whole community of faith.

Johannine Christians are described in terms of family or friends, not of leaders and followers, lords and servants, teachers and disciples. The Johannine community is not even described in terms of its functional interdependence. The images John uses suggest the dependence of each believer on Jesus—in a direct, unmediated way. One wonders whether even the image of the priesthood of all believers would fit the Johannine community. Jesus seems to be the one high priest through whom believers are brought, one-by-one, into the presence of God. As we shall see, the Johannine epistles somewhat expand the imagery to a greater stress on love within the community, and John 13 and 15 stress love and service between Christians. However, the relationship of a Christian to God is direct, individual, through Christ and Christ alone.[29]

---

28. Brown, *Churches*, 90. This does not mean, of course, that the Johannine community has no concern for the fellow Christian. The whole argument of 1 John belies that. Rather the sense of community as organic and interdependent and of church members as diverse in function and service is not nearly so evident. It is almost as if each believer has a one-to-one relationship to Christ and a one-to-one relationship with each other believer.

29. See Eduard Schweizer, *Church Order in the New Testament*, trans. Frank Clarke (Naperville, Ill.: Alec R. Allenson, 1961), 123.

EXCURSUS:
COMMUNITY AND LEADERSHIP IN JOHN 21

Along with many other commentators, I am convinced that John 21 represents a somewhat later addition to the Gospel of John. Its difference from the rest of the Gospel is evident in part precisely in the way it treats issues of church leadership.

We have seen that in the main body of the Gospel, Peter, known in much of the church as a great apostle, is seen in a subservient position to the beloved disciple. The beloved disciple almost certainly represents the faithful believer in his or her direct relationship to Jesus. Peter represents by implication a more "apostolic" and "hierarchical" vision of church leadership, and his role is deliberately downplayed.

John 21, however, is particularly concerned with setting Peter's apostolic leadership within an appropriately Johannine framework. In the first part of the chapter (21:1-14), Peter and the beloved disciple play somewhat customary roles. It is the beloved disciple who needs to tell Peter that the figure they see is the risen Lord (21:7). On the basis of that affirmation by the beloved disciple, Peter acts out his loyalty to Jesus first by jumping into the sea and then by hauling the catch ashore. (The symbolism of the fish is unclear, but they may represent the believers to be brought in from the nations of the world.)

In the second portion of the chapter (21:15-25), however, the focus shifts considerably. The relationship between Peter and the beloved disciple remains an issue. Peter wants to know how he stands vis-à-vis that disciple (21:21), and the author of the chapter testifies that the authority (of this chapter? of the Gospel?) derives from the testimony of the beloved disciple.

However, here for the first time in the Fourth Gospel attention is paid to Peter's particular authority. In John 10, Jesus alone is shepherd of his flock. In John 21, Peter is given some of Jesus' authority: he is called to feed the sheep. This suggests that the Gospel may here be granting some legitimate authority to Peter and to those who stand in the succession of the more "apostolic" and hierarchical church—that church that honors Peter as its founder.

Note, however, that Peter's authority is qualified in appropriately Johannine terms. Like the beloved disciple, Peter is to derive his special status from the fact that he loves Jesus (as all Johannine Christians are to do); and as with the disciples who are Jesus' friends in John 15,

Peter will need to lay down his life for the flock: "No one has greater love than this, to lay down one's life for one's friends" (John 15:13; see John 21:19). Like the good shepherd, Peter will need to make the final sacrifice: "I am the good shepherd. The good shepherd lays down his life for the sheep" (John 10:11).[30] The story also apparently adapts the call story of Mark 1:16-20 to a Johannine context. It is not the pre-Easter Jesus who calls Peter to follow, but the risen Lord who forgives Peter his denial and calls him to follow, a shepherd following the good shepherd.[31]

Raymond Brown suggests a plausible setting for this expansion and addition to the original Gospel. If the Gospel itself represents a clear distinction between Johannine (sectarian?) Christianity and the more "apostolic" office-centered Christianity of the "mainstream church," John 21 may represent a later attempt on the part of the Johannine community to come to terms with the church at large: "In the redactional chapter 21 we may have a more moderate voice persuading the Johannine Christians that the pastoral authority practiced in the Apostolic churches and in 'the church catholic' was instituted by Jesus and could be accepted without denigration of the specially favored place in history given by Jesus to the disciple(s) whom he loved most."[32]

Therefore, we can see in this final recension of the Fourth Gospel a movement toward an acknowledgment (if not an acceptance) of a more official structure of church leadership. However, it is leadership still defined by Johannine norms—love and sacrifice—and it does not replace or diminish the more collegial community represented by the beloved disciple and his heirs.

THE JOHANNINE EPISTLES

Raymond Brown, Jerome Neyrey, and Wayne Meeks come rather close together in providing a persuasive reading of the historical rela-

---

30. See Brown, *Churches,* 93.

31. For the argument that John's Gospel knows and uses motifs from Mark, see Lloyd R. Kittlaus, "The Author of John and the Gospel of Mark," Ph.D. diss., University of Chicago, 1988.

32. Brown, *Community,* 162. See also the preceding discussion of the passage. Edward Schillebeeckx notes that "John 21 indeed underlines the pastoral role and the authority of Peter over all the church, but only after Peter has been subjected to the Johannine criterion of love" (*The Church with a Human Face,* trans. John Bowden [New York: Crossroad, 1985], 98–99).

tionship of the Johannine epistles to the Gospel of John. The evidence of language, interest, and community structure suggests that the Johannine epistles do represent developments within the community of the Fourth Gospel. The author of the Gospel is almost certainly not the author of the epistles; nor is it entirely clear that 2 and 3 John are from the same pen as 1 John. Nonetheless, these four "Johannine" writings can be persuasively argued to address one community. They represent developments within that community and its faith.[33]

Raymond Brown is perhaps most persuasive on the nature of the development of this community and its relationship to the writings under consideration. He argues that the epistles grew out of a time of schism within the Johannine community, probably early in the second century. Two groups, that represented by the elder who writes the epistles and another "heretical" group, compete as interpreters of the Johannine tradition as represented in the Fourth Gospel. Christologically, Brown suggests the opponents did not precisely deny Jesus' humanity—to do so they would have had to ignore too much of their own tradition. What perhaps they did deny was the salvific significance of that humanity—so, for instance, the stress on Jesus coming "by blood" as well as "by water," in John 5:6.[34] Ethically, the opponents come close to perfectionism, to the claim that unity with Jesus protects them from sinning. Eschatologically, the opponents hold to one Johannine theme—realized eschatology—while letting go the emphasis on future judgment that is present in the Fourth Gospel and emphasized in the epistles. Finally, the opponents apparently claim the authority of the Spirit for their own teachings, while the author of the epistles somewhat downplays the stress on the Paraclete evident in the final chapters of the Fourth Gospel. The author suggests, however, that the Spirit is closely bound to the community he represents, to the "we" who have borne witness "from the beginning" (1 John 1:1).[35]

Martin Hengel affirms the relationship between the Johannine epistles and the Gospel but charts the chronology differently. The epistles and Gospel emerge from the same school and from the teaching, if not

---

33. See Brown, *Community,* esp. 93–103; Meeks, "Man from Heaven," 71; Neyrey, *Ideology of Revolt,* 99–100.

34. Ibid., 117.

35. See ibid., 93–144, 166–67. Brown acknowledges that we see the opponents only as the author of the epistle sees them, and that some of the issues raised by the author may have to do with other kinds of community disputes; see ibid., 103–4.

the pen, of John the elder, who may well have known Jesus in Jerusalem in Jesus' last days. The epistles were actually written earlier than the Gospel, though the Gospel (with its various apparent seams and shifts) represents the long development of the elder's oral teaching. Chapter 21 of the Gospel may well represent the hand of a later editor or editors. Hengel also affirms that both Gospel and epistles seek to hold together what the opponents behind the epistles would tear apart—that the Christ, the one from God, is identical with the man Jesus—though Hengel thinks the issue is at least nascent docetism. Hengel's thesis is fascinating, but it depends on moving the Gospel farther from the dispute with the synagogue than the strong stress of passages like John 9 would suggest. While tracing trajectories is always iffy, the move from pre-Johannine tradition to Gospel to epistles still seems a more persuasive track. Whether or not, as Hengel argues, the Johannine writings represent the work or reminiscences of one seminal figure, I affirm with Hengel and Brown that the reflection of one community or—with Hengel—even one school lies behind these works.[36]

If we are right in seeing in the Johannine epistles a further development of the community of the Fourth Gospel, we can draw some inferences about that community. The community is still sectlike insofar as it distinguishes itself sharply from the world and the values of the world. "We know that we are God's children, and that the whole world lies under the power of the evil one" (1 John 5:19). "Many deceivers have gone out into the world, those who do not confess that Jesus Christ came in the flesh: any such person is the deceiver and the antichrist" (2 John 7). I take it that this last passage means not just that there are deceivers around, but that deceivers have gone out from the church into the world—to Satan's sphere. The world, as Brown points out, is not now identified with the synagogue but with the defectors from the Johannine community.[37]

The community of the epistles is also sectlike insofar as it defines Christian obedience primarily in terms of relationships within the community. The great commandment once again becomes: "Those who love God must love their brothers and sisters also" (1 John 4:21; cf. John 13:34-35).

---

36. See Martin Hengel, *The Johannine Question,* trans. John Bowden (London: SCM; Philadelphia: Trinity Press International, 1989).

37. Brown, *Community,* 143–44.

The community is clearly spread among various locales, however. The elder sends emissaries from one town to another. He sends greetings from "children" in one church to "children" in another church, another location. If Abraham Malherbe is right, local "churches" can have several house congregations, as well.[38]

Furthermore, as with other sects in their attempt to be pure, the community has evidently suffered schism:

> Children, it is the last hour! As you have heard that antichrist is coming, so now many antichrists have come. From this we know that it is the last hour. They went out from us, but they did not belong to us; for if they had belonged to us, they would have remained with us. But by going out they made it plain that none of them belongs to us. (1 John 2:18-19; see also 4:1-3)

> Many deceivers have gone out into the world, those who do not confess that Jesus Christ has come in the flesh; any such person is the deceiver and antichrist! (2 John 7)[39]

What is striking is what the author of the epistles does not do in the face of schism and "heresy." He does not refer to the authority of his office, or to any inherited apostolic claim to adjudicate right from wrong. He appeals rather to the tradition (presumably that witnessed in the Fourth Gospel) and to the truths that should be self-evident in the family: that one cannot love God, the parent, without loving the children as well, and that Jesus, the true Christ, came in the flesh:

> We declare to you what was from the beginning, what we have heard, what we have seen with our eyes, what we have looked at and touched with our hands, concerning the word of life—this life was revealed, and we have seen it, and testify to it, and declare to you the eternal life that was with the Father, and was revealed to us. (1 John 1:1-2)[40]

As in the Gospel, in the Johannine epistles there is no stress on apostleship or on the figure of any apostle. The author of 2 and 3 John, however, designates himself as the elder (2 John 1; 3 John 1). It is not clear whether this designation represents any kind of office, as it clearly

---

38. See Abraham Malherbe, *Social Aspects of Early Christianity,* 2d ed. (Philadelphia: Fortress Press, 1983), 70, 104–5.

39. For a plausible reconstruction of the history of schism in the Johannine community see Brown, *Churches,* 108–23. The evidence of the epistles suggests that part of what was at issue was at least perceived by the writer as docetism.

40. The echoes of the Prologue of the Fourth Gospel are surely deliberate.

does in the Pastoral Epistles. The use of familial imagery throughout these epistles suggests that in part the image here is familial too: "the elder" as in elder brother, or revered elder.[41] Certainly, as we see especially in 3 John 9, the elder wishes to claim for himself some genuine authority beyond that of any Christian brother or sister. In that sense the apparent egalitarianism of the Gospel is here augmented or shifted toward some more hierarchical model—though the model is that of a family.

The question of the authority of the elder is pertinent to the question of how conflicts apparently are solved in the communities of the epistles. In reading 3 John (and to some extent 2 John) we get the sense that the elder wishes to claim for himself the authority to determine who is and who is not welcome in the house and the house church to which he writes. However, that authority needs to be tested and validated by the authority of the church itself. (Of course Paul has to argue for his authority, but we have his more extended arguments why his authority is not dependent on the approval of others.) In 2 John, the elder argues that the question of who is or is not welcome depends on the validity of the visitor's doctrine: "Do not receive into the house or welcome anyone who comes to you and does not bring this teaching; for to welcome is to participate in the evil deeds of such a person" (2 John 10-11).

Abraham Malherbe argues persuasively that in 3 John, the elder is fighting the power of Diotrephes, who as host has thrown people out of his house church. Gaius has apparently earlier written a letter of commendation to some traveling Christian. Diotrephes, for whatever reason, not only refused to welcome this Christian but forced more hospitable Christians out of Diotrephes' house and the church that meets there. Gaius is commended for having welcomed these earlier travelers and is perhaps urged to welcome Demetrius now. Malherbe's argument

41. Brown (*Community,* 100–103) suggests that the elder may also have been a member of a "Johannine school," a circle of those particularly close to the beloved disciple and in that sense a validator of inherited tradition. The fact that he has to argue so vehemently for his cause suggests that he was *not* a bishop. See also Campenhausen: "He should not be thought of as a kind of 'superintendent'; he figures rather as a prophet or teacher of the earlier type, one of those 'elders' and fathers to whose testimony Papias and Irenaeus later appealed" (*Ecclesiastical Authority,* 121–22). Similarly, W. Trilling, "Zum 'Amt' im Neuen Testament: Eine Methodologische Besinning," in Ulrich Luz and Hans Weder, eds., *Die Mitte des Neuen Testaments: Einheit und Vielfalt neutestamentlicher Theologie* (Göttingen: Vandenhoeck and Ruprecht, 1983), 323.

depends in part on the suggestion that the "church" of verse 9 includes both Gaius and those who meet at Diotrephes' house.[42]

In these epistles we seem not to have clear lines of authority but rather to have conflicting claims to power. On the one hand, the elder thinks that he has the right to ask for hospitality for his emissaries (or to counsel inhospitality for "heretics"), and he is offended when his claims are not recognized.[43] On the other hand, Diotrephes apparently takes upon himself the power of host and householder. He welcomes whom he chooses to welcome and dismisses those with whom he disagrees. Malherbe defines the situation clearly: "The situation reflected is one in which power rather than ecclesiastical authority is exercised."[44]

The "titles" of church leaders and the images for the church alike reflect a familiar pattern. They are familial, personal. The elder may be more like an elder brother or father than like a "bishop." The author refers to the recipients of the letters as "children"—both *teknia* and *paidia* (1 John 2:1, 12, 18, 28; 3:7; 4:4; 5:21; and 3 John 4). The "elect lady" of 2 John 1 may itself be a personal term for the church to which he writes. The church members are designated as her "children" (2 John 4; see 2 John 13 where members of another church are designated as children of "your elect sister"). In 1 John 3:1, 2, believers are designated as "children of God" (so also 1 John 5:1-2). Children of God are contrasted with children of the devil in 1 John 3:10.

Christians are seen as brothers to one another, again a familial image. The significance of the term is perhaps most pointed in 1 John 4:20—5:1:

> Those who say, "I love God," and hate their brothers or sisters, are liars; for those who do not love a brother or sister whom they have seen, cannot love God whom they have not seen. The commandment we have from him is this: those who love God must love their brothers and sisters also. Everyone who believes that Jesus is the Christ has been born of God, and everyone who loves the parent loves the child. (see also 1 John 2:9, 10, 11; 3:10, 13, 14, 15, 16, 17; 3 John 3, 5, 10)

---

42. Malherbe, *Social Aspects*, 103–12.

43. The NRSV's translation of 3 John 9 ("Diotrephes, who likes to put himself first, does not acknowledge our authority") could read: "Diotrephes, who likes to put himself first, does not welcome us." That is, by refusing to welcome the elder's emissaries, Diotrephes refuses to welcome the elder himself.

44. Malherbe, *Social Aspects*, 109.

As in John 15:15, Christians are designated as friends in 3 John 15, and Christians are addressed as "beloved" in 1 John 2:7; 3:2, 21; 4:1, 7, 11; Gaius is addressed as "beloved" in 3 John 1, 2, 5, 11.

Even more than in the Gospel, the picture that emerges is of a community that the elder, at least, understands in familial, affectional terms. Insofar as authoritative relationships exist, they are modeled on the family: an elder addresses his brothers or his children. Among the children the relationships are those of brother to brother. Though in some sense the children are children of the elder, far more significantly, all Christians are children of God and therefore demand respect from other Christians—as brothers.

Perhaps most strikingly, the elder who writes 1 John, though he himself is clearly a teacher of the community, specifically denies that a community of Spirit-led Christians needs any special order of "teachers." He disputes the false teachers by arguing: "I write this to you about those who would deceive you; but the anointing which you received from him [God] abides in you, and you have no need that any one should teach you; as his anointing teaches you about everything, and is true, and is no lie, just as it has taught you, abide in him" (1 John 2:26-27; RSV).[45]

THE JOHANNINE CHURCH AND MINISTRY TODAY

The picture of leadership and authority in the Johannine community sketched above has pointed to the community's more sectarian nature. In that community there is little or no concern for apostolic authority or for teaching whose validity is guaranteed by succession or structure. The Holy Spirit, the Paraclete, is the true teacher who weds each individual Christian to right tradition and to the living Christ. Because each Christian is directly related to Christ through the Holy Spirit (and through Christ to the Father), no Christian acts as priest or director or teacher for another. The responsibility of Christians is to love one another, not to direct or teach one another. If there is a structure of authority in the Johannine church, it is hidden from our eyes. One's sense is much more of communal concern and decision making than of authoritative instruction or institutionalized leadership. Only John 21 and the instructions to Peter to be a good shepherd hint at a more in-

---

45. See Schweizer, *Church Order,* 127.

stitutionalized leadership—and even here it is not clear whether the Johannine community sees such leadership as appropriate to its life or only acknowledges the validity of apostolic leadership for other Christian churches.

Because, on the whole, the concern for the Eucharist moves to the background, we have little sense of appropriate official leadership at the table—if there was such leadership. Jesus' word, more than the eucharistic bread, becomes the bread of life, and the relationship of the believer is again directly with the Lord, unmediated either by leader or sacrament. The words of institution at the Last Supper give way to the washing of feet and the command to mutual service: here there can be no question of authority or priority. Believers are equal not in their privileges, but in their humility. Raymond Brown suggests how the shift in perspective from the table to the bowl has implications for visions of leadership:

> The washing shows more clearly than does the eucharist the theme of humble service by the Christian. Because it is so sacred, the eucharist has been very divisive in Christian history with almost every aspect having been fought about. Would Christians have argued with each other so fiercely over the washing of the feet? Many Christians vie for the privilege of presiding at the eucharist. How many would vie for the "privilege" of washing another person's dirty feet?[46]

Of course the Gospel of John is not without eucharistic references, but their place in the development and redaction of the Gospel is unclear, and the references provide no clues to the place of leaders in the celebration of the meal (see John 6:51, 53-57).[47]

Overall, therefore, our picture of the Johannine community is of a "family" where membership is egalitarian, and leadership, if it can be called that, is informal. Christians see themselves as individuals bound to Christ and to each other. Their authority is the Holy Spirit, the Paraclete, and not any human figure. The paradigmatic disciple is the one who is loved by Jesus, loves Jesus, and keeps the tradition; that disciple is not so much leader over other Christians as example for them.

46. See Brown, *Churches,* 88 n. 148.
47. If the context in John 6 provides any clues to the significance of these (later?) references to the Eucharist, we recall that Jesus serves the bread and fish directly without any intermediary help from the twelve (John 6:11).

The implications of this picture of the Johannine community for our ministries are several:

1. In some ways the structure of the Johannine churches is even more radically egalitarian than the structure of Paul's churches. Ernst Käsemann has argued that the movement away from egalitarian and charismatic church structure came as expectation of an imminent parousia gave way to institutional patience and ethical resignation to the long haul of history.[48] On the whole, the Johannine communities seem not greatly concerned with Christ's imminent return, though the stress on antichrists in the epistles may carry a stronger apocalyptic flavor than the Gospel. Yet even more than Paul's vision of the church, the Johannine vision of the church is egalitarian. Not only the diversity of authority but the very diversity of gifts is underplayed.

Could it be that John's vision of the church is more like that of the enthusiasts to whom—against whom—Paul writes 1 Corinthians than like the vision of Paul himself? The Corinthian Christians, too, may have lived quite immediately under the direction of the Spirit. Seeing themselves related to Jesus, either individually or with the help of a spiritual leader like Paul or Apollos, they have attended less to their dependence on one another. They think of themselves as vines on a branch, dependent only on the branch. Paul sees them as members of a body, dependent on one another.

The great strength of the Johannine church is that it envisions a unity between Christians and Christ that mirrors the unity between Christ and the one he calls Father. The weakness of such a vision may be that it undervalues the unity among Christians. The Johannine epistles, especially, try to correct this one-sidedness, but even there the love for the brother is a commandment, not a description of the essential nature of Christian community, of what it means to be in Christ.

2. Not surprisingly, a Johannine church that lives under the Spirit has only a tenuous need for spiritual leaders. The beloved disciple, Raymond Brown convinces me, is seen as a paradigmatic Christian, not a paradigmatic Christian leader.[49] The disciple's relationship to Jesus is often only confused by Peter's miscues; Peter is more a foil than a bishop. Perhaps in this way, the Johannine community celebrates the

---

48. See, for instance, Ernst Käsemann, "Paul and Early Catholicism," in *New Testament Questions of Today,* trans. W. J. Montague (Chatham, Eng.: SCM, 1964), 63–94.

49. Brown, *Community.*

equal relationship of believers to the Lord without any dependence on direction from the "official" apostolic leaders, and perhaps without much direction from leaders at all.

By the time of the epistles, some sorts of leadership are beginning to emerge: apparently in conflict with one another. There is the leadership of the elder, who bases what authority he has on his relationship to tradition and, he hopes, on a reservoir of good feeling within the family of faith. There is the leadership of Diotrephes, perhaps of Gaius, and other hosts and patrons of house churches whose authority derives largely from the fact that they can invite or dis-invite people to their homes and to the community that gathers there.

3. The conflict between the elder and Diotrephes, and perhaps the schismatic problems of the Johannine churches, suggest a possible drawback to the Paraclete-led egalitarianism of these communities. When notions of authority and responsibility or interdependence are not drawn from a theological understanding of the church—as for instance in Paul's symbol of the body of Christ—the inevitable conflicts and fusses will be resolved by means that have no particular Christian rationale. Competing voices simply beg for attention; competing powers see who can wield the bigger stick. Here, in the midst of a study that has been pointing toward greater reliance on the Spirit and less obsession with structures, a cautionary note emerges. No community will be without structure. Perhaps communities that are self-consciously structured and that draw theological warrants for their structure have a better chance both at resolving conflicts and at resolving them in ways appropriate to a community of faith than do communities that assume that trust in the Spirit militates against any form of authority.

4. All this is to say that in the Johannine communities, as I have defined them, ministry is most evident by its lack. A Johannine picture would suggest that at best ministry can be a useful tool for the life of the church; at worst it distracts the faithful from their direct relationship to Christ. Even in the most positive view of pastoral leadership, in John 21, where Peter's special authority is acknowledged, his authority is still that of an assistant shepherd, who like the good shepherd tends the sheep and lays down his life for them. There is no sense that Peter's apostolic authority is necessary for the existence of a true church; he is, at best, useful.

5. We have seen that sacraments are underplayed in John's theology. Where there is a hint of Eucharist, in John 6, Jesus serves the

elements—bread and fish—directly to the crowds. No intermediary officiant, no priest or pastor, no disciple stands between Jesus and those who need the bread of life. Where the institution of the Last Supper comes in the other Gospels, here Jesus institutes the washing of feet. Surely Raymond Brown is right in suggesting that just here where we clergy wait eagerly for the words of institution that will institutionalize our authority, the Johannine Christ fools us. What he commands is probably a commandment for all Christians, to serve one another in love. If by any chance Jesus' command can be read as a special word for Christian leaders, the word is to doff our Geneva gowns, our surplice, stole, or alb and put our aprons on. If there is a table in the Johannine church, all have equal place there. If there is any special office at that table, it is not the office of the president but the office of the one who takes the basin and the towel to wash the feet of those who come to eat.

CHAPTER 5

Ministry in Luke and Acts

There is nearly unanimous agreement among New Testament scholars that the Gospel of Luke and the book of Acts were written by the
same person. For convenience I shall refer to the author of the two-
volume work as Luke, without making any judgment whether Luke,
Paul's companion, was in fact the author of these two books.[1]

However we may understand the purpose of this two-volume work,
the very fact that the Gospel is supplemented by a "history" of the
earliest church suggests a somewhat different understanding of Jesus'
ministry and his relationship to his first followers than we have in
Matthew or John. In Matthew and John alike the stories about Jesus
and his followers provided fairly direct reference points for our understanding of the Matthean or Johannine churches. The disciples served
as surrogates, either for first-century church leaders (as in Matthew's
Gospel) or for the whole circle of church members (as in John's
Gospel).

Luke and Acts put the apostles at historical distance from the author
and his church. The twelve apostles are not stand-ins for either church
members or church leaders of Luke's time. They represent the circle of
unique, irreplaceable witnesses to the ministry and resurrection of Jesus.
With their death, apostleship ceases in the church. While the picture of

---

1. For a discussion of the issue see Joseph A. Fitzmyer, *The Gospel according to Luke
I–IX,* AB (Garden City, N.Y.: Doubleday, 1979), 35–53.

the apostles may point ahead to the church leadership of Luke's time, it does so in ways that are indirect—marked as much by distinction as by similarity.

THE HISTORICAL SITUATION FOR WHICH LUKE WRITES

I make the same disclaimer I made in the discussions of the historical situation for Matthew's and John's Gospels. Our knowledge of the immediate history behind the writing of Luke-Acts is always inferential and indirect. Different hypotheses represent different interpretations of the same primary evidence: the texts themselves.

There is general agreement that Luke and Acts were written after the fall of Jerusalem and the destruction of the temple.[2] There is general agreement that the books seek to set the emerging church in the context of its relationship to the Old Testament and to Israel. There is disagreement on whether Luke envisions the (gentile) church as replacing Israel or whether believing Jews are now the ongoing covenant people of God. Along with this there is some question whether Luke writes primarily as a Gentile or as a Hellenistic Jewish Christian.

Jacob Jervell is perhaps the most influential proponent of the claim that the church does not represent a new Israel, but that faithful Israel continues among believing Jews. Jervell summarizes his own work:

> I try to show that Luke never had any conception of the church as the new or true Israel. Luke is rather concerned to show that when the gospel was preached, the one people of God, Israel, was split in two. The result is that those Jews who do not accept the gospel are purged from Israel; the history of the people of God, of the one and only Israel, continues among those obedient Jews who believe in Jesus.[3]

Jervell effectively demonstrates that in the early chapters of Acts the apostles' preaching always divides the Jewish congregation. Many disbelieve but many also believe.[4] The mission to the Gentiles, Jervell argues, does not replace the mission to the Jews but is an extension of

2. See, for instance, ibid., 53–57; Hans Conzelmann, *Acts of the Apostles,* trans. James Limburg, A. Thomas Kraabel, and Donald H. Juel, Hermeneia (Philadelphia: Fortress Press, 1987), xxxiii.

3. Jacob Jervell, *Luke and the People of God* (Minneapolis: Augsburg, 1972), 15. A similar argument is found in David L. Tiede, *Prophecy and History in Luke-Acts* (Philadelphia: Fortress Press, 1980).

4. See Jervell, *Luke,* 43–46.

that mission. What is at issue is the question of obedience to the Torah. Acts argues that Gentiles join the community of the faithful without any requirement that males be circumcised. However, the inclusion of the Gentiles does not contradict Torah and the Prophets but is foretold therein.[5]

For Jervell, the twelve apostles are not guarantors of the traditions about Jesus; they do not represent the beginning of church offices; nor are they prototypes of later church leaders. Their sole function is to serve as signs for the restoration of Israel, as guaranteed through the resurrection of Jesus Christ. The key passage for understanding their function is Luke 22:28-30, where the apostles are promised that they will sit on twelve thrones to judge the tribes of Israel.[6]

Jervell's reminder that Israel continues to include believing Jews is entirely persuasive. His discussion of the function of the twelve seems accurate as far as it goes, though he undervalues the role of the apostles as witnesses who foreshadow later witnesses. Two features of his argument, however, are less immediately persuasive.

Jervell's discussion of the end of Acts (28:23-31) seems too sanguine in its conviction that God's activity has not now turned from the Jews to the Gentiles. To be sure, even in this last recorded preaching of Paul's, "some [Jews] were convinced by what he had said, while others refused to believe" (28:24).[7] However, the citation from Isaiah seems to close the door on further witnessing to Israel, and Paul's closing comment seems a conclusion, not just to the scene but to the two-volume work: "Let it be known to you then that this salvation of God has been sent to the Gentiles; they will listen" (28:28).[8]

More crucially, Jervell's conclusion that Luke-Acts is written by a Jewish Christian for Jewish Christians does not follow even from the most sympathetic reading of his premises.[9] It does seem clear that the

---

5. Ibid., 56–58.

6. See ibid., 75–112.

7. The NRSV's translation seems more tendentious than the RSV's "others disbelieved." The Greek is *epistoun*.

8. See Jervell, *Luke*, 63. Perhaps the clearest statement of a "hard line" reading of the text is Conzelmann's: "The picture of Judaism divided within itself is presented here for the last time. Luke no longer counts on the success of the Christian mission with 'the Jews'" (*Acts*, 227). Similar is Ernst Haenchen, *The Acts of the Apostles: A Commentary*, trans. R. McL. Wilson (Philadelphia: Westminster Press, 1971), 723–24.

9. Jervell, *Luke*, 174–77. To be sure the conclusions here are based largely on Jervell's description of the role and speeches of Paul in Acts.

relationship between Israel and gentile Christians is a major theme for Luke and Acts, but this could be explained in the light of apologetic purposes—as Luke stresses the antiquity and perhaps even the legality of the new.[10] Nils Dahl suggests, more plausibly, that Luke-Acts was written primarily for the "God-fearers" to whom Acts several times refers. If they find Judaism an appealing religious option, why not show that Christianity is the rightful fulfillment of the promises to Israel?[11]

Joseph A. Fitzmyer, in his Anchor Bible commentary, sees Luke-Acts, however, as primarily written for Gentiles. Fitzmyer holds that the author of Luke-Acts was indeed Luke, Paul's companion, a position on which I remain agnostic. He conjectures that Luke was a gentile Christian, perhaps from Antioch.[12] Fitzmyer also convincingly maintains the now widespread view that Luke-Acts was written for a predominantly gentile audience. The evidence for this view includes the following data: (1) Luke's concern to set his work within the context of secular, Roman history; (2) Luke's stress on the inclusion of the Gentiles within the scope of God's promised salvation; and (3) Luke's "elimination of materials from his sources, 'Mk' or 'Q,' that are predominantly Jewish preoccupations."[13]

Fitzmyer also shows that Luke-Acts was written after the fall of Jerusalem, which it presupposes, and before the collection of Paul's epistles (toward the end of the first century), because Luke shows no knowledge

---

10. On this see George E. Sterling, "Luke-Acts and Apologetic Historiography," SBLASP (Atlanta: Scholars Press, 1989), 337; and Douglas R. Edwards, "Acts of the Apostles and the Graeco-Roman World: Narrative Communication in Social Contexts," in that same collection, 366.

11. See Nils A. Dahl, "The Purpose of Luke-Acts," in *Jesus in the Memory of the Early Church* (Minneapolis: Augsburg, 1976), 87–98, esp. 96–98. Similarly Philip F. Esler, *Community and Gospel in Luke-Acts* (Cambridge: Cambridge Univ. Press, 1987), 31. Esler sees the Lukan community as a mixture of Jews and Gentiles, but suggests that the gentile Christians had mostly been previous "God-fearers." A. Thomas Kraabel suggests that the whole notion of "God-fearers" is a Lukan invention, but even without the title it seems likely that Gentiles interested in Judaism might provide at least one of Luke's audiences. See A. T. Kraabel, "Synagoga Caeca: Systematic Distortion in Gentile Interpretations of Evidence for Judaism in the Early Christian Period," in Jacob Neusner and Ernest S. Frerichs, eds., *"To See Ourselves as Others See Us": Christians, Jews, "Others" in Late Antiquity* (Chico, Calif.: Scholars Press, 1985), 219–46.

12. Fitzmyer, *Gospel*, 35–53. Fitzmyer also adds that this identification is not crucial to the interpretation of the Gospel (see p. 53). On Ephesus as an alternative to Antioch, see below.

13. Ibid., 58.

of the material in those letters. Fitzmyer guesses the date of the writing to be 80–85 C.E.[14]

More recent studies by Philip F. Esler and by Peter Lampe add further nuances to our understanding of the situation of Luke-Acts.[15] Esler argues that the gentile features of Luke-Acts combined with Luke's use of the Septuagint as a source for his theological reflection suggest that the community for which Luke writes was a mixture of Jews and Gentiles, the latter (as Nils Dahl also suggested) primarily God-fearers.[16] Two key issues for such a mixed congregation are evident in the concerns of Luke-Acts. First, there is the issue of table-fellowship, central to the whole discussion of Acts 10 and 11. The resolution to the issue of table-fellowship was essential to the viability of a mixed congregation of Jews and Gentiles.[17] Second, there is the issue of the relationship of the church to Roman governing authorities. The evidence of Luke's apologetic sympathy for Roman rule evident in most readings of Luke-Acts points neither to an attempt to persuade the Romans that Christianity was a legitimate religion nor to an attempt to persuade Christians that Rome had legitimate rule. Rather Luke seeks to persuade Gentiles sympathetic to Christian faith that their loyalty to a crucified law-breaker does not conflict with their loyalty to the Roman state. They may become Christian without becoming subversive.[18]

Peter Lampe suggests that the congregations to which Luke-Acts was initially addressed were to be found in Ephesus. Lampe bases this argument partly on the close relationship between Luke-Acts and the Pastoral Epistles. Particularly evident are correspondences between the Pastorals (with the letters to Timothy addressed to Ephesus) and Acts

14. Ibid., 53–57. Conzelmann puts the date between 80–100 C.E. (*Acts,* xxxiii).

15. Philip Francis Esler, *Community and Gospel in Luke-Acts* (Cambridge: Cambridge Univ. Press, 1987), and Peter Lampe, *Lokalisation der Lukas-Leser: Lk/Apg. als Zeugnisse für das ephesische Christentum des ausgehenden l.Jh.* (Tübingen: J. C. B. Mohr [Paul Siebeck], forthcoming).

16. See Esler, *Community,* 31–41. Esler (in chap. 5) also maintains that Luke's ongoing interest in the validity of the law suggests an ongoing issue in a mixed church for which he writes.

17. See ibid., 96–109.

18. See ibid., 208–18. For a similar argument see Vernon K. Robbins, "The Social Location of the Implied Author of Luke-Acts," in Jerome Neyrey, ed., *The Social World of Luke-Acts: Models for Interpretation* (Peabody, Mass.: Hendrickson, 1991), esp. 330. For an alternative reading of Luke's attitude toward Rome, see Paul Walaskay, *"And So We Came to Rome": The Political Perspective of St. Luke* (Cambridge: Cambridge Univ. Press, 1983).

20 (with Paul's speech to the Ephesian elders).[19] The issue that "Paul" addresses in Acts 20, and that is therefore crucial to Luke's own purposes, is the issue of super-Paulinists among the Ephesian churches. These Paulinists may claim to be apostles for a new generation, which is one reason that Luke underplays Paul's own historical role as an apostle. Lampe also holds that Theophilus, as a kind of ideal reader for Luke-Acts, is either a baptized Christian or a sympathizer from the circle of those who visit church and synagogue seeking the assurance of right belief.

Lampe and Esler, following a line earlier suggested by Dahl, help make sense of the diverse data studied by Jervell and Fitzmyer. Luke probably writes for a community that acknowledges its continuity with Israel but is separate from the synagogue and that seeks to grow by appealing to those sympathizers who have been attracted to the synagogue but are now urged to choose the church instead. The church for which Luke writes, precisely because it is a mixed church, is threatened by "heretics" who would outdo Paul by leaving behind not only the synagogue but respect for the Torah.

My sense of the historical setting for Luke-Acts is this: after the fall of Jerusalem, Luke—a Gentile—writes for a church in Ephesus. The church consists both of Jewish and of gentile Christians, but almost certainly with a preponderance of the latter.

One way to read Luke's view of church structure and church leadership is to see it growing out of his twofold stress on the continuity between Israel and the church, on the one hand, and the genuine newness of the postresurrection church living in the Spirit, on the other. What would threaten that church is either a retreat to ethnic separatism, violating the fellowship of the table, or a rush toward extravagant Paulinism without sufficient respect to the Torah. Luke's portrayal of the apostles and his directions for proper church order grow out of these pervasive concerns.

LUKE'S UNDERSTANDING OF APOSTLESHIP

The apostles are central to Luke's narrative of Jesus' ministry and to his narrative of the first years of the church. In Luke and Acts—unlike the other material we have studied—the term "apostle" is reserved for

19. See Lampe, *Lokalisation,* chap. 7, pt. 1.

the circle of the twelve around Jesus, with Judas replaced by Matthias after the crucifixion.[20] The narrative of Matthias's selection in Acts 1:21-26 is indicative of the way in which Luke understands apostleship.

Three features of this story indicate Luke's understanding of apostleship. First, the circle of the apostles is identical with the circle of the twelve. When one of the twelve betrays Jesus and deserts his "place," another must be chosen to complete the requisite number. This indicates not only a historical reminiscence of the importance of twelve followers for Jesus; it also represents the sense that the twelve apostles represent or replace the leaders of the twelve tribes of Israel in the transition to the new community, the church.[21] Second, an apostle must be one who accompanied Jesus on his earthly ministry: "beginning from the baptism of John until the day when he was taken up from us." Third, the primary function of the apostle is not to witness to Jesus' earthly ministry but to witness to Jesus' resurrection. This witnessing apparently means not just "bearing witness" but bearing witness to what one has witnessed (i.e., seen), the appearances of the risen Lord. (While Jesus' resurrection appearances in Luke and Acts are primarily to the eleven, they are not exclusively so. See, for instance, Luke 24:13-35.)[22] The last chapter of Luke and the first chapters of Acts indicate the fundamental role Luke sees for the apostles: they bear witness, testify, to what God has done in Jesus Christ. This testimony begins at Jerusalem, but through the apostles (and those they recognize) it is to spread throughout the world.

After the resurrection, in Luke 24:36-49, Jesus renews the call to the apostles. Jesus becomes the first witness to the meaning of his own death and resurrection and then passes that kerygma on to the apostles (who in turn will pass it to Paul and through Paul to Luke's own church). At his ascension, Jesus says to the eleven: "But you will receive power when the Holy Spirit has come upon you; and you will be my witnesses in Jerusalem, in all Judea and Samaria, and to the ends of the earth" (Acts 1:8; see also Acts 3:14-15; 10:40-42). The apostles, therefore, become both the heirs and the guarantors of Jesus' ministry. Like him they engage in teaching (Acts 2:42) and in the working of miracles (Acts 2:43). They in their turn preach the kerygma that he presents in

20. The exception is the reference to Paul and Barnabas as "apostles" in Acts 14:4 and 14:14, on which more below.

21. See Luke 22:28-30, and Conzelmann, *Acts,* 12.

22. See Eduard Schweizer, *Church Order in the New Testament,* trans. Frank Clarke (Naperville, Ill.: Alec R. Allenson, 1961), 70–71.

Luke 24:45-47, interpreting Jesus' ministry, death, and resurrection in the light of Scripture and calling people to repentance in his name (see, for instance, Acts 2:38-39; 3:17-26; 10:34-43).

What is striking in Luke and Acts, however, is that the office of apostle ceases with the ministry of the twelve. As they fade from the scene halfway through the book of Acts, the apostolic office disappears from view. That is, no one, not even Paul, becomes a new apostle. What remains, however, is the apostolic ministry—or ministry in continuity with the apostles. Such ministry includes teaching, healing, and above all the kerygma.[23]

There is a succession of proclamation—from Jesus, to the apostles, to Paul, to the later gentile church. What is passed on from one generation to the next is not, however, the office or title of apostle—but the message the apostles have been given to proclaim. A new generation bears witness to a story they did not themselves witness.

The succession from the apostles to a larger circle of preachers and missionaries is first signaled in Acts in the transitions from Acts 10 through Acts 15.[24] In Acts 10–11, in his interaction with Cornelius and the vision from God, Peter is persuaded that the gospel is to be preached to Gentiles as well as to Jews. In Acts 11:25-26, Barnabas and Paul are teachers of the church at Antioch. The connection is made delicately but clearly. Barnabas is appointed or acknowledged by the Jerusalem church, which is not simply identical with the apostles but is closely related to them. Barnabas in turn goes to get Saul. The succession from the apostles and the Jerusalem church to Barnabas to Paul is acknowledged, but without any particular speech or ceremony.

In Acts 12:1-3, James, the brother of John, is killed, and the first of the apostolic circle is removed from the church's ministry. No new apostle is appointed to replace him. Peter is imprisoned, and though he miraculously escapes, his imprisonment is a foreshadowing of his imminent disappearance from the narrative in Acts. (At the end of the narrative Paul is imprisoned; it is for the next generation, we presume,

---

23. Using terms from sociological study, Halvor Moxnes describes the role of the apostles in Luke-Acts as that of brokers ("Patron-Client Relations and the New Community in Luke-Acts," in Neyrey, *Social World,* 241–68).

24. Joseph Tyson sets the effective disappearance of apostolic authority from the scene at Acts 12. See his "The Emerging Church and the Problem of Authority in Acts," *Int* 42, no. 2 (1988): 142.

—

to carry on the ministry.) In Acts 13:1-3, the Holy Spirit acknowledges the ministry of Barnabas and Saul, and they are set aside for their missionary work by the laying on of hands—but it is not the apostles who lay hands on Barnabas and Saul. The modest apostolic acknowledgment of their mission is now followed by the explicit affirmation of the Holy Spirit and the "ordination" not by the apostles, but by other church members—prophets and teachers.[25]

In Acts 13:16-41, Paul preaches to Jews and God-fearers, and the kerygma he preaches is very much like that which the apostles received from Jesus. The striking transition comes at Acts 13:30-33: "But God raised him from the dead; and for many days he appeared to those who came up with him from Galilee to Jerusalem, and they are now his witnesses to the people. And we bring you the good news that what God promised to our ancestors, he has fulfilled for us, their children, by raising Jesus." Put most simply, the notion of "witnessing" has now been divided. The original apostles are still the eyewitnesses, but even Paul, who was not an eyewitness, is empowered to "bring the good news." The original witnesses are no longer the sole (or even the primary) evangelists. (Like Jesus and then the apostles, Paul and Barnabas not only teach and preach; they do miracles [Acts 14:3, 8-18].) Then with the apostolic council of Acts 15, Paul and Barnabas have their ministry acknowledged by the apostles and the elders. With this acknowledgment, the center of the narrative passes from the apostles, especially Peter, to Paul. The kerygma moves, if not to a new generation, at least to a wider circle.[26]

All this is to say that the apostles provide the essential foundation for the later ministry of the church, but their own ministry does not continue. It is unique and irreplaceable. Their particular office is not passed on by the laying on of hands, but ends with their death. Their kerygma is passed on and becomes the basis for the mission of the church that succeeds them.

---

25. Conzelmann (*Acts,* 99), probably rightly, denies that this is an ordination at all. It is rather a blessing by equals as Paul and Barnabas begin their mission.

26. R. W. Wall suggests ways in which Acts 12:1-17 prepares the way for this transfer of authority ("Successors to 'the Twelve' according to Acts 12:1-17," *CBQ* 53, no. 4 [1991]: 628–43).

EXCURSUS:
PAUL AND BARNABAS AND "APOSTLES" IN ACTS 14

There is one section of Luke-Acts that uses the term "apostle" in ways different from the consistent usage I have suggested. In Acts 14:4, Luke refers to the conflict at Iconium: "But the residents of the city were divided; some sided with the Jews, and some with the apostles." Here, quite clearly, the "apostles" are Paul and Barnabas. The identification is explicit in Acts 14:14 where Paul has healed the man at Lystra who has been unable to walk. The people think that Barnabas is Zeus and Paul is Hermes and prepare to offer sacrifice. "When the apostles Barnabas and Paul heard of it, they tore their clothes and rushed out into the crowd, shouting, 'Friends [Gk.: Men], why are you doing this?" (Acts 14:14-15a).

Hans Conzelmann's explanation for Luke's unique use of "apostle" in this chapter is that he takes it over from a source.[27] Günter Klein strongly affirms not only the distinction between Paul and the apostles in Acts, but Paul's subordination to the authority of their proclamation. He explains the peculiarity of Acts 14:14 by suggesting that the original reading may be from the "Western" text that omits the term "apostles." Acts 14:4, Klein suggests, does not unequivocally refer to Paul and Barnabas.[28]

Whatever the explanation, the use of the term "apostle" in Acts 14 is unique in Luke-Acts and goes against the quite consistent understanding of "apostle" that we have traced.

RESOLVING CONFLICTS IN LUKE-ACTS

Because Luke appears to take account of the historical distance between the circle of apostles and the church of his own time, the connections between dispute-solving in Luke-Acts and dispute-solving in the Lukan church are not always evident.

The most striking passage in the Gospel of Luke is striking in part because of its differences from similar Matthean material: "Jesus said to his disciples, . . . 'Be on your guard! If another disciple [Gk.: your

27. Conzelmann, *Acts,* 108, 111.

28. See Günter Klein, *Die Zwölf Apostel: Ursprung und Gehalt einer Idee,* FRLANT 77 (Göttingen: Vandenhoeck and Ruprecht, 1961), 210–13. Conzelmann notes Klein's suggestion without comment (*Acts,* 108 n. 3; 111 n. 14). Tyson says the passage is a "puzzle" ("Emerging Church," 143).

brother] sins, you must rebuke the offender, and if there is repentance you must forgive. And if the same person sins against you seven times a day, and turns back to you seven times and says, "I repent," you must forgive' " (Luke 17:3-4). We shall see below that in Luke and Acts the term "disciple" seems to refer not to any particular group of church leaders, but to all faithful Christians. Therefore, this whole passage deals with the issue of Christians' relationship one to another. Christians are enjoined to solve disputes in two ways. When one Christian discovers another sinning, the first is to rebuke the second. If the sinner repents, the fellow Christian is to forgive. The first part of the passage suggests the responsibility of Christians to address any sin and to forgive any penitent sinner. The second part of the passage ("if the same person sins against you seven times a day . . . ") suggests that what is at stake is forgiveness on the part of the particular Christian who has been wronged. In either case (as in Matthew 18), what is striking here is that no cadre of church leaders is put in charge of admonishing against sin or of forgiving penitent sinners. It is the responsibility of each member of the community to be on guard against violations; it is the responsibility of each member of the community to forgive those violators who are truly penitent.[29]

We do not know for sure what sources Matthew and Luke may have had in common. Several features of Luke's discussion of sin and forgiveness are different from Matthew's. In Luke, the admonition to rebuke the sinful brother does not move on to a discussion of further levels of discipline (other witnesses to the rebuke, communal discipline, excommunication) but moves directly to the admonition to forgiveness (cf. Luke 17:3-4 with Matt. 18:15-17). In Matthew it is Peter who is given the admonition about forgiving (seventy times seven, without any specific mention of repentance); in Luke it is the community of disciples who are called to forgive (seven times, for a penitent sinner). Luke lacks any larger reference to the power of the community or its leaders to "bind" or "loose" the sins of community members (see Matt. 18:18).

So, too, the other Matthean passage where Peter is given particular authority and where Jesus confers the power of "binding and loosing" finds no parallel in Luke. In Matt. 16:18-19, after Peter's confession of Jesus as Messiah, the Son of the living God, Jesus confers on Peter the keys of the kingdom of heaven, "and whatever you bind on earth will

29. See chap. 3, above.

be bound in heaven, and whatever you loose on earth will be loosed in heaven." In Luke 9:20, Peter confesses that Jesus is "the Christ of God," but Jesus goes on immediately to warn the disciples to keep silent, without any particular recognition of Peter's authority or any reference to the gift of the keys. Thus in that Gospel where the role of the apostles is most clearly underlined there is no sense that Peter takes a unique role in the apostolic succession.

Issues of rebuke, penitence, and forgiveness seem to be matters between individual Christian believers, not matters for communal discipline and certainly not matters for the intervention by designated leaders. In this way the picture of discipline in Luke's Gospel is quite different from the picture we get in Matthew.[30]

Several passages in the book of Acts give us possible clues to Luke's view of the settling of disputes in the early church. One of those is Acts 6:1-6, a passage that presents a host of historical difficulties, and even as narrative its point is not quite clear.[31] Philip F. Esler is probably right that in the early history of this narrative there is a story of a split between Aramaic-speaking and Greek-speaking Christians in Jerusalem, perhaps having to do with the distribution of alms to Hellenist widows. Luke has reshaped the narrative to maintain his story of churchly harmony (and perhaps also, as we shall see, to give some hints about the nature of authoritative leadership).[32]

The description of what Stephen and the Hellenists actually do after their appointment ill fits the NRSV's suggestion that the seven are to "wait on tables" (Acts 6:2). John N. Collins shows that the notion of *diakonia* as service at table is derivative at most from the more general notion of the *diakonos* as one who is commissioned by another for a particular, often mediating, responsibility. Collins reminds us that the tables could either be tables where people eat or counting tables where people receive their allotment from the community. The passage, he thinks, is not about waiters but about ministers:

---

30. "In Luke the twofold activity [of rebuke and forgiveness] is to be part of the spontaneous life-style of the individual disciple, whereas in Matthew 18 it is a Christian duty ordained in a code of church discipline" (Charles Talbert, *Reading Luke: A Literary and Theological Commentary on the Third Gospel* [New York: Crossroad, 1986], 60).

31. On the difficulties with this text, see Conzelmann, *Acts,* 44.

32. Esler, *Community,* 139–45. Part of Esler's analysis depends on taking *diakonia* as referring to table service, which is what John N. Collins's study throws into question. See the following paragraphs.

The twelve call the task "duty," which is a further indication of how much the passage is about commissioned roles. The duty is the *diakonia* of 6:1. So named, it is a public function under someone's direction already existing in the community; it is a "daily" ministry in contrast with the ministry of Acts 1, which is to take the twelve "to the end of the earth." As ministry it is indeterminate, and we have to make our own estimates of the kind of care extended to the widows; the word says more about Luke's conception of a community with official structures than about how the community cares for its widows.[33]

While I find this explanation largely persuasive, I need to add that the work of the twelve in the *diakonia* of the word (Acts 6:4) is clearly contrasted with the work of the seven in the *diakonia* at tables (Acts 6:2). Therefore, it is not only the daily and local nature of the ministry of the seven that distinguishes it from the ministry of the twelve, it is the function of that ministry. My guess is that Luke sees the primary, though not exclusive, function of the seven to have to do with charitable administration; the primary, if not exclusive, function of the twelve is to preach the word. In the appointment of elders in Acts 20, we shall see that the two functions are combined, in Paul and presumably in the elders as well.

In shaping this story, however, Luke may reflect the practical distinctions within some churches of his own time. Church leaders (Do the apostles now point ahead to later elders?) nominate other church members to serve in the diaconal ministry. Some church leaders are primarily responsible for spiritual direction and proclamation. Commissioned by them, the diaconal ministers perform other functions, perhaps related to providing material help to the community.

The disciples clearly represent the whole community of the church. It is the congregation who chooses the actual "deacons." The apostles ratify that choice by blessing the deacons with prayer and the laying on of hands. The somewhat artificial reshaping of a first-generation conflict therefore serves to validate a third-generation practice.[34]

For the dispute settled in Acts 15, Hans Conzelmann provides the appropriate setting:

---

33. John N. Collins, *Diakonia: Re-Interpreting the Ancient Sources* (New York and Oxford: Oxford Univ. Press, 1990), 231.
34. See Conzelmann, *Acts*, 45.

It is not by chance that the Apostolic Council occupies the middle of the book. It is the great turning point, the transition from the primitive church to the "contemporary" church. From this point on the apostles disappear, even in Jerusalem itself (cf. 21:15-26, etc.). In Jerusalem continuity is represented by James, in the gentile Christian church by Paul.[35]

There are significant questions about the historicity of the story of the Jerusalem Decree, but no doubt about the significance of the incident in the structure of Luke-Acts and in Luke's own understanding of church.[36] In this transitional story, the apostles are joined by the "elders" (Acts 15:2, 4, 6, 22, 23). From now on, however, leadership will shift from the apostles to the elders—whose place as leaders, says Ernst Haenchen, Luke believes to be recognized throughout the church.[37] The resolution of the dispute—whether gentile Christians need to take on the Torah as part of their faithfulness—occurs in three stages.

First, Peter, as representative of the apostles, bears witness to the reality of his own mission to the Gentiles, a mission ordained by God (Acts 15:7-11; see Acts 10). Then, James, presumably as leader of the Jerusalem elders, affirms the testimony of Peter. However, it is James who makes the decision about what is to be binding upon gentile Christians. The apostles bear witness; the elders make decisions.[38] Finally, the whole congregation consents—presumably to the decree, certainly to the sending of a delegation from Jerusalem to Antioch. The leaders act with congregational approbation.[39]

By the time Acts is written, the Jerusalem church has faded from the scene, and with it much of Jewish Christianity. The story of Acts 15 may represent the reminder of a transitional period when the Jerusalem church turned to the elders rather than to the apostles for authority. It may also be that we find here a foreshadowing of the role of elders in the gentile churches as well. Certainly we see attention

---

35. Ibid., 114.

36. For some of the problems, see Esler, *Community,* 98, and Luke T. Johnson, *Decision Making in the Church* (Philadelphia: Fortress Press, 1983), 48–53.

37. Haenchen, *Acts,* 444, 461–62.

38. Conzelmann (*Acts,* 117) reads this differently as representing two "votes," one by Peter and one by James. Then the testimony of two witnesses agrees. If he is right we might have a clue to dispute-settling in the Lukan church. Does the testimony of two elders settle the case—or move the congregational leadership toward consensus?

39. See Robert Tannehill, *The Narrative Unity of Luke-Acts,* vol. 2: *Acts* (Minneapolis: Fortress Press, 1986), 192.

to that problem we have seen was central for Luke's communities: how gentile and Jewish Christians are to be together, especially to eat together.[40]

Luke T. Johnson reminds us that here as so often elsewhere in Luke, the church's reflection depends both on present experience and on the testimony of Scripture. Disputes are solved and unity protected by the theology that includes both tradition and contemporary narrative.[41]

In Acts 20:17-38, Luke acknowledges the authority of these gentile "elders." I shall say more on the issue of "offices" in the Lukan church below, but here I note only that the Ephesian elders are entrusted with the responsibility, if not of settling disputes, at least of guiding the church in right belief and practice.

A clear pattern emerges. The apostles receive their office because they are witnesses both to the ministry of Jesus and to his resurrection. They receive the kerygma from Jesus, and they pass it on to the church, especially to the elders, who with Acts 15 succeed the apostles. The role of the elders, both in Acts 15 and in Acts 20, is to preserve clearly the implications of the gospel for the life of the church. They are to do this against threats from Judaizers (in Acts 15) and from (perhaps gnosticizing) heretics (in Acts 20). There are important issues of succession in the way leaders are chosen to handle disputes in Luke-Acts, but the succession is the succession of true teaching rather than that of office or ordination.

To summarize this study of "disputes" in the Lukan congregation: in issues of offense and forgiveness, each Christian is called to rebuke and forgive his or her opponent. In issues of right teaching, a cadre of leaders—usually called elders, perhaps also bishops—succeeds the apostles by guarding the kerygma that they witnessed and to which they bore witness. In issues of administration—hinted in Acts 6—some combination of authority between leaders (here for the apostles perhaps for once foreshadowing later practice) and the congregation (the disciples) is assumed.

---

40. Luke T. Johnson (*Decision Making,* 83) points out that the stipulations of the decree about diet would make it possible for Torah-observant Jewish Christians to eat the same communal meals as gentile Christians. See also Esler, *Community,* 98–99.

41. Johnson, *Decision Making,* 86–87.

OFFICES IN THE LUKAN CHURCHES

Whereas in studying Matthew's and John's Gospels I suggested that the closest circle around Jesus sometimes was transparent to Matthew's or John's own communities, I have suggested that for Luke, the title "apostle" is reserved for the circle of the twelve and that apostleship ceases with their generation. For that reason, the Gospel of Luke does not really provide much direct material for understanding church leadership in the community of Luke's own time. I turn to Acts for discussion of "offices" in the Lukan churches.

The above survey of the material on apostleship and on disputes in Acts has already suggested that in Acts the leadership role of the apostles is taken over by groups of elders, both in the Jerusalem church and in the gentile churches represented by Ephesus. The first mention of Christian elders comes in Acts 11:30. Agabus has come down from Jerusalem to Antioch and has prophesied a great famine. "The disciples determined that, according to their ability, each would send relief to the believers [Gk.: brothers] living in Judea; this they did, sending it to the elders by Barnabas and Saul" (Acts 11:29-30).[42] Though no mention has been made of the institution of the office of elder in the church, Luke clearly presumes that elders represent a circle of leaders in Judea (where they will appear in Acts 15 at the Jerusalem Council). It may well be that by implication these Judean Christian elders function for the Christian community as the elders of the Jews function for them.[43] The present text, with its stress on channeling relief through the elders, suggests that they may have had some administrative function. Whether this represents a reminiscence of the historical role of elders in the Jerusalem church or Luke's projection of his own church's practice seems impossible to determine.[44]

---

42. For a survey of the use of the term "elder" in Jewish material, see Günther Bornkamm's article on *presbyteros* in *TDNT* 6:651–83. Bornkamm notes that "elder" and *episkopos* come together in Acts 20:28, perhaps a merging of more traditional Jewish and gentile missionary terms, though we have seen that *episkopos* has some Jewish antecedents as well (above, chap. 2). Hans Lietzmann also argues that the use of *presbyteros* in Greek material carries meanings quite different from those that develop in the church ("Zur altchristlichen Verfassungsgeschichte," in Karl Kertelge, ed., *Das Kirchliche Amt im Neuen Testament* [Darmstadt: Wissenschaftliche Buchgesellschaft, 1977], 93–143, esp. 107–25; the article dates from 1914).

43. Conzelmann (*Acts,* 91) thinks the reference to elders may come from a source, precisely because it is not really prepared for in the book.

44. See here Haenchen, *Acts,* 375.

In Acts 4:8, Peter addresses the Jewish leaders: "Rulers of the people and elders...." It may be that "elders" simply elaborates on "rulers of the people," or it may be that the two groups are distinct, functioning somewhat in authority like the "apostles and elders" of Acts 15. In 4:23, the elders are distinguished from the chief priests (so also 23:14; 24:1; 25:15). In 6:12, the Jewish elders are distinguished from the scribes. It would seem that Luke sees the elders as a circle of leaders within Judaism, but not as the only group functioning with authority. Perhaps Christian elders function in ways analogous to these Jewish elders.

The second mention of Christian elders comes in Acts 14:23: "And after they had appointed elders for them in every church, with prayer and fasting they entrusted [the disciples] to the Lord in whom they had come to believe." Here Paul and Barnabas are on their mission to the Gentiles. The apparent assumption is that in the gentile churches, as in the Jerusalem church, the leadership rests with a circle of elders. We can again guess that Luke is not so much presenting historically accurate information about the first generation of churches as he is reflecting the widespread practice of his time. As the authority of the apostles passes to the elders in Jerusalem, so leadership for the church in every place is in the hands of such a group. The term that the NRSV translates "appointed" apparently does not refer to any election by the congregation, but either to an appointment or an installation by Paul and Barnabas.[45]

We have already seen that in the account of the Jerusalem Council, in Acts 15, the elders function alongside the apostles. It may be that in the testimony ratifying a mission to the Gentiles without requirement of circumcision, Peter speaks for the apostles and James for the elders (see Acts 21:18). What is clear is that in the commissioning of men to accompany Paul and Barnabas the apostles and the elders both have a role, and that their commissioning is ratified by the approval of the "whole church" (Acts 15:22).

So, too, the decree sent to the Gentiles comes from "the brothers, both the apostles and the elders" (Acts 15:23; see also Acts 16:4). If the major function of the account of Acts 15 is to show forth the unity of the early church in its commitment to a circumcision-free gentile mission, a secondary function may be to underline the claim that the

---

45. Conzelmann sees this as an "installation" (*Acts,* 112). Haenchen sees it as a "selection" (*Acts,* 436). Both agree that the practice reflects Luke's situation, not Paul's. See Titus 1:5, where Titus is to "appoint" elders "in every town."

elders shared authority with the apostles and now, in Luke's own time, the elders rather than the apostles become the authoritative leaders of the church. Of course from here on it is not the Jerusalem elders but the gentile elders, commissioned and exhorted by Paul, who become the exemplary church leaders, though again at 21:18, Paul visits with James and the Jerusalem elders.

Acts 20:17-38 almost certainly represents Luke's picture of the appropriate role of elders in his own time. Paul represents the model elder and instructs the Ephesian elders, as his successors, in their duties. (The parallels to the Pastoral Epistles are clear.) Paul as model elder has taught right doctrine. This right doctrine includes the call for "repentance toward God and faith toward our Lord Jesus" (Acts 20:21) and "the good news of God's grace" (Acts 20:24). Presumably this good news, gospel, means life, while turning from this gospel means death. Paul insists that he is "not responsible for the blood of any of you, for I did not shrink from declaring to you the whole purpose of God" (Acts 20:26-27). We can guess that Luke cites or composes this claim on Paul's behalf because later "wolves" have led Christians astray, using Paul's teaching as authority for their own false teaching.[46]

Paul as model elder is willing to suffer on behalf of the right teaching he has received and now transmits (see Acts 20:19, 23-24). As model elder Paul is also unwilling to profit from his leadership (see Acts 20:34-35). By implication, therefore, the Ephesian elders and other Christian elders, the church leaders of Luke's time, are to be the inheritors and transmitters of the true apostolic doctrine. They are to be willing to suffer for the truth they proclaim. They are not to take financial advantage of their position of leadership and responsibility.

The central verses of this testament of Paul to his successors makes explicit the responsibility of the elders—presumably the responsibility of leaders in the Lukan churches. They are to serve as guardians (*episkopoi*) of the flock of Christians. Here the term *episkopos* is not a title but represents a function for the elders. They are overseers, but

---

46. See here Klein, *Die Zwölf Apostel,* 183–84, and Heinz Schürmann, "Das Testament des Paulus für die Kirche: Apg. 20:18-35," in *Traditionsgeschichtliche Untersuchungen zu den Synoptischen Evangelien* (Düsseldorf: Patmos-Verlag, 1968), 310–40. Haenchen (*Acts,* 593) treats the opponents as Gnostics. Jacques Dupont refuses to go beyond fairly general and stereotypical language to characterize the nature of the false teaching (*Le Discours de Milet: Testament Pastoral de Saint Paul* [Paris: Les Editions du Cerf, 1962], 219). For P. Lampe's persuasive suggestion see above, pp. 119–20.

their oversight is particularly the task of preserving their flock for the true teaching against the threats of false teachers without and apostates within (Acts 20:28-30). The elders are to be alert, be on watch. And they are to "shepherd the church," presumably with correct teaching (Acts 20:28).[47] The elders are also to follow Paul's example in "supporting the weak" (presumably among church members). They help the weak by not exacting monetary payment for their work—and perhaps by ministering to those in need as well (see Acts 20:34-35).

If the role of elder includes some care for the poorer or needier brothers and sisters, then we see here among the gentile elders a role similar to that presumed for the Jerusalem elders when money is sent to relieve the needy in Acts 11:30. It may also be that the responsibilities assigned to the seven in Acts 6 here have passed on to the elders as well (see Acts 6:1-3).

What seems clear in this passage is that Paul's mission and teaching have been validated by his relationship to the apostles—and by extension to the Jerusalem elders. Now he validates the teaching of the elders of Ephesus, who stand as surrogates for the church leaders of Luke's time.[48]

The final reference to Christian elders in Acts comes in Acts 21: "When we arrived in Jerusalem, the brothers welcomed us warmly. The next day Paul went with us to visit James, and all the elders were present" (Acts 21:17-18). Conzelmann points out that the absence of the twelve is probably historically accurate and certainly accords with Luke's scheme wherein the leadership of the church passes from the apostolic to the postapostolic generation with the Jerusalem Council of Acts 15. James represents the postapostolic generation in Jerusalem. Paul represents that generation among the Gentiles.[49]

The elders seem to represent the authoritative leadership of the Jerusalem church. They decide what it is appropriate for Paul to do and beseech, or require, him to do it. How far we can generalize this story (which affirms the continuity between Israel and Paul) to suggest that

---

47. See Conzelmann, *Acts,* 175, on the background for the title. Haenchen sees here clear signs of presbyterial, not monarchical, leadership (*Acts,* 592–93).

48. For a helpful discussion of Acts 20 as a sign of post-Pauline problems in the church and a structural solution, see Hans von Campenhausen, *Ecclesiastical Authority and Spiritual Power in the Church of the First Three Centuries,* trans. J. A. Baker (London: Adam and Charles Black, 1969), 80–81.

49. Conzelmann, *Acts,* 180.

elders in all the churches could make authoritative decisions is unclear. Taken with the other passages we have examined, this seems one more clue to the claim that the practice in Luke's time was to have congregations whose teaching leaders were designated as elders. These elders had certain decision-making power as well, and they probably had administrative responsibility for alms and for the care of the needy brothers and sisters. Overwhelmingly, therefore, the implied title for church leaders in Luke's own time is "elders," and their functions are best understood by examining the passages we have just interpreted.

If "deacon" is already emerging as a title for Christian leaders with specific functions, there is scant evidence of that in Acts 6:1-2. More likely, as we have seen, the diaconal function there suggested passes on to the elders (see Acts 11:30; 20:35). So, too, the word *episkopoi* in Acts 20:28 refers to a function of the elders and not to a distinct title for a church leader. The term "disciple," as we shall see, is used not for church leaders but for the whole community of believers.

The "prophets and teachers" of Acts 13:1-3 seem to be Christians designated by their charismatic functions within the community. Saul and Barnabas are apparently included among these. Agabus in 11:27-28 is apparently a traveling prophet, gifted by the Spirit with the power to predict. Judas and Silas in Acts 15:32 are marked as prophets again by their speech, this time a speech that encourages rather than predicts. One suspects in these passages a tantalizing hint of pre-Lukan church structure, but the evidence is exceedingly slim.

IMAGES OF THE CHURCH IN LUKE AND ACTS

THE COMMUNITY OF THE SPIRIT

Luke and Acts both stress the activity of the Spirit. It is the Spirit that rests on Jesus as he begins his ministry in Luke 4:18, and it is the Spirit that fills the disciples on the day of Pentecost in Acts 2:1-4. The gift of the Spirit is the sign that the days of promise have arrived (Acts 2:17). Baptism, membership in the community of faith, includes the gift of the Spirit (Acts 2:38; 10:44-48). Here indeed the gift of the Spirit precedes baptism and is itself the primary "sacramental" gift.[50]

---

50. On the inaugurating gift of the Spirit both for Luke and Acts, see Tannehill, *Narrative Unity,* 50.

The Spirit is also the church's guide in making decisions and resolving conflicts. When the Jerusalem church sends word of its decision concerning circumcision to the churches in Antioch, Syria, and Cilicia, the decision begins with these words: "For it has seemed good to the Holy Spirit and to us to impose on you no further burden than these essentials . . . " (Acts 15:28).

In his farewell address to the elders at Miletus, Paul makes clear the role of the Holy Spirit, not only in calling and empowering the church but in calling and empowering church leaders: "Keep watch over yourselves and over the flock, of which the Holy Spirit has made you overseers, to shepherd the church of God that he obtained with the blood of his own Son" (Acts 20:28).

DISCIPLES

I will begin by looking at the use of the term "disciples" in Acts and then move to a discussion of the term in the Gospel of Luke. My thesis is simple: while for Luke the apostles are the circle of twelve who witnessed Jesus' ministry and resurrection and then bore witness, the disciples are the whole community of believers, both in Acts and in Luke. Because there is continuity in the community of faith, the term "disciples" can be transparent to Luke's own community in a way that the historically bound term "apostle" cannot.

A central passage for understanding Luke's use of the term "disciples" is found in Acts 11:26: "So it was that for an entire year [Barnabas and Saul] met with the church, and taught a great many people, and it was in Antioch that the disciples were first called 'Christians.' " It seems quite clear here that the term "disciples" does not refer exclusively to Jesus' early followers or to Jewish Christians, but rather refers to the whole company of believers, of whatever generation, whether gentile or Jew. Similarly, in Acts 6:2 (where "the twelve called together the whole community of the disciples") the word "disciples" is a term for Christian believers (see also Acts 9:1, 26).

In Acts 14:22-23, the disciples, as the community of faith, are distinguished from their leaders, the elders. Paul and Barnabas are in Antioch where they "strengthened the souls of the disciples. . . . And after they had appointed elders for them in each church, with prayer and fasting they entrusted them to the Lord in whom they believed." This identification of believers as disciples seems to be perfectly consistent throughout Acts (see also Acts 6:1, 7; 9:38; 11:29; 13:52; 14:20, 28; 15:10; 16:1;

18:23, 27; 19:1, 9). In fact, the term "disciple" seems by far the most pervasive term for a believer in the book of Acts. We shall ask below what the image of believers as disciples might mean for Luke's understanding of the church.

Moving back from Acts to Luke's Gospel we can see that the term "disciples" in that Gospel refers to the larger group of those who follow Jesus. The apostles are called forth from the larger company and are distinguishable from it: "Now in those days [Jesus] went out to the mountain to pray; and he spent the night in prayer to God. And when day came, he called his disciples, and chose twelve of them, whom he named apostles" (Luke 6:12-13; see Luke 6:17).[51]

The sequence of episodes in Luke 9 is harder to read in a manner consistent with the depiction of disciples as believers in Acts. In the story of the feeding of the five thousand, in Luke 9:10-17, it would seem that "the apostles" (v. 10), "the twelve" (v. 12), and "his disciples" (v. 14) are all the same people. If, as Fitzmyer suggests, this is a foreshadowing of the Eucharist, then the disciples here represent those church leaders who provide the elements to "the crowd"—presumably the company of believers.[52] The use of the phrase "[he] blessed and broke them" may point toward a eucharistic motif here (see Luke 22:19).

If, however, Luke is consistent in his use of "disciples" as a term for all Christian followers, what happens in the feeding of the five thousand is that the company of believers (not just the twelve) takes the food that Jesus miraculously multiplies and provides it to the crowd—presumably the world. The disciples thereby imitate Jesus who, as the passage begins, has provided for the crowds the bread of his own mercy—through teaching and through healing.

If this reading is correct, then the question to the disciples that follows the feeding ("Who do the crowds say that I am?" [Luke 9:18]) is not a question for the apostles only but for the whole company of believers. The crowds at the feeding are therefore not believers receiving the Eucharist but undecided folk hearing teaching and receiving healing—foreshadowing the undecided multitudes of Acts. The disciples are

---

51. In Luke 9:54, James and John are "disciples," but of course that is not inconsistent with their being "apostles" too.

52. On the identification of apostles, twelve, and disciples, see Fitzmyer, *Gospel,* 761–63 and Eduard Schweizer, *The Good News according to Luke,* trans. David E. Green (Atlanta: John Knox Press), 154–55. For the scene as foreshadowing the Eucharist, see Fitzmyer, *Gospel,* 764.

the believers who are called to claim who Jesus really is. Then the in-junction of Luke 9:23-24—still addressed to the disciples—is addressed to all believers, of Jesus' time and of Luke's as well: "If any want to become my followers, let them deny themselves and take up their cross daily and follow me. For those who want to save their life will lose it, and those who lose their life for my sake will save it" (cf. Luke 14:25-33). Certainly in other key passages the disciples foreshadow the whole community of believers of Luke's time and do not represent either the apostles or the later circle of the elders (see, for instance, Luke 8:9-10; 10:23-24; 11:1-13; 16:1-13; 18:15-17).

More puzzling is the shift from Luke 17:1 to Luke 17:5. In Luke 17:1, a passage examined above, Jesus says "to his disciples, 'Occasions for stumbling are sure to come; but woe to anyone by whom they come.'" The passage goes on to discuss the importance of forgiveness among believers in the community. What is odd is the shift with 17:5: "The apostles said to the Lord, 'Increase our faith!' The Lord replied, 'If you had faith the size of a grain of mustard seed, you could say to this mulberry tree, "Be uprooted and planted in the sea," and it would obey you'" (Luke 17:5-6).

The possible connection between apostles and the next injunction is clearer. Here Jesus reminds the apostles: "So you also, when you have done all that you were ordered to do, say, 'We are worthless slaves; we have only done what we ought to have done'" (Luke 17:9-10). With 17:22, the audience for Jesus' teaching becomes the company of the disciples once again (as again in 22:45).

In Luke, the disciples, not (just) the apostles, accompany Jesus to the Mount of Olives, and the disciples sleep through Jesus' agonized prayer. Does Luke here conflate the disciples and the apostles—who have been present in the upper room? Or are the disciples "transparent" to later believers who still need to hear Jesus' injunction: "Why are you sleeping? Get up and pray that you may not come into the time of trial" (Luke 22:46)?[53]

Though the pattern is not quite so consistent in Luke as in Acts, still

---

53. The word Jesus gives Peter and John to share with the householder ("The Teacher says to you, Where is the guest room, where I am to eat the passover with my disciples?" [Luke 22:11; RSV]) does not fit clearly into our scheme, either. The next passage (Luke 22:14) brings the "apostles" to the guest room for the supper. They are, of course, also disciples, but the word to the householder may point ahead to Luke's own time when all disciples eat the Lord's Supper with Jesus.

the predominant use of the term "disciples" suggests that it refers to the larger company of those who followed Jesus—including the apostles but not restricted to them. If we start with the evidence in Acts—that is, that disciples are believers and that the term "disciples" is the predominant image for the church—we can move back to the picture of discipleship in Luke's Gospel and get some sense of what Luke understands the church to be. Disciples are those who acknowledge Jesus as Messiah, over against the crowds who do not know quite what to make of him. They are those who listen to his words, and who have received the secrets of the kingdom of God. They are those who obey him faithfully, even when that means taking up the cross—separation from family, from personal security, perhaps even martyrdom. In Acts the community of disciples is led first by the apostles and then by the elders, but their primary loyalty is to Jesus, whose disciples they are.[54] The term, then, probably still carries something of its root meaning: disciples learn from Jesus. They are under his discipline.

BRETHREN

Another term for believers suggests a familial image for the church. At a number of points in Acts, Christians are referred to as "brethren." In the following discussion I will quote the RSV rather than the NRSV. In its laudable attempt to be inclusive, the NRSV loses the familial connotations of the Greek text, translating *adelphoi* by terms such as "believers."

There are two slightly different uses of the term "brethren" in Acts, and both are evident in the first reference, Acts 1:15-16: "In those days Peter stood up among the brethren (the company of persons was in all about a hundred and twenty), and said, 'Brethren, the scripture had to be fulfilled, which the Holy Spirit spoke beforehand by the mouth of David, concerning Judas who was guide to those who arrested Jesus.'" Peter's address to his fellow believers suggests that the term "brother" was used in salutations to one's fellow Christians as in the Pauline epistles (see, for example, Phil. 3:1; 1 Cor. 10:1). Unlike Paul, Luke here uses two Greek words for the address, *andres adelphoi*.[55] The introductory phrase by Luke, however, also suggests that "brethren" was a

---

54. The only alternative use of the term "disciple" for a believer comes in Acts 9:25, where *Paul* has disciples.

55. For the use of "brethren" as an address to Christians, see also Acts 6:3, here using only *adelphoi*, and 15:7, 13, using *andres adelphoi*.

term used for the community of faith. Christians were "the brethren [*hoi adelphoi*]." It is with this usage that the term "the brethren" occurs most frequently in Acts.[56]

When Ananias greets Paul under the direction of his vision, he welcomes Paul into the community of believers: "Saul, brother..." (Acts 9:17). The word is not only a salutation; it is also an acknowledgment, almost an initiation (see also Acts 21:20). In Acts 11:1, the "brethren" are distinguished from the apostles in the Judean church, presumably as the community of believers is distinguished from the inner circle of twelve original witnesses: "Now the apostles and the brethren who were in Judea heard that the Gentiles also had received the word of God." In 15:23, in the apostolic decree, the brethren include (or consist of?) the apostles and elders in the Jerusalem church.

Acts can also use the term "brethren" as a form of address when a word is directed by a Jew to fellow Jews. So in his Pentecost speech Peter addresses the Jewish community gathered in Jerusalem: "Brethren, I may say to you confidently of the patriarch David that he both died and was buried, and his tomb is with us to this day" (Acts 2:29). The term translated "brethren" again represents the two Greek words—*andres adelphoi*. The penitent Jews address Peter and the apostles with the same phrase: "Brethren, what shall we do?" (Acts 2:37).[57] In Acts 13, the Jewish leaders address Paul and Barnabas as "brethren" (*andres adelphoi*), and Paul in turn refers to the Jews by the same address (Acts 13:15, 26, 38).

Stephen's address to the Jews in Acts 7:2 suggests both that the term "brethren" was used by one Jew speaking to another and that there is a familial—clan—connotation to its use: "Brethren and fathers, hear me. The God of glory appeared to our father Abraham." The familial imagery continues in Stephen's testimony to Moses: "When he was forty years old, it came into his heart to visit his brethren, the sons of Israel" (Acts 7:23). In that same speech, when Moses seeks to stop the fighting among the Hebrews, he says: "Men, you are brethren, why do you wrong each other?" (Acts 7:26). There is a strong implication here that familial terms are appropriate to the people Israel—and we

56. See also Acts 9:30; 11:12, 29; 12:17; 14:2; 15:1, 3, 22, 32, 33, 36, 40; 16:2, 40; 17:6, 10, 14; 18:18, 27; 21:7, 17; 28:14, 15.

57. Peter refers to his fellow Jews as brethren (here *adelphoi*) again in Acts 3:17. The Jewish leaders refer to Paul and Barnabas as "brethren" (*andres adelphoi*) in Acts 13:15.

shall suggest can therefore be taken over by the church that succeeds, if it does not supplant, Israel in God's purposes. (The familial imagery continues in Acts 7:37, 39.)

So, too, Paul's address to the Jews in Acts 13 draws on the sense that Israel is a family, of which he, too, is a member: "Brethren, sons of the family of Abraham, and those among you that fear God, to us has been sent the message of this salvation" (Acts 13:26). In Acts 22:1-3, part of Paul's defense depends on his "familial" relationship to his Jewish audience. Then, in Acts 22:5, in a manner not underlined but nonetheless significant, it is the Christians who have become "the brethren," and in 22:13, as in 9:17, Ananias welcomes Saul as "brother."[58]

Several uses of the term "brother" or "brethren" in Luke indicate that the Gospel can use the term to foreshadow the life of the later church. Luke 6:41-42, apparently looking toward life among believers, warns the "disciples"—forerunners of the church—not to worry about the speck in the brother's eye while ignoring logs in their own eyes. In Luke 17:3-4, in a passage I have already discussed, church discipline is discussed in terms of the brother: "If your brother sins, rebuke him, and if he repents, forgive him." In Luke 8:21, "brethren" are not brothers (and sisters) to one another only but to Jesus: "My mother and my brothers," Jesus says, "are those who hear the word of God and do it."

Therefore, in Luke-Acts the use of the term "brethren" for the community of believers suggests two understandings of the church. First, implicitly the church becomes a family. Though the implications of this image are not thoroughly developed, the early idealized portrait of the Christian community is familial (see also Acts 2:43-47). The believers may also be seen as the family of Jesus, in the light of Luke 8:21. The second understanding is more explicit. Israel has been understood as a community of brethren, a family, a clan. Peter and Paul address their fellow Jews as brethren. Now the church becomes the new family or clan, and while Peter and Paul do not cease addressing their Jewish opponents as brothers, the overwhelming use of the term suggests that the new family—a family of both Jews and Gentiles—is now the family of those who believe in Jesus. While this is not the forthright claim that

---

58. Paul continues to address the Jewish leaders as "brethren" in Acts 23:1, 5, 6; in 23:1 and 23:6, he uses the more formal opening address: *andres adelphoi;* see also 28:17.

the church replaces Israel in God's purposes, it does suggest that for Jewish believers a new family supplants the old.

THE WAY

There are several references in Acts to the Christian community as "the Way." In Acts 9:1-2, the term is clearly used as an identifying title for the community of disciples: "Meanwhile Saul, still breathing threats and murder against the disciples of the Lord, went to the high priest and asked him for letters to the synagogues at Damascus, so that if he found any who belonged to the Way, men or women, he might bring them bound to Jerusalem." As Conzelmann suggests, the term "the Way" both here and in other references in Acts seems to refer both to the Christian movement or group and to the teaching that Christians follow.[59]

In the passage from Acts 9, "the Way" seems especially to refer to the community of believers. This is equally true of Acts 22:4, where Paul testifies to his own role as persecutor. In Acts 19:23, however, where "about that time no little disturbance broke out concerning the Way," the explanation of this uproar suggests that "the Way" is evident in Paul's teaching. Demetrius complains that "not only in Ephesus but in almost the whole of Asia this Paul has persuaded and drawn away a considerable number of people, by saying that gods made with hands are not gods" (Acts 19:26). Acts 24:22 also implies that the Way at least includes teaching, doctrine, with which Felix is familiar.

In a passage where "the Way" refers at most indirectly to the community of believers, and may not be a title at all, its connotations as a walk, a set of teachings, is particularly clear:

> Now there came to Ephesus a Jew named Apollos, a native of Alexandria. He was an eloquent man, well versed in the scriptures. He had been instructed in the Way of the Lord; and he spoke with burning enthusiasm and taught accurately the things concerning Jesus, though he knew only the baptism of John. He began to speak boldly in the synagogue; but when Priscilla and Aquila heard him, they took him and expounded to him the Way of God more accurately. (Acts 18:24-26)[60]

59. See Conzelmann, *Acts,* 71. He also suggests analogies with some Qumran usage. Haenchen (*Acts,* 320) stresses the communal aspects of the term. It is a self-designation by Christians as opposed to the designation "sect" provided by their opponents (as in Acts 24:14).

60. Haenchen (*Acts,* 320) sees the "way of the Lord" or the "way of God" here as being "the saving action of God."

A passage from Luke also suggests an understanding of "the Way" as direction, teaching. The spies of Jesus' enemies speak sarcastically but truly: "Teacher, we know that you are right in what you say and teach, and you show deference to no one, but teach the way of God in accordance with truth" (Luke 20:21).[61]

In Acts 19:8-9 and Acts 24:14 the term "the Way" seems to refer both to the community of believers and to the teachings they believe. Insofar as the Way is a "sect," it seems to represent the community. Insofar as following the Way includes worshiping and believing in particular ways, the Way seems to represent a teaching, a walk.

We can suspect that the use of the term "the Way" to refer to the church was inherited and not invented by Luke. It suggests not only a community, but a community engaged in a particular walk, a "way of life."

Though there are no passages that discuss how leaders might function for a church understood as on "the Way," we can guess that right leaders would be those who themselves walked according to the Way, and led others on that same path.

THE *EKKLĒSIA:* THE CHURCH

Paul already uses the term *ekklēsia,* or "church," without explanation as the self-evidently appropriate term for a gathered community of Christians. In Luke and Acts the term is also used without particular elaboration or explanation. However, we may be able to get some sense of the background and meaning of this term for the group of believers.

Hans Conzelmann points out the evidence of an Old Testament background for the church as *ekklēsia* in Stephen's speech of Acts 7:

> This is the Moses who said to the Israelites, "God will raise up a prophet for you from your own people [Gk.: brethren] as he raised me up." He is the one who was in the congregation [*ekklēsia*] in the wilderness with the angel who spoke to him at Mount Sinai, and with our ancestors; and he received living oracles to give to us. Our ancestors were unwilling to obey him; instead, they pushed him aside, and in their hearts they turned back to Egypt. (Acts 7:37-39)

---

61. Compare Acts 16:17. Joseph Fitzmyer suggests that the praise rings hollow on the lips of these opponents and recalls that the "Way" is here taken from Mark 12:14 (*The Gospel according to Luke, X–XXIV,* AB [Garden City, N.Y.: Doubleday, 1985], 1295).

In the passage as a whole Moses is clearly a forerunner both of Jesus and of the leaders of the early church. Moses, like Jesus and the church, presented oracles to the people of Israel, and as with Jesus and the church, many turned aside. The familial imagery we have seen in our examination of the church as "brethren" fits here. Stephen stresses the continuity of present-day Israel with the contentious Israel of the wilderness, "our ancestors." The suggestion is that the clan of Israel of Stephen's time lives out the rebellion of its ancestors. By implication the new clan, the new family of brothers, the Christian church, is the newly obedient community. Hans Conzelmann's discussion of this passage at least implies that the antecedent references in Deuteronomy refer to the people of Israel gathered to receive the law.[62]

By extension it may be that Luke sees the Christian *ekklēsia* as that community gathered to receive the new oracles of God proclaimed by Jesus (and the apostles?). If so we have here the suggestion that the church stands in continuity with Israel and in contrast with it. This new assembly also receives God's commands and promises, but unlike the former assembly, the church will not turn away.

In Acts the term *ekklēsia* is also used for the gentile gathering at Ephesus where the outraged people accuse Paul of undermining their economy. The term is used here in two senses. On the one hand, the *ekklēsia* is the crowd gathered to protest Paul's activity (19:32, 41). On the other hand, there is apparently an official *ekklēsia* that has the power to decide on civic issues, the "regular" (*ennomos*) assembly (19:39).[63] This would suggest that not too far behind the more conventional use of *ekklēsia* as a term for the community of believers there is the more general notion that an *ekklēsia* is a gathering.

Ernst Haenchen suggests that in Acts 9:31 the term has become the technical term for "the church." "Its being 'edified'—consolidated— strikes no longer an apocalyptic or Messianic, but an ecclesiastical note."[64] Certainly the validity and growth of the *ekklēsia* are seen here

---

62. Conzelmann (*Acts*, 54) finds antecedents for this use of *ekklēsia* for the people of Israel in Deut. 4:10; 9:10; 18:16. In each case the root of the term for assembling or assembly is *qahal* in the Hebrew; in Deut. 4:10 the verb is used, in the other two instances the noun. The *ekklēsia* is here the community of Israel as they are gathered together. The purpose of their gathering, their assembly, in each case is to receive the law.

63. On 19:39, see Conzelmann, *Acts*, 166.

64. Haenchen, *Acts*, 333.

as the work of the Holy Spirit, an expansion of Lukan motifs evident throughout, and perhaps especially in Acts 2. Whether or not it is fair to say that the apocalyptic and messianic note has dropped out altogether from the notion of the *ekklēsia,* clearly throughout most of Acts the term is used not only in continuity and contrast with Israel's called community but also as a standard term for Christian communities.

Most often the term refers to a particular, local gathering of Christians. That is perhaps most evident in Acts 14:23 and Acts 15:3-4.[65] In several instances, however, the term *ekklēsia* apparently refers to the larger community of Christians—if not the church universal, at least the church extensive. A few examples of these passages are: "So the church throughout all Judea, Galilee, and Samaria had peace and was built up" (Acts 9:31). "About that time Herod the king laid violent hands upon some who belonged to the church" (Acts 12:1; perhaps also 12:5). Further, in Paul's speech to the Ephesian elders he addresses leaders of the specific local church in Ephesus, but in his instructions the term *ekklēsia* seems to take on a broader meaning: "Keep watch over yourselves and over all the flock, of which the Holy Spirit has made you overseers, to shepherd the church of God that he obtained with the blood of his own Son" (Acts 20:28).

The term *ekklēsia* therefore has both gentile and Old Testament antecedents. Within a gentile context it can apparently refer to a general gathering of people or to a more official deliberative assembly. Within the pertinent Old Testament passages the term refers to the people of Israel gathered to receive the law and the oracles of God.

For Luke the Christian *ekklēsia* may also be a gathering and sometimes (as in Acts 15) a gathering for deliberative purposes. The Christian *ekklēsia* stands both in continuity and in discontinuity with Israel. As Israel gathered before Moses to receive the law and oracles of God, so the Christian community gathers before the words of Jesus and the preaching of the apostles. However, Israel (for the most part at least) turned away from Moses (see Acts 7:35-43). The Christian church (for the most part at least) lives "in the fear of the Lord and in the comfort of the Holy Spirit" (Acts 9:31).

Again, as in the previous discussion of the familial imagery for the church, we can see that Luke employs terms originally appropriate for

---

65. For other apparent references to *ekklēsia* as a local community of faith, see Acts 5:11; 8:1; 11:22; 13:1; 14:27; 15:22, 41; 20:17.

the clan or kinship structure of Israel and now applies them to the church: the new assembly, the new gathering, the heir to Israel in the promises of God.

CHRISTIANS

Acts twice uses the term "Christians" for those folk who belong to the Way. In each case (11:26; 26:28) the term is used by nonbelievers to refer to the followers of the Way. There is no sense that Luke finds it either troublesome or particularly helpful as a designation for the community whose beginnings he portrays.[66]

SUMMARY

Close examination of the images for the church strengthens our sense of the role of leadership in Luke and Acts. To begin, we can say that since all believers are understood as "disciples" under the one master, Jesus, the apostles and the elders who follow them are not set apart either as super-Christians or as uniquely called to sacrifice and martyrdom. They teach, and they shepherd, but they do not represent a special, separate group of Christians. All believers are set apart from old ways to join on the way of the cross.

Since the church is understood as a family, relationships may perhaps better be seen as patriarchal than hierarchical. "Elders" becomes not only a technical term for church leaders but a familial term. Elders take on the responsibilities of fathers and older brothers in a structure of mutual dependence and love.

Since the church is understood as a clan, a new community succeeding if not supplanting Israel, some of the images of leadership appropriate to Israel are now appropriate to the church. The twelve apostles represent the twelve thrones. Jesus succeeds Moses as the mediator between God and the family of Israel, but the apostles and the elders also take leadership: they preach, they teach, they shepherd God's people.

Since the church is also the Way, both a community and a walk, we can suppose that leaders of such a community are followers of the Way—folk who walk in the paths of righteousness. We can also suppose

---

66. See Conzelmann, *Acts,* 88–89. Haenchen (*Acts,* 371–72), however, offers the observation that 11:26 may mark the point where the discontinuity between Judaism and Christianity became clear to outsiders, and thus a problem for Christians themselves.

that they lead and teach other Christians the Way that they themselves follow. They live and teach the right path of faithfulness.

Since the church succeeds Israel as the assembly called for hearing and obeying the law and oracles of God, we can suppose that the leaders of such an *ekklēsia* also hear and declare the true oracles of God as found in Jesus Christ and in the teaching of the apostles. It may also be that they assemble under the guidance of the Holy Spirit to make those decisions that are appropriate to the life of this assembly (as in Acts 15). Again the church succeeds, if it does not supplant, Israel. Just as for Israel, elders become the appropriate leaders of this new assembly.

LUKE-ACTS AND MINISTRY TODAY

The apostles provide the link between the promise to the twelve tribes of Israel and the inclusion of the Gentiles. Peter's recognition of Cornelius validates both the continuity and the expansion of God's promise. While the apostles are not in any simple way prototypes of later church leaders, they are the indispensable connection between God's covenant with Israel and God's ongoing relationship to the church. Luke-Acts gives no evidence for hierarchical apostolic succession but does give modest evidence for a succession of the apostolic kerygma. It does affirm that the first circle of church leaders was the necessary bridge between Israel, Jesus, and the later community.

While the term "apostle" is reserved for the historical circle of twelve (then eleven, then twelve), the term "disciple" is used for believers both during Jesus' ministry and after his resurrection and ascension. Because Luke wants to show the continuity between the first (Jewish) community of believers and the largely gentile community of his own time, he uses the term "disciple" as a way of describing believers of both generations.

The sense that the church consists of "brethren" recognizes its continuity with the people Israel who were brothers and sisters to one another and who had Abraham for their father. It also claims familial or clan status for this new community, opening to the Gentiles the promises given to Israel.

Jervell persuasively argues that Israel remains Israel in Luke and Acts, and that the true Israel is not so much the church as that group of Jews who accept Jesus as Messiah. Luke's reference to Christians as people of the Way provides a larger category that can include both Jewish and gentile Christians. The Way, Jesus' way, has continuity with Moses' Torah, but also goes beyond it to open the way for faithful Gentiles.

The clearest indication of church office we have in Acts, the groups of "elders," may relate both to the church's roots in Israel and to its new status as the community of the Way. Elders are to function like good teachers and shepherds, as in the best traditions of Israel. They are also elders within the family context where Christians are brothers and sisters to one another. And while they do not simply replicate the function of the apostles, the elders do have the same kind of responsibility for right testimony that the apostles bore in their generation.

In all these ways Luke portrays a community where the promises to Israel are affirmed and claimed—the promises not only that Jewish believers will know salvation, but that salvation is also extended (from Israel) to the whole world.[67] Joseph Tyson well summarizes the picture of leadership and authority that emerges in Acts:

> The point to be stressed is that in Acts no permanent form of authority is indicated. Luke seems to be sensitive to changing conditions that might require changing structures, and so he does not continue apostolic authority beyond a particular time and place.... Luke thinks in terms both of continuity and change in the exercise of authority. The emphasis on change shows that Luke is sensitive to historical development and would probably not want to impose the structures of an earlier age on a later. The emphasis on continuity suggests that whatever changes might be considered legitimate in the church, there is a sense in which later structures emerge from earlier ones and do so with the concurrence of the earlier leaders.[68]

Luke's openness to change is most evident in the way he moves from the apostles to other forms of church leadership and quite possibly in the differences between elders in Jerusalem and those in the gentile churches. Luke's emphasis on continuity is present in the way that later generations of church leaders are faithful to, tested by, the apostolic witness. The content of the gospel remains constant, while the forms of church supporting the gospel are open to change. In the midst of such Lukan variety, three major themes are constant.

First, with the stress on the church as brethren (fellow disciples) and *ekklēsia* (assembly), there is a stress on the community of the church.

---

67. On this worldwide thrust, see also Edwards, "Acts of the Apostles," esp. 371–73.
68. Tyson, "Emerging Church," 144–45.

Issues of discipline or decision often presuppose shared responsibility (in the forgiving of sins of Luke 17, in the appointment of the seven in Acts 6). The familial or ecclesial images often draw on Old Testament parallels and suggest that church is a new family, a new clan, heirs to the promises to Moses fulfilled in Jesus Christ. While it would be anachronistic to call this an egalitarian image of the church, it is certainly a cooperative and communal image.

Second, the description of church as the Way, as *ekklēsia* (like the congregation on Sinai), and as disciples suggests that a major function of the community is to hear the oracles, teaching, truth, and witness of God. Apostles are the first proclaimers (after Jesus) of this testimony. The elders are guardians of the proclamation they receive. Decision-making, authoritative roles are derivative from this role as teacher.

Third, the life of the church and of its leaders is lived under the direction of the Spirit. The formula of the Acts 15 decree ("It seemed good to the Holy Spirit and to us . . . " [Acts 15:28]) is not merely formulaic but reflects the conviction of Luke that the Spirit that rested on Jesus at the beginning of his ministry came upon the Jerusalem church at Pentecost and upon the gentile church with the conversion of Cornelius (Acts 10:44). At the end of the two-volume work, Paul quotes the Holy Spirit as the true author of the definitive words from Isaiah that (apparently) shift the church's mission decisively from Jews to Gentiles.

The following implications therefore emerge for our understanding of the church and its leadership today:

1. The specific shape of church leadership may differ from time to time and from place to place without thereby forfeiting faithfulness to the gospel. The discussion of the role of religious leadership today is not in order to find the appropriate style of leadership for all time but to ask what is faithful today—in the light of our tradition but also in the light of emerging circumstances.

2. The church continues to be seen as kin, clan, family. Leadership does not substitute hierarchical authority for the more mutual responsibilities of a community.

3. The continuity of the church rests in the continuity of its message. The faithfulness of church leaders (elders?) lies not in the fact that they proceed in an unbroken line of ordination from the apostles but that they are faithful to the apostolic witness. We may well decide that a different view of apostolic succession more appropriately continues the great tradition of the church and more effectively meets the need for

authority in our time—more faithfully follows the Spirit's leading. We will not find that sense of apostolic office as inheritance in Luke or Acts.

4. The role of church leaders is therefore, like the apostles, to declare the message that other "disciples" need to hear, and, like the elders, to preserve that message against attacks from within and without. We do not reinvent the gospel for each generation, however much we may need to reinterpret it. A great line extends from Jesus to Peter to James and Paul to the Ephesian elders—to us.

5. Again there is slight evidence in Luke or Acts that any cadre of church leaders had special sacramental privileges. (The only possible foreshadowing is in the feeding story of Luke 9.) The significance of the service at tables or "ministry" at tables in Acts 6:2 is, we have seen, not very clear. It does not seem possible to extrapolate any eucharistic ministry from this puzzling passage.

6. For Acts and for us the Holy Spirit not only establishes the church but guides the church. Along with the apostolic witness, the Holy Spirit provides both continuity and flexibility. In Acts 15 the church leaders and the Holy Spirit affirm a brand new implication of the gospel, yet one consistent with the promises implicit in Luke 4 and Acts 2. The church and its leaders live out of the past but into God's future, the Holy Spirit being our guide.

7. If Esler is right, part of the work to which the Holy Spirit calls the church is the work of unity. To be sure, with Paul in Acts 20 contemporary ministers may need to be on guard against deception from without or defection from within. But with Peter in Acts 15 we shall also ask what seems good to the Holy Spirit in our time, and seek to be true to Peter's vision of Acts 10 that runs counter to every attempt to close and bar the doors of the church against strange people, or the stirrings of the Spirit.

CHAPTER 6

Ministry in the
Pastoral Epistles

Any discussion of the significance of the Pastoral Epistles as a model for contemporary ministry depends on our judgments concerning the authenticity and historical circumstances of these letters. Therefore I begin my discussion in this chapter with attention to those questions and then move to the other issues pertinent to my argument.

THE HISTORICAL CIRCUMSTANCES
OF THE PASTORAL EPISTLES

WHO WROTE THESE LETTERS?

The initial question any study of the Pastorals must face is whether these letters were written by Paul or were written by a later Christian author pseudonymously. For reasons of clarity it is perhaps most helpful to begin with the reasons most often cited by those who think that the Pastoral Epistles were not written by Paul.

1. A primary reason has to do with style and vocabulary. Comparative studies of style and vocabulary are tricky. Different interpreters read the same statistics in different ways, and there can be no denying that Paul sounds rather different in Romans, say, than he does in 1 Thessalonians. Skeptics use the statistics to bolster an almost intuitive sense that we have moved into a different linguistic world than that of the apostle. More than in Paul, sentences are shaped according to the norms of

Hellenistic parenetic discourse, and telltale Pauline idiosyncrasies are missing.[1]

2. The Pastoral Epistles seem to presuppose variations of "heretical" Christianity later than Paul's own time. Martin Dibelius and Hans Conzelmann argue that the heresy the author here combats is a kind of Judaizing Gnosticism that is almost certainly later than Paul.[2] One plausible reading of the Pastorals also sees in them the fading of eschatological expectation to the far horizon. History and the church will go on for the foreseeable future, and provisions must be made for that future.[3]

3. Related to this is the claim put forth especially by Hans von Campenhausen but affirmed by others that the church structure envisioned by the Pastorals must be later than Paul.[4] There can be no doubt that the Pastorals move toward a more rationalized, structured picture of church leadership than that suggested or idealized in the undeniably genuine epistles. It also seems clear that church structures do not yet include the kind of strong episcopate reflected in the letters of Ignatius. Consequently, if church organization moves on a kind of trajectory from charisma to order, the Pastorals come after Paul and before Ignatius.[5]

4. Those who doubt the authenticity of the Pastorals further argue that the implied chronology and geography behind the Pastorals do not fit well with what we can piece together of Pauline chronology.[6]

5. Part of the purport of Lewis Donelson's study of the Pastorals is to argue that a right discernment of the genre of these epistles suggests that they are pseudepigraphal. Donelson draws on a broad range of ancient literature to find analogues for the Pastorals with their mixture of forewarning, personalia, and generalized exhortation. He argues that

---

1. See Jerome D. Quinn, *The Letter to Titus,* AB (New York: Doubleday, 1990), 6; Martin Dibelius and Hans Conzelmann, *The Pastoral Epistles,* trans. Philip Buttolph and Adela Yarbro; ed. Helmut Koester (Philadelphia: Fortress Press, 1972), 3–4.

2. See, for instance, Dibelius and Conzelmann, *Pastoral Epistles,* 17.

3. Eduard Schweizer makes this claim most persuasively in *Church Order in the New Testament,* trans. Frank Clarke (Naperville, Ill.: Alec R. Allenson, 1961), 77.

4. See Hans von Campenhausen, *Ecclesiastical Authority and Spiritual Power in the Church of the First Three Centuries,* trans. J. A. Baker (London: Adam and Charles Black, 1969), 108. His argument is further cited in Dibelius and Conzelmann, *Pastoral Epistles,* 4.

5. See Quinn, *Letter to Titus,* 18–19, who consequently dates the Pastorals in the period from 80–90.

6. See Dibelius and Conzelmann, *Pastoral Epistles,* 3.

the Pastorals fit what we would expect of forgeries, intended both to fool and to direct their readers.[7]

For each of these arguments against authenticity, there is an opposite, if not necessarily equal, counterargument.

1. The argument for the authenticity of the style of the Pastorals takes at least two forms. Some argue, reading the same slippery statistics as their opponents, that the differences between one of the Pastoral Epistles and the other Pauline letters is not sufficiently out of line to require positing a non-Pauline author. What differences there are between the Pastorals and the other letters can be explained by changes in Paul's age and in the situation he addresses in the letters themselves. Others argue that the Pauline mode of "writing" letters was not to write them at all but to dictate them to amanuenses. Those who helped write the Pastorals developed them in somewhat different style than those who helped write the undeniably authentic epistles.[8]

2. The question of a probable date for the opponents addressed in the Pastorals, the heretics, depends simply on a different historical reconstruction. If the issues addressed in the Pastorals can plausibly be dated within Paul's lifetime, there is no reason to deny Paul as the author.[9]

3. The issue of church organization depends in part on how sanguine one can be of our knowledge of the "inevitable" direction of the evolution of church leadership. Is there as big a gap as the doubters suggest between the "bishops and deacons" of Phil. 1:1 and the "bishops, elders, and deacons" of the Pastorals?[10]

4. One way to explain the apparent divergences between the Pastorals and the Pauline chronology derived from the evidently genuine epistles and from Acts is to say that Acts does not tell the end of the story, and that the Pastorals derived from a time after that Roman imprisonment Acts relates, when Paul is again imprisoned.[11]

5. Finally there is a kind of ethical argument for the authenticity

---

7. See Lewis Donelson, *Pseudepigraphy and Ethical Argument in the Pastoral Epistles* (Tübingen: J. C. B. Mohr [Paul Siebeck]), esp. 54–66.

8. For the former argument, see Thomas Oden, *First and Second Timothy and Titus,* IBC (Louisville: John Knox Press, 1989), 13; on the second, Gordon D. Fee, *1 and 2 Timothy and Titus,* NICNT (Peabody, Mass.: Hendrickson, 1988), 24, and J. N. D. Kelly, *The Pastoral Epistles,* Black's New Testament Commentaries (London: Adam and Charles Black, 1963), 25, 33–34.

9. So Kelly, *Pastoral Epistles,* 12.

10. See ibid., 14–15.

11. See ibid., 6–10; Fee, *1 and 2 Timothy,* 4–5, with somewhat different reconstructions,

of the Pastorals. Thomas Oden writes: "If not Paul, the surrogate had to be blatantly fabricating when he instructed Timothy to 'bring the cloak that I left with Carpus at Troas, also the books, and above all the parchments.' "[12] But that begs the question rather than answering it. Donelson has shown persuasively that these references to "realia" are typical of pseudonymous literature, which, of course, is blatantly fabricated from the first word to the final salutation.[13]

While the arguments concerning authenticity are helpful and by no means simply question-begging, there is also no doubt that scholars' views on the Pastorals are often correlated with their theological positions. Ernst Käsemann with his strong reading of Paul as the exponent of Christian freedom is glad to let the Pastorals go. American scholars who find in some of the structures envisioned by the Pastorals a counterbalance to the excesses of individualism are more apt to attribute the letters to the apostle (e.g., G. D. Fee) or at the least to applaud their canonicity (e.g., L. T. Johnson). Whether or not one sees the Pastorals as genuinely Pauline depends in part on how one reads the genuine Paul.[14] Nonetheless, when I read the Pastorals, I feel as if I have stepped into another thought world than that of the undoubtedly genuine epistles. I am also persuaded that this is a later world, not a century later, but decades later.

Someone else writes in Paul's name, whether out of the most open of intentions or, as seems likely, out of motives more dubious. We can guess that this later writer seeks to honor Paul, at least to the extent of trusting or rehabilitating his authority. And this later writer presents a plausible, though again perhaps idealized, model of what church leadership can be as the church moves toward the end of the first century.

One obvious trajectory of theological and institutional development runs from the early Pauline letters to the late Pastorals or, more probably, from the genuine Pauline letters to the pseudonymous Pastorals.

---

and P. C. Spicq, *Les Epîtres Pastorales*, 2 vols. (Paris: Librairie Lecoffre, J. Gabalda et Cie, 1969), 1:126–46.

12. Oden, *First and Second Timothy*, 15.

13. See Donelson, *Pseudepigraphy*, 54–57.

14. See, for instance, Ernst Käsemann, "Ministry and Community in the New Testament," in *Essays on New Testament Themes*, trans. W. J. Montague (London: SCM, 1964), 63–94, esp. 85–89; Fee, *1 and 2 Timothy*, 14–23; Luke T. Johnson, *Decision Making in the Church: A Biblical Model* (Philadelphia: Fortress Press, 1983), 1–3.

Another trajectory runs from the Pauline farewell address of Acts 20 to the Pastorals and especially to the farewell testament, 2 Timothy.[15]

Acts 20 and 1 and 2 Timothy both presuppose a "real" or a fictionalized description of the church at Ephesus. In each case, we can guess that the "Pauline" description in fact represents a list of the dangers and possibilities of a later generation, the generation in which these works were written. In each case, the church is threatened from without by false teachers and from within by heretics (Acts 20:29-30; 2 Tim. 3:6-9). In each case, safety for the Ephesian church lies in the correct teaching of its leaders, the elders (of whom Timothy in 2 Timothy is probably a prototype) (see Acts 20:28-31; 1 Tim. 5:17; 2 Tim. 3:14-17). In each case, what concerns "Paul" is not only that the elders and leaders teach rightly but that they live rightly (Acts 20:35; 1 Tim. 5:17; 2 Tim. 2:22-26; and, perhaps, if bishops are also elders, 1 Tim. 3:1-7). In each case, Paul himself becomes a model of the right teacher (Acts 20:33-34; 2 Tim. 1:11-14). In each case, using similar words and images, Paul makes his farewell to the Ephesians through their leaders (see Acts 20:24; 2 Tim. 4:6-8).[16]

In fact the relationship between Acts 20 and the Pastorals (especially 2 Timothy) helps us in estimating the historical situation out of which the Pastorals grew. It is possible that the author of Acts 20 knew the Pastorals or vice versa; it is even possible that the author of Acts 20 was the author of the Pastorals—that the Pastorals represent the third volume of a work that included Luke and Acts.[17] In any case, what we see in these last chapters of Acts and in the Pastorals is a similar situation. The author takes the figure of Paul and uses Paul to predict what will happen in a later time, in fact the author's own time. What Paul prescribes for the church of the future is what the author wishes for the church of the present: a church toward the end of the second generation of Christians.[18]

---

15. In his commentary, Jerome Quinn alludes to the possibility that the author or editor of Luke-Acts may also have been the author-editor of the Pastoral Epistles. See Quinn, *Letter to Titus*, 19, and idem, "The Last Volume of Luke: The Relation of Luke-Acts and the PE," in C. Talbert, ed., *Perspectives on Luke-Acts* (Macon, Ga.: Mercer Univ. Press, 1978), 62–75.

16. Dibelius and Conzelmann (*Pastoral Epistles,* 121) cite other partial parallels for the 2 Timothy verses but somehow miss Acts 20:24.

17. See note 15, above.

18. It is a nice question, perhaps unanswerable with current evidence, whether Acts and the Pastorals were also written to defend Paul. If so the authors took on a courageous

In reading Acts we have very little sense of what specific heresies or false teachings the author wishes to combat. In reading the Pastorals, we have some clearer ideas, and these help us in our discussion of the historical setting for those letters.

WHO ARE THE FALSE TEACHERS THE PASTORALS ADDRESS?

As any number of scholars have noted, the language of the Pastorals is polemical when the author addresses the mistakes of his opponents. Clearly we have hyperbole, caricature. What is less clear is whether, as with good caricature, we can discern something of the actual lineaments of the teachers the Pastorals caricature, or whether the descriptions function more like expletives, showing the spleen of the author but little of his opponents.

Abraham Malherbe, who looks at similar strains of polemic among Hellenistic philosophers, argues persuasively that typically, for all its hyperbole, such polemic is directed against specific philosophical and personal characteristics of the opponent.[19] Similarly, studies with greatly diverse perspectives, such as those by Luke T. Johnson, Martin Dibelius and Hans Conzelmann, Jerome Quinn, and Lewis Donelson, argue that we can discern something of the nature of the "heresies" the Pastorals combat and on the basis of this discernment make some judgments about the historical milieu out of which they arise.[20]

Lewis Donelson points out two methodological difficulties in describing the opponents condemned by the Pastorals. First (as with the genuine Pauline correspondence), we have the account of only one side of the argument. Second, we have two "layers" of opposition as portrayed by the Pastorals. The one layer is that of Paul's, Timothy's, and Titus's opponents, and even here Paul's enemies are used to foreshadow the enemies of his younger companions. The other layer is that of the opponents "Paul" predicts will come "in the last days." Here we can assume that the author portrays the opposition of his own time, as if they

---

task: to rehabilitate Paul's authority before they relied on it. My guess is that might be one feat too many. But see Quinn, "Last Volume," 71, and idem, *Letter to Titus,* 19.

19. Abraham Malherbe, "Medical Imagery in the Pastoral Epistles," in W. Eugene Marsh, ed., *Texts and Testaments: Critical Essays on the Bible and Early Church Fathers* (San Antonio: Trinity Univ. Press, 1980), 19–35.

20. See Johnson, *Decision Making,* 8–9; Dibelius and Conzelmann, *Pastoral Epistles,* 17; Quinn, *Letter to Titus,* 15; Donelson, *Pseudepigraphy,* 116–28. Johnson, unlike the others, suggests that the different epistles may envision different opponents.

had been authoritatively foreseen by the apostle.[21] Nonetheless, if we are allowed to see the opponents in all three groups and across the fictive chronological limits as representing one set of ideas or problems, here is what we would include:

1. In the Letter to Titus it is clear that the opponents come from Jewish-Christian roots: "There are also many rebellious people, idle talkers and deceivers, especially those of the circumcision" (Titus 1:10). It may also be that the concern with right interpretation of the "law" in Timothy reflects the claims of the "heretics" that the law has binding force on Christians, while "Paul" wants to maintain that the law's validity is only for outsiders (see 1 Tim. 1:6-9a).[22] If the Pastorals present a consistent description of a single group of opponents, then we may guess that the references to myths and genealogies may also represent an argument with Jewish-Christian interpreters of the Torah who use it as the ground for their speculations (see 1 Tim. 1:3-4; 4:7; 2 Tim. 4:3-4).

The Letter to Titus seems to bring misinterpretation of the law together with the love of speculative theology as characteristic of the opponents (Titus 3:9). Again, one way of reading Titus 1:13-14 is to see a link between myth and law (commandment) in the opponents' interpretation of Scripture.[23] The author of the Pastorals acknowledges the validity of Torah, but its validity is as a check on the unfaithful, not as a guide to the faithful. Whether or not the opponents of the epistles to Timothy and that to Titus are all Jewish-Christian, they do seem to share in common a particular way of interpreting Torah.

A second characteristic of the opponents, at least as we see them depicted in 2 Timothy, is that they believe that the general resurrection has already occurred. This claim assumes that Hymenaeus and Philetus, whatever their historical standing, serve in 2 Timothy as typical of false teachers: "Among [the false teachers] are Hymenaeus and Philetus, who have swerved from the truth by claiming that the resurrection

---

21. See Donelson, *Pseudepigraphy*, 117–18.

22. Dibelius and Conzelmann (*Pastoral Epistles*, 22) argue that 1 Tim. 6:8 is a quotation from Paul but misreads Paul's paradoxical understanding of law. Be that as it may, these claims of 1 Timothy do seem to be based on a reading of Paul. Oden (*First and Second Timothy*, 38) reads the passage as a further elaboration by Paul of themes introduced in Romans 7.

23. Jerome Quinn (*Letter to Titus*, 109) argues interestingly that the "myths" or "tales" represent Haggadah and the "commandments" Halakah. Jewish Christians by their midrash are misinterpreting Scripture for their own false purposes.

has already taken place" (2 Tim. 2:17-18). The closest Pauline parallel to concern with such a misunderstanding is probably 1 Corinthians, where a plausible reading suggests that part of the Corinthians' "mistake" rested in the view that the conditions of the resurrection already obtained for believers (see esp. 1 Cor. 4:8-9; 15:12-14). It also seems plausible that for some Corinthian Christians the claim that the resurrection has already occurred means that the ascetic strictures regarding sex that Paul thinks ought to be reserved for the kingdom are appropriate to the present (see 1 Cor. 7:1-3). In 1 Timothy, "Paul," foreseeing the future, which is surely the Pastorals' present, warns against inappropriate asceticism, not only regarding sex, but regarding food: "They forbid marriage and demand abstinence from foods, which God created to be received with thanksgiving by those who believe and know the truth" (1 Tim. 4:3).

As is often the case in philosophical arguments with opponents, the author of the Pastorals accuses the "heretics" not only of theological mistakes but of ethical failings. While this undoubtedly serves a polemical function it also is congruent with what we shall see is the Pastorals' concern that right teaching and right conduct go together for legitimate church leaders. Some of the descriptions of the opponents' misconduct do, however, seem to be more hyperbolic flourishes than helpful characterizations. The "prophecy" of 2 Tim. 3:1-5 and the doggerel of Titus 1:12 fit this rhetorical category.[24]

Less "typical" and therefore more persuasive as genuine characterizations, however sharpened polemically, are the claim that the opponents make money from their religion, and the claim that they seduce gullible believers, especially gullible women. The description in Titus 1:10-11 begins, as we have seen, apparently putting the opponents within the school of Jewish Christians but then goes on to accuse them of mercenary motives.[25] In 1 Timothy 6 it is not altogether clear that false teachers have instructed believers that godliness can be a means of financial gain, but certainly some misled Christians have come to believe just that:

---

24. See Dibelius and Conzelmann, *Pastoral Epistles,* 115–16.

25. Jerome Quinn suggests that it is because the opponents teach falsely that their teaching is obviously for personal gain. If they taught aright it would be legitimate to pay them; but since they lie, their motive is obviously mercenary (Quinn, *Letter to Titus,* 106).

Of course there is great gain in godliness combined with contentment.... But those who want to be rich fall into temptation and are trapped by many senseless and harmful desires that plunge people into ruin and destruction. For the love of money is a root of all kinds of evil, and in their eagerness to be rich, some have wandered away from the faith and pierced themselves with many pains. (1 Tim. 6:6-10)

The concern that the opponents have the power to seduce the minds of foolish believers, especially women believers, is represented in 2 Tim. 3:6-7. In 2 Tim. 4:3-4, the description of gullible believers is not confined to women but gives some clues to the way the opponents work among the people. Again "Paul" looks forward to the time of the Pastorals: "For the time is coming when people will not put up with sound doctrine, but having itching ears, they will accumulate for themselves teachers to suit their own desires, and will turn away from listening to the truth and wander away to myths."

Related to the claim that the opponents betray the faith by their love of money and their intellectual seduction of "silly" women, is the claim that they bring division within the church. In a list of criticisms of the opponents, 1 Tim. 6:4 includes the claim that they have "a morbid craving for controversy and for disputes about words. From these come envy, dissension, slander, base suspicions, and wrangling among those who are depraved in mind and bereft of the truth" (1 Tim. 6:4-5; see Titus 3:9-11). In all these ways the problem with the opponents is not just that they teach wrong doctrine but that their own lives (unlike the lives of right teachers) are not upright but crooked, bent.

Finally, it may be important to note that a brief word may be a fundamental clue or a red herring. In 1 Tim. 6:20, Paul concludes his warning to Timothy with these words: "Timothy, guard what has been entrusted to you. Avoid the profane chatter and contradictions of what is falsely called knowledge [*gnōsis*]." Given later developments in Gnosticism, some of them growing out of speculation about the Old Testament and Jewish texts, it would not be impossible for us to find behind the Pastorals a kind of nascent Gnosticism. This hint is perhaps not sufficient to such a hypothesis, but other elements of the Pastorals make such a line of development at least suggestive.

The characteristics of the "opponents" seem fairly consistent and fairly clear. They come from Jewish-Christian circles and portray themselves as true interpreters of Torah as it is a guide for Christians. To the author of the Pastorals, at least, their interpretations smack of myth and quibble; perhaps allegorical tendencies are to the fore, though of course we have no clear evidence of this. Believing that Christians already participate in the resurrection state, they argue for asceticism regarding marriage and meals.

According to the Pastorals the lives of the opponents, however, are neither ascetic nor exemplary. The opponents are out for monetary gain. They presumably know that they speak falsely, yet blatantly seduce others to their side. They sow dissension in the church, presumably by turning away from true teaching and from true (Pauline) churches as well.

The crisis consists in the fact that the numbers of the heretics' followers may well be growing, and while one always holds out hope that the blasphemers may be persuaded to repent and return, even more important is to hold fast to right doctrine and right practice for the sake of those who remain. The purport of the positive argument of the Pastorals is to show forth that right doctrine and that right practice. Both are closely related to a particular picture of the church's structure and its ministry.

APOSTLESHIP IN THE PASTORALS

As in Luke-Acts the notion of apostleship in the Pastorals is apparently limited to the first generation of Christian leaders. Unlike Luke-Acts, however, the circle of apostles includes Paul, normatively and preeminently. In the Pastorals, the primary function of Paul's apostleship is to provide authority for the doctrinal and practical teachings the Pastorals embody.[26] Secondarily, Paul himself, as Lewis Donelson points out, provides a paradigm for third-generation Christians and perhaps especially for third-generation Christian leaders.[27] It may also be that in the references to laying on of hands there is, in the Pastorals, an implicit claim that the church leaders of the third generation stand in a succession with Paul as apostle.

In the Pastorals, the apostle Paul stands as the preeminent guarantor of right Christian tradition. It is an unanswerable question whether the author of the Pastorals thinks of himself as representing a tradition he

26. It is evident that one's decision about the date and authenticity of the Pastorals once again affects one's reading of their theology and purpose, and the reverse is obviously also true.

27. See Donelson, *Pseudepigraphy,* 100–106.

received indirectly from Paul or whether he uses Paul to validate a theology that he himself has consolidated. In any case, within the world of the epistles themselves, right tradition is apostolic tradition is Pauline tradition, passed on from Paul to Timothy and Titus and by implication to the correct teachers of the congregations addressed in the Pastorals.

APOSTLESHIP AND AUTHORITY

The opening salutations of the letters indicate what the rest of the Pastorals make clear—Paul's particular apostolic authority as teacher and guarantor of true faith and practice. The relationship between Paul's apostolic office and his role as guarantor of teaching is perhaps clearest in 2 Tim. 1:11-14:

> For this gospel I was appointed a herald and an apostle and a teacher, and for this reason I suffer as I do. But I am not ashamed, for I know the one in whom I have put my trust, and I am sure that he is able to guard until that day what I have entrusted to him [or: "what has been entrusted to me"]. Hold to the standard of sound teaching that you have heard from me, in the faith and love that are in Christ Jesus. Guard the good treasure [*kalēn parathēkēn*] entrusted to you, with the help of the Holy Spirit living in us.

The gospel Paul has received is identified with the sound teaching he passes on. Timothy becomes guardian of that sound teaching for the next generation, the generation for whom the Pastorals are written. The gospel, the sound teaching, is not something to be inferred behind the Pastoral Epistles; it is that treasure that the Pastorals themselves contain (see also 1 Tim. 1:11; 2:7; 4:6; 2 Tim. 2:1-2; 3:14). Furthermore, the very fact that Paul is able to give orders to Timothy and Titus and through them to the churches indicates that apostleship carries with it teaching and ordering authority.

In its exhortation on prayer, 1 Tim. 2:1 begins with the Pauline *parakalō*, that verb combining apostolic authority and parental urging with which Paul often addresses issues of churchly conduct. The apostle permits or refuses to permit (1 Tim. 2:12); he warns (1 Tim. 5:21—in the presence of God, Christ, and the angels); and, finally, he charges (1 Tim. 6:13). Not only does Paul assume his authority to teach on matters of faith and practice; he also assumes his authority to dictate church structure (Titus 1:5). And Paul assumes his authority to invoke (apostolic) punishment on blasphemers (1 Tim. 1:19-20; cf. 1 Cor. 5:5). At least by inference, Paul refuses to bless Phygelus and Hermogenes as he blesses the hospitable Onesiphorus in 2 Tim. 1:15-18 (see also Titus 1:10-11, 13).

If I am correct that the Pastorals are pseudonymous writings addressed to the third Christian generation, then apostleship becomes a device of that pseudonymity. Whether because he is loyal to Paul, or because his opponents have cited Paul as their authority, or simply because he thinks Paul's name and reputation will carry particular weight, the author clothes himself in brief apostolic authority.

THE APOSTLE AS PARADIGM

Lewis Donelson has shown that the Pastorals not only use the fiction of apostleship to deepen their own authority; they also use Paul, the model apostle, as a paradigm for the behavior of church people and perhaps especially of church leaders in the Pastorals' own time.[28]

In two ways Paul's paradigmatic status is not surprising and is indeed consistent with Paul's self-portrait in other acceptably genuine epistles and with some of the material in Acts. First, Paul is portrayed as a true teacher whose faith and conduct are appropriate models for Timothy, Titus, and later generations of Christians. In 2 Tim. 1:11-12, Paul as true teacher is paradigm for Timothy's own sound teaching (and that sound teaching for which the Pastorals plead). The first part of the paradigm in 2 Tim. 3:10 holds Paul up as a model for later faithful Christians, especially Christian teachers: "Now you have observed my teaching, my conduct, my aim in life, my faith, my patience, my love, my steadfastness."

Second, Paul is portrayed as one who has to suffer for the sake of the gospel, and in this way as an example to church members and leaders of the Pastorals' own time (see 2 Tim. 3:11). Indeed, 2 Tim. 1:11-12 combines Paul's commitment to true teaching, the knowledge that persecution will follow such commitment, and faithful confidence in the God who will rescue Paul, Timothy, and all such faithful teachers: "For this gospel I was appointed a herald and an apostle and a teacher, and for this reason I suffer as I do." The closing testament of 2 Tim. 4:6-8

---

28. Ibid., 100; see also Dibelius and Conzelmann, *Pastoral Epistles,* 98. One might argue that in 1 Tim. 6:13-14, Jesus with his good confession before Pontius Pilate becomes a paradigm for "Timothy" and therefore for later Christians or Christian leaders. See Ernst Käsemann, "Das Formular einer Neutestamentlichen Ordinationsparänese," in *Exegetische Versuche und Besinnungen* (Göttingen: Vandenhoeck and Ruprecht, 1964), 1:103.

ties Paul's faithfulness to his implied suffering and to his confidence of eschatological reward both for him and for those who follow his example. In particular, Paul may represent one who remained faithful though he was deserted by many, an encouragement to later church leaders who find their followers deserting them for false teachings (see 2 Tim. 1:15-18; 4:11).[29]

The one surprising feature of the portrayal of Paul as paradigm is evident in the first extended paradigmatic section, 1 Tim. 1:12-16 (with a doxology in 17). The surprising feature is the emphasis on Paul's former life as a blasphemer. However, in the context of the Pastorals and especially of 1 Timothy, the significance of this paradigmatic reference to Paul's life becomes clear. The letter is written to deal with heretics, blasphemers (whose own paradigms are Hymenaeus and Alexander: 1 Tim. 1:20). Paul's hope is that blasphemers may not be excluded forever from the community of true faith; he hopes that if they repent, they may return to the teachings of the right church (see also Titus 1:13). The paradigmatic Paul provides them with an excuse from his own life: he was ignorant. He provides them with hope from his own story: the grace of God rescued him from blasphemy. The reason God rescued Paul from blasphemy was so that Paul might do precisely what he does in this epistle, become "an example to those who would come to believe in Christ for eternal life."[30]

THE APOSTLE AND ORDINATION

One other function of the "apostle" in the Pastorals can here only be mentioned. Its significance awaits our discussion of the variety and function of church officials in the Pastorals.

In 2 Timothy, "Paul" reminds Timothy of his goodly heritage, through his grandmother and mother and finally through Paul himself: "[Because of your sincere faith] I remind you to rekindle the gift of God that is within you through the laying on of my hands; for God did not give us a spirit of cowardice, but rather a spirit of power and of love and of self-discipline" (2 Tim. 1:6-7). The question is: How does the apostolic laying on of hands here function? Is this a sign of ordination? If so, does Paul's apostolicity validate the ordination, or does his orthodoxy do so, or does the Spirit do so, Paul only bearing witness?

---

29. See Donelson, *Pseudepigraphy,* 106.
30. See the discussion of this passage in ibid., 101–3.

RESOLVING CONFLICTS IN THE PASTORALS

It seems evident that the Pastoral Epistles reflect conflicts within the churches to which they are addressed. First and Second Timothy deal with "false" teachings from two perspectives. First Timothy indirectly addresses the entire congregation with guidelines for right teaching and right structure. Second Timothy more directly addresses the leaders of divided congregations, encouraging them to hold fast even as many fall away. Titus is apparently directed toward churches at Crete that also suffer dissension and (from the author's perspective) heresy. The most important way in which at least one church leader seeks to resolve these conflicts is by writing the Pastoral Epistles themselves. The devices of pseudonymity, continuity, and apostolic authority are brought together in the attempt to end the dissensions and disputes evident in our description of the "opponents" of Paul, above.

Put most baldly, the way to end conflict within the church, so the author hopes, is to appeal to the authority of Paul. If one takes the more sanguine view of pseudonymity, a Pauline disciple draws on his master to provide lessons for a generation later than Paul's own. If one takes the less sanguine view, a frustrated Christian teacher, not trusting in his own authority to end corrosive conflict, forges three letters in the name of the apostle. Perhaps he does this because his opponents cite Paul for their own purposes. The way to end their foolishness is to find the "real" Paul who (because he is an invention of the author) agrees in every way with what the author proposes.

In addition to using the epistles to draw upon apostolic authority, the author draws on a familiar technique of pseudepigraphal literature. He has the "author" (sometimes a seer, sometimes a prophet, here an apostle) foretell events purportedly far in the apostle's future but actually taking place in the author's own time and communities. Included here are probably 1 Tim. 4:1-4, 2 Tim. 3:1-9, and surely 2 Tim. 4:3-4.[31]

In two ways this prophetic material strengthens the argument of the Pastorals' claims against dissenters. First, Paul's authority is further strengthened. Not only was he a great apostle; he also foresaw, like a

---

31. Luke T. Johnson (*Decision Making,* e.g., 28, 82) apparently concludes that Paul himself lives in these later days, since the foretold opponents are also his real opponents. A further alternative explanation is that Paul does look ahead to developments of the later church in ways sufficiently perspicacious that the Pastorals proved immensely useful to later generations of Christians. See, for instance, Spicq, *Les Epîtres Pastorales,* 1:494; Oden, *First and Second Timothy,* 57–58.

great prophet, the actual events of the Pastorals' own time. Second, the
foolishness of those who follow the "false" teachers is underlined. Not
only are they making a huge mistake, but they also were warned long
ago not to do so.[32] Their little heresies are in fact part of the apostasy
of the end times.

One other literary technique in the pseudonymous letters works to
end disputes (in ways favorable to the author, of course). Helpers of
Paul become illustrative paradigms for those believers the Pastorals
seek to encourage (see, for instance, 2 Tim. 4:11, 16-17). And, of
course, Timothy and Titus, Paul's "legitimate" children, stand as positive examples for believers and teachers (see 1 Tim. 1:2; Titus 1:4).
Opponents of Paul become paradigms in a negative way for the opponents of the Pastorals' own time (see 1 Tim. 1:20; 2 Tim. 1:15). Those
who read wisely see themselves or their enemies foreshadowed in the
enemies of Paul.[33]

Not only does the genre of pseudonymous literature (and last testament) provide a means of resolving disputes in the congregation; the
right teaching that the Pastorals embody will itself also help to provide
healing and direction for a broken community. Timothy and Titus as
paradigmatic church teachers are enjoined to hold fast, guard, and pass
on that teaching they have received from Paul. The author's hope is
apparently that the teaching itself will persuade the straying to return
to the flock and will strengthen those who might be tempted to stray.
The author's confidence is that the teaching of the Pastorals and its ad-
herents will be vindicated by the judgment of God (see 1 Tim. 4:16;
2 Tim. 4:1-2, 7-8).

Equally important, the church leaders whom Paul describes and instructs in these epistles by their upright conduct and correct teaching
provide a means to the solution of disputes. A fuller discussion of their
qualifications and functions follows in this chapter, but in regard to the
question of disputes one feature of the relationship between right conduct and right teaching among church leaders is especially interesting.
One reason Paul wants church leaders to live upright lives is so that the
dissenters will have no reason to slander them, no appropriate grounds
for ethical outrage to excuse their own apostasy: "Show yourself in all
respects a model of good works, and in your teaching show integrity,

---

32. See Dibelius and Conzelmann, *Pastoral Epistles,* 64.
33. Donelson, *Pseudepigraphy,* 107.

gravity, and sound speech that cannot be censured; then any opponent will be put to shame, having nothing evil to say of us" (Titus 2:7-8; cf. 1 Tim. 3:7; 2 Tim. 2:16-17).

Finally, two specific sets of injunctions deal with divisions within the church—injunctions concerning women and injunctions concerning censure and forgiveness for apostates. In particular the injunctions to women regarding their role in the church seem to represent the author's attempt to solve what he thinks is a dilemma in his congregations, the disruptiveness of certain women. We can assume that 2 Tim. 3:6-7 represents something of the dilemma "Paul" wishes to solve: "For among [those who go astray in the last days] are those who make their way into households and captivate silly women, overwhelmed by their sins and swayed by all kinds of desires, who are always being instructed and can never arrive at a knowledge of the truth."[34] This polemical prophecy may well reflect the author's reading of the situation of his own churches. For whatever reasons (he suggests both theological and psychological ones) large numbers of women in the community have been persuaded by the "false" teachers. The author's way of handling this perceived problem is not only to deal with the false teachers; he also sets limits on the communal participation of women.

In this light the injunctions of 1 Tim. 2:11-15 are more explicable, if no more edifying, than they might otherwise appear: "Let a woman [perhaps 'wife'] learn in silence with full submission. I permit no woman ['wife'?] to teach or to have authority over a man [or 'her husband']. She is to keep silent. For Adam was formed first, then Eve, and Adam was not deceived, but the woman was deceived and became a transgressor." Here Eve serves as an illustrative paradigm for the mistaken women of the Pastorals' own time.[35] Titus 2:4-5 advises older women to "encourage the young women to love their husbands, to love their children, to be self-controlled, chaste, good managers of the household,

---

34. See Dibelius and Conzelmann (*Pastoral Epistles,* 116) for further guesses on how "Gnosticism" might be involved in this conversion of women.

35. Regarding this text, Norbert Brox makes connections to the putative status of women in Gnosticism (*Die Pastoralbriefe,* RNT [Regensburg: F. Pustet, 1969], 133). Luke T. Johnson, who holds the text to be genuinely Pauline, explains it in the light of the distinction between prophetic utterances in the church—permissible to women—and the role of scriptural interpretation that Paul, as a Pharisee, would still restrict to men (*Decision Making,* 69–70). Thomas Oden argues that the text is more about learning with proper feminine tranquility than about silence or submissiveness to males (*First and Second Timothy,* 96–97).

kind, being submissive to their husbands so that the word of God may not be discredited."[36] Thus, seeing the numbers of women who have been tempted away from true teaching, "Paul" responds not only by trying to combat false teaching, but also by trying to limit the leadership and independence of the women in the Pastorals' communities.

We can see, then, that in dealing with apostasy, these epistles employ a mix of firmness and compassion. First Timothy 5:19-20 suggests that church leaders deal with elders who wander from true faith first cautiously, then firmly and publicly. The meaning of 1 Tim. 5:22 is uncertain. The reference to laying on of hands may be a warning not to ordain elders without due testing and circumspection, or it may mean not hastily to lay the hand of reconciliation on elders who have gone astray: "Do not lay hands on anyone hastily, and do not participate in the sins of others; keep yourself pure" (NRSV margin).

A picture of the church leader who mixes firmness with considerable gentleness is provided in 2 Tim. 2:24-26. It is not clear whether these instructions regarding apostasy also refer to elders who have gone astray, or to all erring Christians: "And the Lord's servant must not be quarrelsome but kindly to everyone, an apt teacher, patient, correcting opponents with gentleness. God may perhaps grant that they will repent and come to know the truth, and that they may escape from the snare of the devil, having been held captive by him to do his will."

Titus 3:10-11 either provides harsher dictates for a different congregation or shows forth the limits of acceptable mercy: "After a first and second admonition, have nothing to do with anyone who causes divisions, since you know that such a person is perverted and sinful, being self-condemned."[37] The claim that the wrongdoer is self-condemned nicely underlines the interplay between false teaching and behavior and its consequent judgment.

I have already noted that by the use of paradigms, "Paul" uses biographical details and literary memorabilia to reinforce a picture of discipline toward blasphemers that is firm but finally also merci-

---

36. Quinn sees here another indication of the concern that the conduct of "Paul's" Christians should not lead to scorn, either among unbelievers or among Jewish Christians—scorn because of the anarchy of believing households (see Quinn, *Letter to Titus,* 138). The issue of how the order of family interrelates to church order will be discussed below.

37. Jerome Quinn argues that this passage in Titus may not be as harsh as it appears, since the admonition is only for Titus as representative church leader to cut himself off from the offender, not for all Christians to do so (Quinn, *Letter to Titus,* 248, 251).

ful. Hymenaeus and Alexander are to be delivered to Satan (rebuked and excommunicated?) not for their eternal destruction, but in hope of their repentance (1 Tim. 1:20). The apostle himself was once a blasphemer: "But I received mercy because I had acted ignorantly in unbelief... making me an example to those who would come to believe in Christ for eternal life" (1 Tim. 1:13, 16).

Clearly, therefore, church order is to be maintained by public rebuke, perhaps limited to two occasions, but with the hope that those who wander from the truth will be shamed or graced into repentance.[38] In this way "Paul" instructs the churches to deal with dissension and move toward order and unity.

OFFICES IN THE CHURCHES OF THE PASTORALS

The Pastoral Epistles not only mention a number of types of church leader; more than any other New Testament literature they spell out in some detail the qualifications and tasks of such leadership. I shall look at each of the apparent offices, then address the issue of the relationship between leadership and upright Christian living, and finally attend to the function of ordination in the Pastoral Epistles.

TITLES AND FUNCTIONS

A preliminary issue, not easily sorted out, is the relationship between elders and bishops in the Pastorals.[39] In Titus the solution seems clearest: "elders" and "bishops" are different names for the same office or function in the community. The discussion fits within the "fiction" of Paul passing authority to Titus, who passes authority to the third-generation church leaders in Crete:

> I left you behind in Crete for this reason, so that you should put in order what remained to be done, and should appoint elders in every town, as I directed you: someone who is blameless, married only once, whose children are believers, not accused of debauchery and not rebellious. For a bishop, as God's steward, must be blameless. (Titus 1:5-7)

---

38. Contra Schweizer, *Church Order,* 82.

39. Von Campenhausen (*Ecclesiastical Authority,* 106–7) points out that while bishops, elders, and deacons are all listed as leaders in the Pastorals, the three never occur together in the same context. His guess is that the references represent an interweaving of traditions.

Either the two terms are simply equivalent, or, as Jerome Quinn argues, noticing the syntactical shift from plural "elders" to singular "bishop," the author uses "bishop," a traditional term for leadership in some of the Cretan communities, to show the congruence between local views of leadership and the view represented by the Pauline "elders."[40] Abraham Malherbe further points out that the elders or bishops apparently have leadership responsibility for all the churches in a city, not just for an individual house church.[41]

First Timothy has separate passages referring to bishops and elders: "The saying is sure, whoever aspires to the office of bishop desires a noble task" (1 Tim. 3:1). But, "Let the elders who rule well be considered worthy of a double honor, especially those who labor in preaching and teaching" (1 Tim. 5:17). (The issue is further complicated by the question of whether the reference in 1 Tim. 5:1 is to an elder [official] or, as the NRSV has it, to an "older man.")

Three options seem possible, and it seems impossible to adjudicate with any certainty among them.

1. Bishops and elders are the same persons. The Pastorals perhaps draw on different traditions, a tradition of bishops within the local churches and a tradition of elders among those who draw especially on a particular strain of Pauline authority.

2. Bishops are a particular subset of the council of elders, whether themselves elders entrusted with particular responsibilities or as ex officio members of the council of elders due to their discrete duties as overseers.[42] Hermann von Lips, seeing the term "elder" as derived from the synagogue and the term "bishop" as derived from Hellenistic circles, suggests that the most likely explanation is that the bishop was a (the?) leader of the circle of elders, first among equals.[43] Norbert Brox nicely explores the possibilities and acknowledges the limits of the evidence but hypothesizes that bishops were members of the council of elders but were simply equals among equals, without any primacy. The

---

40. See Quinn, *Letter to Titus,* 88.

41. See Abraham Malherbe, *Social Aspects of Early Christianity,* 2d ed. (Philadelphia: Fortress Press, 1983), 70, 101.

42. This seems to be what Dibelius and Conzelmann conclude in their excursus (*Pastoral Epistles,* 54–57).

43. Hermann von Lips, *Glaube, Gemeinde, Amt: Zum Verständnis der Ordination in den Pastoralbriefen* (Göttingen: Vandenhoeck and Ruprecht, 1979), 111–13.

Pastorals may represent the last stages before clearer distinctions both of function and of authority were made in the early church.[44]

3. Bishops are distinguished from elders in the communities represented by 1 and 2 Timothy but are the elders in the community to which Titus is written.

Whatever the precise relationship between elders and bishops in the Pastorals, two facts seem reasonably clear. First, bishops have the same responsibilities that (other?) elders do, while any unique responsibilities pertaining to the bishop are impossible to specify clearly. Second, bishops and elders are expected to lead the same kind of exemplary lives. I shall therefore discuss the apparent functions of the elders in the Pastorals' communities, suggesting that whatever other responsibilities bishops may have, they at least have the same responsibilities as the elders.

First Timothy includes a discussion of the responsibility of certain elders: "Let the elders who rule well be considered worthy of double honor, especially those who labor in preaching and teaching: for the scripture says, 'You shall not muzzle an ox while it is treading out the grain,' and, 'The laborer deserves to be paid' " (1 Tim. 5:17-19). Functions appropriate to elders include "ruling," which might also be translated "supervising." For this job elders are apparently to be compensated financially.[45] Some, but presumably not all, elders are also responsible for preaching and teaching.

By implication, the earlier list of qualifications for a bishop in 1 Timothy suggests that the bishop does have supervisory, administrative responsibility in the church (1 Tim. 3:4-5). Titus's description of the bishop, who is also an elder, stresses the teaching function, and along with it the concomitant responsibility for correcting error (Titus 1:7).

As we shall see, the references to ordination and laying on of hands, as well as the whole literary device of the Pastorals, suggest that Timothy and Titus are themselves prototypical elders or bishops. As paradigms they receive instructions that give clues to the functions of the actual presbyters in the churches to which the Pastorals were written.

"And the Lord's servant must not be quarrelsome but kindly to everyone, an apt teacher, patient, correcting opponents with gentleness" (2 Tim. 2:24-25a; see also 2 Tim. 2:15; 4:1-2, 5). Here, especially in

---

44. Brox, *Die Pastoralbriefe,* 147–52.

45. See Dibelius and Conzelmann, *Pastoral Epistles,* 78; Brox, *Die Pastoralbriefe,* 199.

2 Timothy, the instructions to the paradigmatic church leader are surely also to be read as applicable to third-generation church leaders who follow Paul and Timothy. If this is correct, then the appropriate functions for an elder (and at least for some bishops) are clear. Primarily the elder teaches true faith and corrects those who go astray, rebuking them and hoping to bring them back (see also Titus 2:1; 3:10-11). Bishops, therefore, apparently have supervisory responsibilities, somewhat comparable to those of the father of a household. Some bishops and most (all?) elders are responsible for right teaching and preaching, and for the disciplinary charge that goes with that: to reprove and correct the mistaken and to bring them back to right faith and the true community.

The functions of deacons are considerably less clear. They are required to be "orthodox," but whether that is because they teach or only because all servants in the church are to be right believers is unclear. They are not to be greedy for money, but whether that is because they have fiscal responsibilities or only because they are to conform to the ethical standards for Christian people is likewise unclear. "Deacons likewise must be serious, not double-tongued, not indulging in much wine, not greedy for money; they must hold fast to the mystery of faith with a clear conscience" (1 Tim. 3:8-9).

It may be that there are women deacons; it may be that instructions are included for the wives of deacons. The text and its meaning remain ambivalent: "Women, likewise, must be serious, not slanderers but temperate, faithful in all things" (1 Tim. 3:11).[46]

"Widows" are apparently real widows, that is, women of a certain age who have neither husbands nor children to support them. For real widows the church takes financial responsibility (1 Tim. 5:16). It is clear that widows take a pledge to remain unmarried (1 Tim. 5:12). Those who are enrolled as widows show their worthiness of support by their history of good works. Is a particular responsibility for intercession, visitation, and other good works in the community included in the use of the title (see 1 Tim. 5:9-10)?[47]

---

46. Jouette M. Bassler acknowledges the puzzles, citing other studies that claim the "women" may also be equated with the "widows." If so this passage would be an indication that the widows are also officers. See Jouette M. Bassler, "The Widows' Tale: A Fresh Look at 1 Timothy 5:3-16," in *JBL* 103, no. 1 (March 1984): 23–41, esp. 40.

47. On intercession as a responsibility of the widows, see Schweizer, *Church Order,* 86.

Jouette M. Bassler suggests that the widows may have included women who took earlier Pauline claims of Christian freedom earnestly and consequently were felt by the author of the Pastorals to require some more disciplined reaction. Bassler thinks the widows might include not only those who have outlived their husbands but also those who have divorced unbelieving husbands; they might perhaps also include never married women who have taken vows of chastity (see 1 Tim. 5:12).[48]

The author of the Pastorals seeks to deal with this problem by limiting the number of "real" widows who had genuine need (see 1 Tim. 5:3-8, 16). Further, as Bassler suggests, widows are chosen from among those who have lived acceptably traditional domestic lives.

> Thus a potentially objectionable office has been tamed, for even though the behavior of the widows may continue to deviate from society's expectations, the office itself now extols and rewards the expected virtues. Beyond this, the requirement that younger widows marry and bear children (v 14) not only encourages them to conform to society's expectations, but it also has a distinctly anti-ascetic thrust that was probably intended to counter the influence of the heretical camp.[49]

Widows constitute a group with special needs. It is less clear whether they constitute a group with particular responsibilities in the community. The worry that widows who are too young, as they "gad about from house to house," may turn into "gossips and busybodies" may well suggest that household visitation was a job of the official widows. The prayerful life enjoined in 1 Tim. 5:5 is clearly a widow's responsibility, less clearly her job.[50]

In all these cases the term "office" is probably anachronistic when applied to the world of the Pastorals. Particular functions and responsibilities were recognized, sometimes with ceremony (see below). Among these were the functions of bishop and presbyter, closely interrelated. The responsibilities of bishops and presbyters might include teaching, preaching, reproof, and administration or oversight. Deacons were also

---

48. See Bassler, "The Widows' Tale," 34–36.

49. Ibid., 38–39

50. So Dibelius and Conzelmann, *Pastoral Epistles,* 75. Brox (*Die Pastoralbriefe,* 186–87) sees responsibilities for "real widows," but not really an "office" here. Bassler ("The Widows' Tale," 41 n. 60) does not think there is sufficient evidence to think of any official role.

recognized, and their function may have included particular kinds of teaching and fiduciary responsibilities, but this is far from clear. Widows were indeed widows, and childless in their family status, but they also may have had special responsibilities for visitation, intercession, and charitable deeds within the church community.

ORTHODOXY AND ORTHOPRAXIS

We have already seen that a particular family situation and strong charitable commitments were requirements for those who served as widows. Strikingly, correct behavior is equally enjoined for those who serve as deacons and for those who serve as bishops or elders. There is a strong correlation drawn between the responsibilities of right teaching and those of right behavior, especially at home.

This is evident in the one passage in the Pastorals that deals with the requirements for deacons:

> Deacons likewise must be serious, not double-tongued, not indulging in much wine, not greedy for money; they must hold fast to the mystery of the faith with a clear conscience. And let them first be tested; then, if they prove themselves blameless, let them serve as deacons. Women [deacons, or deacons' wives] likewise must be serious, not slanderers, but temperate, faithful in all things. Let deacons be married only once, and let them manage their children and their households well; for those who serve well as deacons gain a good standing for themselves and great boldness in the faith that is in Christ Jesus. (1 Tim. 3:8-13)

We see here a general concern for the morality of deacons (and their spouses), and a particular concern that they manage their households well, presumably as signs that they are capable of managing well at church. There may be some hint that concern for the opinion of the world in part motivates this concern for right Christian behavior. The good standing that deacons gain may include recognition by neighbors outside the church itself; all the more reason that the deacons should live upright lives. (We have already noted the possibility that financial responsibility could be included in the diaconal tasks and provide its own particular temptations.)

In 1 Tim. 3:1-7, the injunctions for bishops and elders are even more thorough and specific.[51] Here again right teaching is closely correlated with right practice. There is major concern for the correspondence

---

51. Commentators differ on whether the injunction to have one wife means one wife

between responsible householding and responsible church leadership. There is worry lest outsiders find reason for slander in the behavior of a bishop. Two more specific, practical concerns emerge. The church is warned against trusting new believers with major responsibility prematurely. Lovers of money are to be avoided, perhaps because church leadership involves decisions about funds.

Titus includes a similar list of instructions in Titus 1:5-9. Jerome Quinn shows how the image of the household functions in this passage from Titus:

> The parenthetical description of a bishop as "God's steward" takes up the familial or household paradigm, implicit in the preceding catalog, and explicitly compares a bishop to an *oikonomos,* a Greek compound referring literally to house regulation. The church is a family in which God is Father; a bishop is compared to the man, often a slave, who administered the property of the head of the house.[52]

The bishop must control his own children, or (implicitly) how will he provide strong leadership for the flock entrusted to him? There is to be a congruity between his firm adherence to the word and his staunch morality. As regards the outside world, he must be "blameless."

The Pastorals also envision the possibility of elders going astray. While it is not clear whether heretical or unethical behavior is the major concern here (the two are obviously interlinked), there may be some particular stress on moral misdeeds:

> Never accept any accusation against an elder except on the evidence of two or three witnesses. As for those who persist in sin, rebuke them in the presence of all, so that the rest also may stand in fear. In the presence of God and of Christ Jesus and of the elect angels, I warn you to keep these instructions without prejudice, doing nothing on the basis of partiality. Do not ordain anyone hastily, and do not participate in the sins of others; keep yourself pure. (1 Tim. 5:19-22)

The concern for fairness on all sides is evident. No accusation is to be taken hastily; elders or bishops (represented here by Timothy) are not to give personal favoritism any play in their decisions concerning discipline. The rebuke is for the sake of the offender and for the sake of

---

at a time or only to marry once in a lifetime, widowed or not. See Dibelius and Conzelmann, *Pastoral Epistles,* 52.

52. Quinn, *Letter to Titus,* 88.

potential offenders. "Do not ordain anyone hastily" might mean "Do not lay hands of forgiveness or reconciliation on anyone hastily." In either case the hope is to act against sin, either preventively or after the fact.

Again Timothy and Titus are employed as paradigms for right behavior among their successor church leaders. In the passage we just examined, Timothy is told as representative elder or bishop how to deal with other elders who err. In 1 Tim. 6:11 and in 2 Tim. 2:22 and 4:5 the recipient of the letter is enjoined to combine piety and godly behavior, a model for other church leaders.

Our analysis of these passages suggests that at least three issues are at stake in the correlation between right behavior and right teaching among church leaders.

1. There is a congruence between the argument for right leadership and the argument against the "heretics." The false teachers not only lead people astray; they also demonstrate a variety of moral misbehavior. Those who stand in the tradition of Paul, Timothy, and Titus are called to do just the opposite: to combine right teaching with the behavior that fits with godliness.

2. As we shall see, there is a congruence between the argument for right behavior and the governing image of the church in the Pastorals, the image of the household. The right functioning of a household, according to the Pastorals, depends on the strong leadership of a father (or a steward) who not only teaches what is right but also behaves decorously and responsibly toward the rest of the family. So, analogously, the health of the church depends on leadership that is correct doctrinally and responsible ethically.

3. The church that adheres to the Pauline tradition, according to the Pastorals, lives a precarious existence, dependent in part on the goodwill of its secular neighbors. Wrong behavior becomes an object for scorn and derision among outsiders and therefore endangers the life of the church. For reasons of shame and prudence, church leaders are to behave responsibly.

For all these reasons, in discussing "official" church leaders, the Pastorals make a very strong connection between duties (largely didactic) and behavior (irreproachably upright).

Ordination and Charisma

Two passages in the Pastoral Epistles refer directly to the laying on of hands in some sort of service of ordination, installation, and transmission of tradition; and the meaning of another passage is even less clear.

The first of the two more direct statements is 1 Tim. 4:14: "Do not neglect the gift that is in you, which was given to you through prophecy, with the laying on of hands by the elders." Three features mark the authorization of Timothy's ministry as set out in this passage. First, there is the gift (charisma) that he has received. Second, there is the claim that this gift was given him through prophecy. Hermann von Lips admits that the significance of this phrase is unclear: Does it mean that Timothy's ministry was foreseen by the prophets or (we should think more likely) that prophecy was part of the rite of ordination?[53] Third, there is the laying on of hands by the elders. Whether or not this rite can be properly described as sacramental, it does represent a legitimizing recognition by church leaders that the gift given is indeed a gift from God. It implies at least recognition if not empowerment. As Brox points out, in an epistle eager to stress the continuities between Paul, the elders, and the churches of the Pastorals, this view of ordination becomes a way of reinforcing those ties of tradition and lineage.[54]

The second pertinent passage is 2 Tim. 1:6-7: "For this reason I remind you to rekindle the gift of God that is within you through the laying on of my hands; for God did not give us a spirit of cowardice, but rather a spirit of power and of love and of self-discipline." While the language here shifts somewhat from 1 Timothy, there is still considerable continuity. Instead of the stress on charisma there is now stress on the spirit (or Spirit) that was given Timothy, perhaps at the time of "ordination" itself. Now it is not the elders who lay on hands but Paul. Brox argues convincingly that the distinction lies not in different understandings of ordination but in the genre of the two letters. First Timothy represents a more general discussion of appropriate church leadership, including attention to the council of elders. Second Timothy,

---

53. See von Lips, *Glaube, Gemeinde, Amt,* 243. Dibelius and Conzelmann (*Pastoral Epistles,* 71) see the prophecy as part of the rite itself. Brox (*Die Pastoralbriefe,* 180) appropriately finds the best background in 1 Tim. 1:18 where Paul refers to prophecies made earlier about Timothy (one would assume prophecies by Christian, not pre-Christian, prophets) and made at the time of the "ordination" itself.

54. Brox, *Die Pastoralbriefe,* 182. Von Campenhausen sees ordination here as "sacramental" (*Ecclesiastical Authority,* 115; so also von Lips, *Glaube, Gemeinde, Amt,* 247–48), while Schweizer (*Church Order,* 84) thinks the laying on of hands recognizes charisms already bestowed.

as Paul's last testament, stresses the paradigmatic relationship between Timothy and Paul: Paul lays on hands as the prototypical elder. Again, continuity between the apostle and the disciple (and the church of the Pastorals) and the legitimacy of Timothy's teaching are symbolized by this appropriate succession.[55]

The more ambiguous text concerning laying on of hands, which follows a discussion of elders who have persisted in sin, is 1 Tim. 5:22: "Do not ordain anyone hastily, and do not participate in the sins of others; keep yourself pure." Literally the text reads: "Do not lay hands on anyone hastily. . . ." Given the context, in a discussion of church discipline, the admonition may be a warning not to forgive an erring elder too easily. Or it may be that the reference is again to ordination, with the warning not to lay hands on untested candidates.[56]

The texts are disappointingly brief. My reading suggests this: the understanding of ordination and laying on of hands is not a fully developed sacramental understanding. It is not that the office is conveyed by the laying on of hands, but the rite does mediate the church's authoritative recognition of the prophecy and the gifts of the Spirit that accompany ordination. The church is able to recognize those fit for ordination because the church knows what faith and what conduct are required of its leaders: those requirements were passed down by "Paul" through Timothy and Titus in the very epistles these third-generation churches now read.

In summary: distinct functions are moving toward distinct offices in the churches of the Pastorals. Especially the offices of elder and bishop begin to take on definition, with some stress on leadership and some stress on teaching as central responsibilities. For a variety of reasons the conduct of the church leader is as important as his or her orthodoxy. Indeed right practice and right belief are inseparably joined.

It is for elders to recognize other elders and their gifts through the laying on of hands. "Paul" and the elders have laid hands on Timothy. Timothy is called to lay hands on those elders of a later day who meet the requirements of right teaching and conduct, and to delay laying hands on candidates who do not. Presumably those church

---

55. See Brox, *Die Pastoralbriefe,* 181–82.

56. If Ernst Käsemann is right, 1 Tim. 6:11-16 is a portion of an address used at an ordination; Timothy becomes a paradigm of other church leaders, ordained like him for teaching and directing the congregation. See Käsemann, "Das Formular," 101–8.

leaders who read the Pastorals see themselves and their responsibilities foreshadowed, directed.

IMAGES OF THE CHURCH IN THE PASTORALS

As Hermann von Lips points out, the governing image of the church in the Pastorals is the image of the household.[57] The most explicit use of the image is found in 1 Tim. 3:14-15: "I hope to come to you soon, but I am writing these instructions to you so that, if I am delayed, you may know how one ought to behave in the household of God, which is the church of the living God, the pillar and bulwark of the truth."

Not only is there the clear implication that God is the head of this household; there is the further implication that church order and order-liness are directly related to household orders. The passage is preceded by these instructions for a bishop: "He must manage his own household well, keeping his children submissive and respectful in every way—for if someone does not know how to manage his own household, how can he take care of God's church?" (1 Tim. 3:4-5). The bishop therefore serves as a kind of surrogate father in the church, bringing God's own order to God's own family.

In the stress on authority, mutual respect, appropriate submission, upright standards, and clear discipline throughout the Pastoral Epistles, the author shows forth a vision of the church that is informed by his vision of the proper, orderly, unified family.

The image is used similarly in Titus 1:7 where the description of the bishop as good steward sounds in many ways like the appropriate description of an upright and loyal steward in a well-run household: "For a bishop, as God's steward, must be blameless; he must not be arrogant or quick-tempered or addicted to wine or violent or greedy for gain; but he must be hospitable, a lover of goodness, prudent, upright, devout, and self-controlled."[58]

The image extends to the paradigmatic relationship between the apos-tle and his disciples, Timothy and Titus. As we have seen, each of these recipients of one of the letters is referred to as Paul's loyal child

---

57. Von Lips, *Glaube, Gemeinde, Amt,* 96–98.

58. Abraham Malherbe (*Social Aspects,* 98–100) argues that the evidence is incon-clusive whether bishops in the communities of the Pastorals were regularly heads of households that hosted house churches.

(1 Tim. 1:2), beloved child (2 Tim. 1:2), and again loyal child (Titus 1:4). Further, the term "loyal child" may in fact better be translated "true child" or "legitimate child," part of Paul's true family as opposed to those who claim him illegitimately as their father in Christ. Also, the relationship between Timothy and his mother and grandmother may foreshadow the way in which, at the time of the Pastorals, familial relationships and churchly relationships enrich and inform each other (2 Tim. 1:5).

In the discussion of right relationships among different generations in the church in 1 Tim. 5:1-2 the familial categories explicitly inform the ecclesiastical ones: "Do not speak harshly to an older man, but speak to him as to a father, to younger men as brothers, to older women as mothers, to younger women as sisters—with absolute purity." (We may wonder whether the use of the term "elders," whatever its Jewish or Pauline antecedents, may not also include some allusion to the parallels between familial and church orderings.)

All these uses are both familial and hierarchical, or, in context, hierarchical precisely because they are familial. Authority in God's house is parallel to authority in any well-run household, and the well-being of the church, like the well-being of a family, depends on order and on those leaders who provide it.

Other images add in passing to our impression of the Pastorals' vision of the church, though none is developed in any thorough way. In 1 Tim. 3:15, the church is not only God's household; it is "the pillar and bulwark of the truth." There are other images that suggest the church as a kind of fortress, a gift of great worth but a gift that needs to be protected against the onslaughts of the enemies and of the Enemy. So Paul instructs Timothy: "Hold to the standard of sound teaching that you have heard from me, in the faith and love that are in Christ Jesus. Guard the good treasure entrusted to you, with the help of the Holy Spirit living in us" (2 Tim. 1:13-14). The idea of the young church leader as "guard" of the "treasure" or the "bulwark" entrusted to his care may feed the image of the apostle, of his disciples, and of later church leaders as brave soldiers in a great cause (1 Tim. 1:18-19; 6:12; 2 Tim 4:7).[59] And loosely related to this is the image of the church leader as athlete, training for the course of the faithful life: "Train your-

---

59. Dibelius and Conzelmann discuss this imagery in an excursus (*Pastoral Epistles,* 32–33).

self in godliness, for while physical training is of some value, godliness is valuable in every way" (1 Tim. 4:7-8; see 2 Tim. 2:5).

What emerges from all these images is quite consistent with the theology and the admonitions of the Pastorals. The author is concerned with holding the church together, as one might want to hold a family together. The author is concerned with holding fast the faith in a fight against the enemies, or on a course toward divine reward. The church is embattled, but its hope lies in reaffirming both its faith and its appropriate structure of faithful orders and loyal subordination. Right teachers keep the faith, assert their authority, and lead the battle against the forces of dissolution and moral decay.

THE PASTORALS AND MINISTRY TODAY

The Pastorals have represented a fertile basis for a discussion of the appropriate grounds and functions of Christian church leaders. For some scholars and theologians, like Ernst Käsemann, Hans von Campenhausen, and Eduard Schweizer, the Pastorals represent the shift from the more vital charismatic ministry evident in the indisputably Pauline epistles toward a more rigid structure soon evident in the monarchical episcopate envisioned by Ignatius.[60]

The controlling devices and images of the Pastorals may in fact point toward an ecclesiology more settled and therefore stuffier than the ecclesiology advocated in 1 Corinthians or Romans. Apostleship functions less as a charism and more as a legitimation of the authority of particular theological claims and community practices. The image shifts from the lively interdependence of the body of Christ to the more stable and hierarchical model of a Hellenistic household.

If there is a link between Paul and the Pastorals, on a kind of trajectory from charism to structure, that link is represented by Luke-Acts and especially by Acts 20. Paul's authority is passed on to the elders, who in turn presumably will pass it on to the churches of Luke's own day (nearly contemporary with the churches of the Pastorals). The Lukan

---

60. See Käsemann, "Ministry and Community in the New Testament," in *Essays on New Testament Themes,* trans. W. J. Montague (London: SCM, 1964), 85–88; see also von Campenhausen, *Ecclesiastical Authority,* and Schweizer, *Church Order.* Peter Lampe doubts that Ignatius actually yet knew a monarchical episcopate. See Lampe, *Die stadtrömischen Christen in den ersten beiden Jahrhunderten* (Tübingen: J. C. B. Mohr [Paul Siebeck], 1987), 336–38.

stress on witnessing the gospel shifts to the Pastorals' stress on guarding the deposit of faith. However, the whole device of pseudonymity represents the attempt to structure authority for the author's own theological and ethical stance.

As Käsemann himself points out, the stress on structure and tradition in the Pastorals is not just a result of the fading eschatological excitement behind Paul's writings and Matthew's too. The church the author of the Pastorals' seeks to save is torn apart by theological controversy and moral confusion. That church is attacked from without and subverted from within, and so the author draws the wagons in a circle.[61]

How pertinent the Pastorals are to our own situation will depend in large measure on how we read that situation. That the churches lie under threat no one will deny. Is that a threat from a world out there, best defeated by strengthening the fortress of faith and traditional morality? Do we need clearer structure so that we can have guidance against the slings and arrows of outrageous secularism? Or is the threat more to be found in the very institutionalization the Pastorals foreshadow? Have we quenched the Spirit by our love of organization and public relations campaigns? Does hope lie more in locking the doors or in opening the windows?

However we decide, a ministry that seeks to find light for its practice from the Pastorals will need to reflect on at least these issues:

1. Despite the cries that the Pastorals move us rapidly toward the rationalization of "early catholicism," the Pastorals, structurally the farthest "right" of any New Testament writing, still stand far "left" of most contemporary church practice.[62] Church leaders are clearly not full-time professionals but serve in this capacity along with other responsibilities, though it is clear that—as with the apostles other than Paul—some compensation is expected for elders.[63] There is no sense that those who receive gifts for leadership are to receive special training that sets them apart from the others. More than we acknowledge

61. Käsemann, "Ministry and Community," 85–86.

62. "Early catholicism" is Käsemann's phrase; he explains its origin and its connection with the Pastorals in the first note in "Paul and Early Catholicism," in *New Testament Questions of Today,* trans. W. J. Montague (Philadelphia: Fortress Press, 1969), 236–37. See also Joachim Rogge and Gottfried Schille, eds., *Frühkatholizmus im ökumenischen Gespräch* (Berlin: Evangelische Verlagsanstalt, 1983).

63. See 1 Tim. 5:17. Von Campenhausen notes the "professional" nature of ministry here but seems to forget that it is already evident in the church of Paul's time (1 Cor. 9:11-12; 2 Cor. 11:8-10). See von Campenhausen, *Ecclesiastical Authority,* 113.

in our own practice, the distinction between teacher and learner is still more charismatic than institutional.

So, too, ordination is not yet a sacrament but at most a mediation of grace given by the Spirit and confirmed by prophecy. I am tempted to say that ordination recognizes gifts of leadership but does not bestow them. The evidence here is not clear, but the texts still point in that direction.

2. A ministry defined by the Pastorals will include a strong stress on continuity. While I do not see here any sense of apostolic succession, there is clearly a succession of both right doctrine and right leadership. Though it may be true that the author of the Pastorals defines his version of Pauline theology for the very first time, he defends it by insisting that it is nothing new at all. Ministry defined by the Pastorals will therefore look less to management theory and demographic projections and more to our fathers and mothers in the faith, finding in those older traditions the resources we need for our own time.

3. Ministry defined by the Pastorals will include public recognition of the gifts of community leadership, including the laying on of hands. Whether "ordination" is the best term for this recognition depends on how much other theological and liturgical baggage the term "ordination" is seen to bear. We have no sense here whether ordination is for life or for a term. What does seem clear is that the ceremony acknowledges the function of the one ordained and his (or her) spiritual gifts. Above all, those who are ordained are ordained to teach. The test of their competence is both the genuineness of their call and the correctness of their claims. In that sense today's ordination councils and presbytery interrogations may not be far from the Pastorals' own mark.[64]

4. The leadership to which the Pastorals attend most closely is the leadership of the elder or bishop, and the responsibility of the elder or bishop is primarily to teach right faith and, as a corollary, to discipline those who go astray.

The Pastorals draw very close to the older American Presbyterian definition of clergy as "teaching elders." What is taught is to be in continuity with the faith as it is received. "The faith" has content. The church does not only entice trust in the God of Jesus Christ; it also

---

64. Von Campenhausen (*Ecclesiastical Authority,* 118), who stresses the increasing "professionalization" of church leadership in the Pastorals, nonetheless acknowledges that the fundamental authority rests with the correctness of the teaching rather than with ordination or structures.

teaches right doctrine about that God against dangerous misreadings. That is to say, there is a shift in the definition of Christian faith from the radical trust and obedience that characterize Pauline teaching to a stress on right doctrine, which is not unrelated to such radical trust but is nonetheless a significant extension of Pauline notions of faith or faithfulness.

Right teaching consists of loyal interpretation (orthodox interpretation) both of Scripture (the Old Testament) and of the apostolic tradition. Scripture and tradition rightly interpreted provide a safeguard against the corrosive influences of worldliness and heresy.

Ministry today that is modeled on the Pastorals therefore takes seriously the didactic responsibilities of the minister. There is a tradition, a faith, to be interpreted and passed on. There is a disciplinary role for a church leader: to name false teaching and to chastise mistaken faith.

My suspicion is that this model of ministry is alive and well particularly in more "conservative" churches, both Protestant and Catholic, where the pastor or priest takes seriously his or her role as guardian of the faith. In such churches right doctrine can be fairly clearly defined, faith is a matter of community convictions rather than individual choice and interpretation, and the community is safeguarded by recognized strategies for discipline (shunning among some Amish Christians, for instance, or pastoral decisions about excommunication).

As with every other body of New Testament literature we have studied, the Pastorals are striking for their silence on issues of the sacramental responsibilities of the elders, bishops, or deacons. Of course, the Pastorals are strikingly silent on issues of liturgy and sacrament, save insofar as communal confessions of faith may lie behind some of the credal affirmations in these letters. There is no evidence here, however, that among the particular responsibilities of elders or deacons was the responsibility to baptize or to preside at the Lord's Table.

5. The Pastorals stress the congruity between right teaching and right practice on the part of the elder or deacon (or widow). It would be anachronistic to see here any claims to donatism, but there is a stress on the moral uprightness of the right teacher. It is not that the sacrament would be made invalid by immoral practice; that issue does not arise. It is rather that teaching might be thrown into question by irresponsible behavior, the elder's authority weakened within the church and jeered from without.

The Pastorals pose vexed questions for ministry today. Is there a particular conduct that is appropriate for church leaders? Is this the same conduct appropriate for all Christians, as I think the Pastorals might say, or are there even "higher" standards for clergy than for others?

The issue surfaces in different ways in different churches. Clearly within the Catholic church the question of clerical celibacy is in part the issue of whether particular standards of conduct are required of "religious" that are not only not required but are discouraged among lay people.

In many denominations the difficulty that clergy have in keeping or getting pastoral positions after they have been divorced represents an ongoing conviction that clergy of all people ought to live up to the Gospels' injunctions on divorce and remarriage and probably to the Pastorals' insistence that an elder should be husband of only one wife, till death do them part.

The vexed question of ordination for gay men and lesbian women is complicated by the fact that many church people who welcome homosexual people into church membership draw the line at ordination. Whether or not such Christians are right in seeing homosexuality as an unacceptable orientation, it is striking that the unacceptability often represents sanctions for clergy but not for lay people. Different standards are supposed for, or imposed on, those who seek ordination.[65]

On the one hand, there is much to affirm in this insistence that clergy practice what they preach, or preach what they practice. Hypocrisy is an ancient and dishonorable problem in every denomination. On the other hand, one must ask about the definition of ordination that presupposes a kind of two-tiered Christianity: the relatively moral lay people and the astonishingly moral clergy. Especially for those for whom the gospel consists centrally in the proclamation of God's choice to justify the ungodly, it becomes odd to define that by the heroic godliness of the preacher. (Though, of course, as Paul reminds us, this does not mean that we sin the more that grace may abound.)

Further, while we want to acknowledge the validity of a congruity between the pastor's personal life and his or her churchly responsibilities, we will want to ask whether the only model of good parenthood, for instance, is the kind of subordinationist, hierarchical model the Pastorals

---

65. My own argument for an accepting stance toward gays and lesbians, including openness to ordination, is found in "A Biblical Perspective on Homosexuality," in Harold L. Twiss, ed., *Homosexuality and the Christian Faith* (Valley Forge, Pa.: Judson, 1978), 23–40.

presuppose. And conversely is the only good elder or pastor a kind of model *paterfamilias* or *Hausvater,* whose word is law and whose service is far from perfect freedom?

6. Finally, the Pastorals provide one option for dealing with dissolution within the church and disapproval without. The strategy is to stress the structures of church authority: to define the constitution and its offices, to make sure that the standards are sufficiently stringent. While the Spirit is cited in the Pastorals, the Spirit seems there to validate the tradition and to sanction the structures, not to stir and certainly not to stir revolt or even much rethinking.

Again it is a matter of discerning the times: if the threat is anarchy then perhaps we need to build better barricades. If the threat is morbidity, then we pray the freeing Spirit. To state the issue that way is to confess a bias. Yet one can only acknowledge that we do live in a time when the church is under stress. The call for stronger order may not be sufficient to our day, but it is understandable. And in the Pastorals that call finds scriptural ground.

CHAPTER 7

New Testament Ministry
and Ministry Today

SERVICE

In various ways the New Testament writings we have studied bear this witness: God gives us the gospel, and then the church, and then the church's ministers. Put the other way around: ministers serve the church; the church serves the gospel. Some contemporary ecclesiologies almost make it sound the other way: the church is constituted by its ministers; the church preaches the gospel for its own upbuilding.

The apostle Paul will have the first and last word in this chapter. His first word is this: "So if anyone is in Christ, there is a new creation: everything old has passed away; see, everything has become new! All this is from God, who reconciled us to himself through Christ, and has given us the ministry of reconciliation" (2 Cor. 5:17-18). The gospel is preached for the redemption of the world; the church exists for the world's sake in the service of the gospel; ministry exists for the church's sake in the service of the gospel for the sake of the world.

While Vatican II's document on the church, *Lumen Gentium,* appropriately begins with a discussion of the church as Christ's own sheepfold, when the document moves to discussing the role of laity in the church, there is the clear sense that the role of God's people is subsidiary to the role of their priests:

An individual layman, by reason of the knowledge, competence, or outstanding ability which he may enjoy, is permitted and sometimes even obliged

185

to express his opinion on things which concern of the good of the Church. When occasions arise, let this be done through the agencies set by the Church for this purpose. Let it always be done in truth, in courage, and in prudence, with reverence and charity toward those who by reason of their sacred office represent the person of Christ.[1]

Baptism, Eucharist, and Ministry, a document of the World Council of Churches, at some points also implies that Christ designates clergy to represent his person at the table, and in that sense, at least to constitute the church as eucharistic community:

> In the celebration of the eucharist, Christ gathers, teaches and nourishes the Church. It is Christ who invites to the meal and who presides at it. He is the shepherd who leads the people of God, the prophet who announces the word of God, the priest who celebrates the mystery of God. In most churches, this presidency is signified by an ordained minister.[2]

For Paul, to turn again to our earliest witness to the meaning of church, it is the church itself that is Christ's body, and from the church certain people as members of the body perform functions, including ministerial functions. The notion that one member of the body could somehow "signify" Christ's presidency or "represent" Christ's person strikes one as being impossible. The head cannot say to the foot, "I have no need of you"; nor can the head say to the foot, "*I* represent Christ; therefore, in virtue of my sacred office, treat me with reverence and charity."

Even in Acts, where Christ's ministry is carried on through the apostles, they are witnesses whose job is to serve him by building up the larger community of disciples, of believers. Even in the Pastorals, where of all the writings we have examined official leadership is most fully delineated and honored, the bishop's role is functional: he is to "take care of God's church" (1 Tim. 3:5), for whose sake he is called to ministry. And the church prays for the world, for whose sake Christ died: "For there is one God; there is also one mediator between God and humankind, Christ Jesus, himself human, who gave himself a ransom for all" (1 Tim. 2:5-6).

---

1. *Lumen Gentium,* in Walter M. Abbott, ed., *The Documents of Vatican II* (New York: Herder and Herder; Association Press, 1966), 4, 37.

2. *Baptism, Eucharist, and Ministry,* Faith and Order Paper no. 111, World Council of Churches, Geneva (St. Louis: Association of Evangelical Lutheran Churches, 1982), 3, 29, 27.

I suspect that in our churches of all denominations, two quite different views of the minister vie with one another. In one view, the minister is sent from God to fill the pulpit or appointed by Christ to take Christ's place as host at the table. In the other view, the minister is called out from among the people to help interpret Scripture by preaching and to help serve at a table where Christ alone is host.

While there may be a few New Testament hints pointing to the former view and considerable churchly practice supporting it, the sources we have examined from Paul through the Pastorals point to ministry that is called forth in the church (not from the church), for the sake of the church, for the sake of the gospel, for the sake of the world.

All this points to some of the difficulty with the models of pastor as professional, on the one hand, and as practical theologian, on the other. For all its positive values, the claim that the minister is professional can suggest that he or she is credentialed and validated by the approval of peers—fellow professionals. We are helpers called in to provide clinical or legal advice to that poor client, the church. For all its positive values, the claim that the minister is a practical theologian can make it sound as if the minister works for the sake of a discipline rather than in service of a people. If we define our field, we shall define our task. That is perhaps fair enough in the academy but scarcely fair *enough* for the people of God.

Like every other church person, the minister is first of all a Christian. The minister's baptism provides the identity that ordination only elaborates. Like every Christian the minister is credentialed and validated by the gospel and by service to the people who cherish and share that good news for the sake of the redemption of the world.

STRUCTURES

From my youth I have been influenced, challenged, and enticed by Ernst Käsemann's view that somewhere as early as a bad day in Paul's apostleship, when Paul ever so slightly lost his grip on Christian freedom, the church has been slipping toward early catholicism. Then, of course, the church slipped into real Catholicism, and for Käsemann, every church stands in danger of that slippage every day.

It is not just my ecumenical sympathies that make me wish we could find another way to talk about emerging church structure and doctrine than to call it "early catholicism." It is partly my realization that every church structure we discover in or behind the New Testament documents stands far to the left of establishment American churches today—Catholic and Protestant alike.

As we looked at the foreshadowings of ordination in the Pastoral Epistles we discovered that they were indeed foreshadowings: laying on of hands seemed to be a way of acknowledging charismatic gifts of ministry, not a way of bestowing or conferring ministry. As far as we can tell no one save the apostles was a church leader full-time. If today one gap runs between those who preside at Eucharist and those who only receive, another great gap runs between those who are paid to serve the church full-time and those who are not. One can guess that in ways that may have been highly salutary, early Christian "elders" or "bishops" worked side by side with, or even under the supervision of, other Christians in day by day occupations. There were no seminaries, no continuing education, no pension plans.

The New Testament's most structured view of ministry, foreshadowed in Acts 20 and delineated in the Pastorals, was still more charismatic than the ministerial leadership of most contemporary Assembly of God churches. There were fewer hoops to jump through, fewer authorities to please, fewer professional standards.

We are who we are, a specialized people living in a specialized world, but the occasional morbidity of the church results in part from a twofold confusion. The first is the minister who thinks that he or she is not only set apart but set above, who thinks that being paid to be Christian makes it especially virtuous to do so. The second is the congregation who sees that minister as hired hand, not fellow Christian, fellow pilgrim, but management: easy come, easy go.

More than the fading of eschatological hope or the recurrent threat of heresy, the movement toward rationalized institutional structures in a complex world causes the church legitimately to call some people to provide leadership in teaching, administering, enabling care, and preaching. (This is not a call to full-time Christian service. What in God's name is part-time Christian service? What days does one get off?) The danger is that those of us who are paid for churchly jobs will so lose touch with other Christians that we will think ecclesiastical issues are the main issues and the bright new paraments a sign of redemption for the pain of the world.

The New Testament from left (Paul) to right (the Pastorals) shakes us from our careful institutional rigidity lest we miss the moving of the

Spirit and the reality of our fellow Christians. I am not sure how we receive that Spirit, save by prayer, self-criticism, and a healthy skepticism toward any too high view of our own calling.

UNITY AND DIVERSITY

The apostle Paul writes to the Romans: "Besides this, you know what time it is, how it is now the moment for you to wake from sleep. For salvation is nearer now than when we became believers; the night is far gone, the day is near" (Rom. 13:11-12a). Christians and Christian ministers always need to ask what time it is. In the New Testament different forms of ministry emerged in part because Christian people and communities answered that question differently.

Paul, eagerly waiting the Lord's return and rejoicing in the power of the Spirit, stressed our interdependence as Christians and nodded to authority but did not structure it, save in the case of his own apostolic ministry. Matthew, sorting out the difference between his community and the synagogue, envisioned the leadership of scribes who would interpret both the Torah and the new Torah of Jesus, but in his vision the teachers were to be seen as equal with those they taught.

The Johannine community looks like it started as a community led by the Paraclete and its memories of its own traditions about Jesus and was very wary of anything verging on official leadership. Even by the time of the Johannine epistles, the elder does not seem able to draw on his official authority but only on his sense of rectitude and loyalty to the tradition. Luke does think about what happens as the witness of the apostles draws (or has drawn) to an end, and he writes a history that links the apostles through the elders to the church of his own time. The elders seem to have had care-giving and supervisory responsibilities, but above all they held forth right teaching against encroaching heresy. The Pastorals watch the heresies encroach faster and stronger yet. They envision a group of leaders who combine right teaching with upright lives, some order, and some limits on the freedom of the Spirit to stir up as well as to stir.

We cannot mix those all together and say: "There it is, New Testament ministry," as if our time were all those times and our needs were all those, quite disparate, needs.

Both *Lumen Gentium* and *Baptism, Eucharist, and Ministry* sometimes seem to assume that there is somehow *the* New Testament answer to what time it is and what kind of ministry is appropriate to that time. Both documents take themes and injunctions freely from here and there in the canon to find the evidence to bolster their own, perhaps quite plausible, views of what ministry for our time might be. Both hold up a threefold picture of ministry—bishop, priest or elder, and deacon. However, the evidence is very slight that such a threefold ministry existed in *any* New Testament community, though of course each title or function or office is evident in some community or another. Even the Pastorals, where the three designations are used, may use "bishop" and "elder" interchangeably, and they never use "priest."

There is, of course, a kind of discernment of the times behind *Baptism, Eucharist, and Ministry*. What the Faith and Order Commission discerns, I hope quite rightly, is that the time has come for Christian churches to move closer together. It is not clear, however, that the way to move toward that unity is to impose a false uniformity on the New Testament documents and then devise for our time a threefold form of ministry whose fundamental function seems to be—to serve our unity.[3]

Perhaps we need rather ask how the church serves the gospel for the sake of the world as we move into the twenty-first century. Perhaps the division of our churches is a scandal to the world, though I suspect not as much as it is a scandal to us. My guess is there are larger scandals to which we might attend with quite different results in our doctrine of ministry. Of many possible results of such a study I can suggest two, not necessarily mutually exclusive.

On the one hand, we might decide that unity lies more in mutual recognition of diverse ministry than in trying to find any model of ministry that will suit us all. There were reasons that one form of leadership arose in the Johannine community but not in the Lukan and reasons why some Paulinist did not think Paul's prescriptions sufficed for the churches in Ephesus when the Pastorals were written. Maybe the needs of Hispanic Christians in Mexico are different from those of Hispanic Christians in Chicago or Euro-American Christians in the suburbs of New York.

To take examples we have noted before: the base communities may want and need a different kind of leadership than St. Bridget's around the block, and the charismatic Presbyterian fellowship may with good

---

3. Note, for example, the fuzziness on the role of deacon in both *Lumen Gentium* and *Baptism, Eucharist, and Ministry*.

reason think about the presbytery a little differently than the elders of Brick Church do. Of course tradition and Scripture will help us find what is appropriate, but there will not be just one answer.

On the other hand, we might actually find some models of ministry that we all can acknowledge. I would suspect that bishop-elder-deacon will not suffice.[4]

SACRAMENTS

To the Corinthians, Paul writes: "For all who eat and drink without discerning the body, eat and drink judgment against themselves" (1 Cor. 11:29). For Paul the scandal was that wealthy Christians, who could arrive early, separated themselves at the meal from poorer Christians, who arrived late and had less. Discerning the body meant, in part, discerning that the whole community gathered around the table is Christ's body. His body for his body.

We too come to the table as a people divided. In most churches economic divisions do not include a division at the Eucharist, but there is a division: between those who are ordained and those who are not; between those who have the authority to preside, to say the words, and those who do not; between those who give and those who receive. Our words say, "We are all the body of Christ and individually members of it." But only a few of us say: "This is my body, broken for you; this is my blood, shed for you." Sometimes the referent of the possessive pronoun is not as clear as it ought to be.

We Protestants sometimes say that we are behind the table for the sake of good order. Churches I have served have always been full of orderly people, articulate, able to say the sacred words loud and clear so everyone can hear them, less apt than I to bungle the appropriate gestures of distribution.

If the New Testament knows a particular ministry of presiding at the table, that is a theme so underplayed as to be barely visible. It may be there as a lesser motif in the feeding stories of Mark, Matthew, and Luke. If so it is a motif that John handles differently, when Jesus shares the bread directly with the people, without intermediaries. Eucharistic

---

4. Also note that if John N. Collins (*Diakonia: Re-interpreting the Ancient Sources* [New York and Oxford: Oxford Univ. Press, 1990]) is right, the line between deacon and elder in the early churches represented, say, by Acts, is extremely unclear.

ministry is almost certainly not in view in the still unclear picture of ministry in Acts 6.

If we are in danger of clericalism in our churches, the confusion of clergy as the church's servants with clergy as the church's essence, it may be in part because clergy are paid. It may be in part because only clergy preside at sacraments. The radical response would be to say: "Let different Christians preside at the meal at different times." We clergy do it decently and in order, of course, but any clergyperson who knows how to preside decently and in good order can teach others to do the same in less than three years of full-time study. The less radical response would be to remind ourselves, our denominations, and our people that whatever officiating role the elders or ministers had in the New Testament, it was almost certainly derivative from their role as preachers and teachers, a kind of convenient extension of responsibility, not a recognition of some generic superiority in handling the mysteries of faith.

Responding to an early version of some of this study, two pastors explained their practice. One pastor trains church members to take turns presiding at the weekly Communion. Another pastor invites a church member who serves as sponsor for a baptismal candidate to perform the baptism. For these aberrations it helps that both are pastors of congregations in (different) denominations that pride themselves on local autonomy and congregational polity. Are these the first winds of anarchy or the blowing of the Spirit?

We can put it somewhat differently. The ordination the New Testament clearly recognizes is baptism. What counts for all of us as Christians is not the vestments we put on before we preach or administer sacraments, but the one whom we put on in baptism, the Lord Jesus Christ. Since we all put him on, we will want to find ways to acknowledge our oneness. The table and the water of baptism bring us together. When they mark any of us as separate, has not something gone amiss?

GIFTS

"Now there are varieties of gifts, but the same Spirit; and there are varieties of services, but the same Lord," writes Paul (1 Cor. 12:4-5). The gifts are given to the body, but not to any one individual in the body—not even pastor, priest, bishop, deacon. The legitimate claim that a good minister is a generalist becomes the astonishing demand that the good minister be a superstar.

One would guess that the church at Corinth was smaller and perhaps more dedicated than most churches served by contemporary clergy. Yet no one was asked to be apostle, prophet, teacher, miracle worker, healer, leader, tongue-speaker, and keeper of the emergency fund for special needs. Maybe because we clergy claim to be engaged in full-time Christian service, both ministers and people eagerly search for jobs to fill the time. Instead of displaying Christian serenity, we display professional frenzy, trying to do it all. Instead of honoring other people's gifts, we justify our salaries by showing off our own. Though it may well be that one sister can administer rings around us, and one brother provide pastoral care beyond our deepest sensitivities, we are reluctant to share responsibility.

I will suggest that the one clearest "ministerial" function for the New Testament was that of proclamation and teaching, and I believe that that function is still most often best served by persons trained for professional ministry. (I still search for the better word.)

Along with this, most churches will require the gift of *kybernēseis*—piloting, administering (1 Cor. 12:28). We will pilot best when we pay close attention to who else is on board and find ways to acknowledge, cultivate, and inspire their gifts for the sake of the church for the sake of the gospel for the sake of the world.

APOSTLESHIP

Both *Lumen Gentium* and *Baptism, Eucharist, and Ministry* evidence the concern of contemporary churches to share ministry that is genuinely apostolic. I have noted that in the New Testament the idea of apostolic authority differs somewhat from place to place. In the material we have studied neither Matthew nor John has any particular place for the notion of apostleship, though as we have seen there are occasional references either to the term itself or to the idea of being "sent" by another. Paul designates himself as "apostle" along with other apostles. His apostleship depends on the fact that he has seen the risen Lord and on the call he received from Jesus. It is validated by his relationship to his churches.

There is no evidence that apostleship itself will extend beyond the lifetime of the first circle of apostles. Paul says: "Last of all, as to one untimely born, he appeared also to me. For I am the least of the apostles, unfit to be called an apostle, because I persecuted the church of God" (1 Cor. 15:8-9). Paul presumably means that he really is last of all the apostles, last to see the risen Lord until he comes. Apostleship is not a gift to the church for eternity but for the moment, though of course Paul thought the moment would end in glory sooner than it did. Paul's function as apostle is made clear in the verses that succeed this brief reference to his call: "But by the grace of God I am what I am, and his grace to me has not been in vain. On the contrary, I worked harder than any of them—though it was not I, but the grace of God that is with me. Whether then it was I or they, so we proclaim and so you have come to believe" (1 Cor. 15:10-11).

The apostles are those who proclaim. They have seen Christ risen and they declare Christ risen and crucified. Though Paul does not explicitly raise the issue, we can presume that though the apostles die, the apostolic responsibility to preach the gospel will extend beyond their circle—to other people and then to other times. The apostolic function for our time, therefore, is to take care that the gospel is preached faithfully, that the crucified and risen Christ to whom the apostle bore witness is declared in our churches, for the service of the gospel in the re-creation of the world.

What happens to apostolic *authority* in a post-Pauline time is less clear. Paul himself urges that certain deference be given to his companions and to his associates. We do not know whether he assumed or his churches assumed that these companions and emissaries would in later years exercise authority in his name.

When we are honest, we acknowledge our distance from Paul's experience and his faith. Many sermons go awry when the preacher identifies with the faithful Paul and berates the modern-day Corinthians (or Galatians) out there in the pews. Perhaps we can claim his authority when we have learned to be imitators of him as he is of Christ. In the meantime, we do well not to confuse whatever role we have with that of exercising the authority Paul earned, and had to fight for time and again.

Both Acts and the Pastorals try to find ways to claim the apostolic function for later generations. In Acts, Paul's own ministry is validated by the approval of the twelve apostles, and he is almost never himself called an apostle. He passes on the apostolic mission to the elders of Ephesus in Acts 20. Apostolic authority seems to include some pastoral care, some supervision, and a considerable amount of right teaching against heretics within and without the church.

For the Pastorals, assuming that they are pseudonymous, Paul's apostolic authority, however reinterpreted, becomes the grounds for the authority the letters themselves seek to presume. Paul's companions and children in the faith, Timothy and Titus, become surrogates for late first-century Christian leaders. They, too, hold apostolic authority by their claim to keep firm the faith that the apostle had first proclaimed.

What is lacking in the New Testament is any sense that the apostolic office itself is passed on from generation to generation. That may be theologically a valid development from the first-century communities, but there is scant evidence for any such vision of apostolicity in the communities themselves.

In different ways the documents we studied that are later than Paul's letters see themselves in a time that is postapostolic. The church's relationship to Christ through the apostles is a relationship carried on through the continued preaching of the gospel and through teaching right doctrine and perhaps enforcing the discipline that can go with that doctrine.

In our churches today the sense of what it means to be part of the "apostolic" church varies widely from communion to communion. Appeal to the New Testament will not solve the question of what apostolic authority might mean for our time. Even free churches, however, can acknowledge that apostolic authority from the earliest time meant the authority of the gospel to stand in promise and judgment over against even our most Spirit-filled schemes and the claim that, however new our approaches to interpreting the faith, they stand in a continuity that is as old as the church itself.

We may not need the apostolic office of bishop, but we do need the apostolic concern to be true to Christ crucified and risen and to honor our fathers and mothers in the faith—all the way back to Peter and Paul and Junia and Phoebe.

Ecumenical discussion surely will include the question of whether apostolic continuity and order require episcopal office. The New Testament will not settle that question for us. We need to discern the times as well as the tradition.

DISCERNING THE TIMES

It is perhaps just as well that the rush to professionalism did not entirely overtake contemporary understandings of ministry. Suspicion now extends to every profession, and the popular media's condescending remarks about preachiness are outstripped by popular suspicion of medicine for profit and the rush toward expensive litigation. There are more lawyer jokes and doctor jokes in the popular press than clergy jokes, and the jokes are less benign.

Physicians and attorneys of integrity are working to get their houses in order, and we clergy are freed to look at our own, built on the foundation of the prophets and apostles. The reasons for ministry are first of all theological and biblical, though of course those are not to be divorced from either sociological or psychological concerns.

Different commentators will discern the times differently and find within the New Testament diverse models for the renewal of our ministry. I have argued that we are not invited to derive from all the diversity of the New Testament a kind of hybrid mix of ministry, as if we could hold to all the options simultaneously and with equal zeal. Nonetheless, my appraisal of the times suggests that motifs from various New Testament witnesses can provide images and possibilities for our own ministry.

As a number of quotations in this chapter make clear, my first perspective owes much to the apostle Paul. Not only because he wrestles more directly with issues of church and ministry does he seem to me a primary resource for contemporary understanding. Two other themes also link him to our time.

Paul writes for a church seeking to be inclusive without being vacuous. As the apostle to the Gentiles, he struggles against traditional exclusions and against any law or custom that separates faithful Christian from faithful Christian. But as 1 Corinthians shows most poignantly, Paul does not believe that every Christian response builds up the church or serves the faith. His combination of inclusiveness and zeal for fidelity seems to me exemplary for our own time.

Some churches excel in zeal but are deficient in openness. The ministry of such churches may reflect dogmatic clarity but can be short on the humility that acknowledges the variety of the church. Other churches reach out broadly from shallow soil. All are welcome not because faith matters so deeply, but because we want to be nice. Faith without charity grows flinty; charity without faith turns to mush. Clergy reflect the churches where they serve. Paul seeks to keep the tension between openness and rigor alive.

Further Paul writes to a church in crisis. It is the crisis of excitement, of new possibilities bursting forth on every hand. More than some of the Corinthian enthusiasts, Paul wants to give some order to the creativity, but more than the Galatian legalists, he knows that Christ has set us free. Mainline Christians, both Catholic and Protestant, note the crisis of our times and assume that the shift from Christendom in its various American guises can only mean decline. My strong guess is that the challenge from churches and theologians who are not white and male, the growth of a lively charismatic movement in the traditional churches, the increasing stress on a variety of lay ministries, and the suspicion of clerical authority both in pulpit and society are signs of a crisis that is, if not eschatologically redemptive, historically healthy.

We cannot be Pauline Christians, of course. We can learn from Paul. We can learn that proclamation is still at the center of the church's life and that insofar as ministry serves church, it will serve preaching. Preaching has a bad press it often richly deserves, but it depends on the assumption that words have power to hurt and heal and that words interpreting the gospel have power to heal now and for eternity. The foolishness of God that is wiser than humankind.

We can learn that the church as a sign of the kingdom cannot be bound by distinctions between Jew and Greek—or male and female. Whatever was going on with the women of Corinth, Paul acknowledged Phoebe as a fellow minister in Rom. 16:1; and in Gal. 3:28 he reminded us that the barriers do come tumbling down.

To deny ordained ministry to women does not come from faith but from fear, and whatever does not come from faith is sin. We who have received word and sacrament from women who are ordained ministers bear our witness to the rest of the church. God has called your sisters to ministry.

From Paul, we certainly learn that ministry is the work of all the body of Christ, and we are exceedingly wary of all-star ministry, clerical perks, two-tiered redemption, and maybe even titles like "Reverend." Sympathizing with an ordained Roman Catholic friend over the decline of priestly vocations, I was amazed to hear him say: "It's the best thing that ever happened to the Catholic church. We're finally learning what it means to be the body of Christ."

While the Pauline church knew the ministry of healing, the more directly therapeutic strategies of pastoral care and counseling waited later developments in intellectual history. While the Pauline church knew the struggles of being a Christian in society, the hope for Christ's return and the relative powerlessness of the institutional church guaranteed that larger issues of social and political ministry were not directly addressed.

Churches that seek to discern faithfulness in our time will be grateful that counseling and social action ministries are among our gifts and our responsibilities. Again I would guess that not many clergy are equally adept at social analysis and strategy, helpful counsel, faithful preaching, and institutional administration. Different members of the body will usually serve different ones of these functions. Whether ordination is appropriate for all such ministries is a question Paul never would have raised: if ordination is a recognition of gifts provided by the Spirit for the upbuilding of the church, then I should think that ordination would be fitting for those providing a whole range of services to the body of Christ.

My guess is that in a Pauline church, Christian people take turns serving at a table where only Christ is host, and maybe even take turns baptizing new believers. None of that do we know for sure. There is clearly a kind of ministry of the word; it is not clear whether that was a ministry of word and sacrament, provided by particular church leaders. We do know that Paul says much about baptism and nothing about ordination. He knows that different people have different gifts, but their identity rests in their baptism: into Christ, into one body.

Matthew provides a kind of counterweight to Paul in the canon and in my discerning of the times. This also for two reasons. First, to be church is in part to be traditioned: to know the stories and the commandments and to interpret them anew in the light of our times, like the scribe discipled for the kingdom in Matt. 13:52. We do need teaching ministers, though their authority—as Matthew's Gospel makes absolutely clear—rests in the fact that they interpret our only true rabbi, not in any claims to special wisdom of their own. Churches both Protestant and Catholic are in danger of washing out for lack of inspiring Christian education or catechesis.

We need Matthew, second, because his concern for the practical implications of the gospel, for Torah if you will, helps to anchor us in an age where we know perfectly well that not everything goes but we are not at all sure what does go, what helps, what is faithful. William

Muehl has written a very Matthean book on preaching, and among his concluding dicta are these words:

> When rightly understood, judgment gives structure and dignity to human existence. Lay men and women understand this and can be demoralized rather than comforted by preaching which overemphasizes unequivocal compassion.
>
> The current proclamation of divine "acceptance" contributes significantly to the anomie characteristic of our time, because it suggests the lack of consequence in relative human achievements.[5]

What Matthew's Gospel often suggests, John's Gospel dramatizes. In John 13, just when readers of the Synoptics would expect Jesus to speak the words that institute the Lord's Supper, instead Jesus institutes the practice of footwashing, not perhaps as a rite for regular worship but as a sign of true discipleship. Those who minister are also those who serve.

Luke and Acts demand that we give attention to tradition, that we remember that neither church nor ministry was invented yesterday nor will fade away tomorrow. While we may not draw the links to the past exactly as Luke draws them, we will draw the links and acknowledge the roots, lest our ministry be faddish, silly, and impertinent precisely in its attempt to be pertinent.

From the Pastorals we learn the legitimate concern for the link between religious leadership and a life of integrity. We will not be able to picture integrity quite as the Pastorals do; their picture depends too much on patterns of masculine dominance and perhaps too much on a dogmatic certainty that for better or for worse eludes so many of us who minister today. Nor, I hope, will we think that integrity is the special concern of Christian priests and pastors. The difficult call to live out our faith applies exactly as much to clergy as it does to other Christians, and to every lay person as much as to every cleric.

The truth is that in the light of the New Testament, it is not absolutely clear what role ordination should play. In the light of our history and of our needs, I presume that we will still ordain and that under the Spirit we will ordain faithfully.

Because we see the church from a Pauline perspective we will ordain, from among the faithful, people who will count themselves as members of Christ's body, not as its head. Many of them will be people who have

---

5. William Muehl, *Why Preach? Why Listen?* (Philadelphia: Fortress Press, 1986), 94.

the gift of proclaiming the gospel, whether they do that from the pulpit or not. Some will have the gift of discerning other peoples' gifts, and some will provide particular services of pastoral care or social action. The whole church, perhaps with the leadership of the ordained, will celebrate the sacraments.

Because we see the church from a Matthean perspective, we will acknowledge the role of teachers among us, some of them also our preachers and some not. Seminary education at its best provides the ways that we can acknowledge the tradition so that we can apply it afresh for the needs of God's people and the world in our own time. Seminary education is not sufficient to preparation for ministry, and it may not even be necessary. It is useful; it has proved its usefulness.

Because the church always stands under the Johannine judgment that we are all brothers and sisters and all servants of one another, we will be wary of any ministry that calls itself "set apart" or any minister who acts that way.

Perhaps it is because Luke-Acts teaches us to honor our apostolic and presbyterial fathers and mothers that we acknowledge the value of ordination at all.

And while I do not suppose I shall ever love the Pastorals as perhaps I should, they do remind me that we are called to practice what Paul preaches, if not always what some later disciple writing in his name thinks is required of us.

These are confusing and perhaps frustrating times for those of us who grew up thinking we were on our way to a kind of majoritarian Christian triumph in North America. We cannot be sure whether the current upheaval represents the devastating winds of secularism or the powerful breath of the Spirit. Some Christians tell us to bolt the door and others to open the windows.

I still honor the apostle who kept arguing for his apostleship: "Now the Lord is the Spirit, and where the Spirit of the Lord is, there is freedom. . . . Therefore, since it is by God's mercy that we are engaged in this ministry, we do not lose heart" (2 Cor. 3:17; 4:1).

Index of Modern Authors

Index of Scripture References